# You're Entitled!

## A DIVORCE LAWYER TALKS TO WOMEN

## SIDNEY M. DE ANGELIS

CB
CONTEMPORARY
BOOKS
CHICAGO · NEW YORK

Library of Congress Cataloging-in-Publication Data

De Angelis, Sidney M.
    You're entitled! : a divorce lawyer talks to women / Sidney M. De
Angelis.
        p.    cm.
    ISBN 0-8092-4339-3 : $18.95
    1. Divorce—Law and legislation—United States—Popular works.
2. Women—Legal status, laws, etc.—United States—Popular works.
I. Title.
KF535.Z9D36    1989
346.7301'66—dc20
[347.306166]
                                                        89-7056
                                                        CIP

The focus of this book is to help the reader understand the legal
concepts concerning divorce. Though the insights of the author
offer a contextual overview of the issues concerning divorce, it
should be noted that divorce codes differ in each state. Futhermore,
the laws concerning divorce often vary according to each party's
individual circumstances. The publisher does not offer any legal
advice in this book and in no way warrants or represents the
accuracy of the opinions and/or conclusions contained in this book.
Names, dates, and places have been changed, and any resemblance
is coincidental.

Copyright © 1989 by Sidney M. De Angelis
All rights reserved
Published by Contemporary Books, Inc.
180 North Michigan Avenue, Chicago, Illinois 60601
Manufactured in the United States of America
Library of Congress Catalog Card Number: 89-7056
International Standard Book Number: 0-8092-4339-3

Published simultaneously in Canada by Beaverbooks, Ltd.
195 Allstate Parkway, Valleywood Business Park
Markham, Ontario L3R 4T8 Canada

# Dedication

When I began writing *You're Entitled!* a few years ago, my dear secretary, Marjorie Estep, had been my friend and right-hand for more than twenty years. She'd been at my side through all of the good and bad times, the triumphs and tragedies, and was more like a member of my family than an employee.

She helped me with the manuscript, typed the exhibits, and, of course, was the "Marge" in the Henderson case you'll read about. She was completely supportive throughout the period when I was working as a divorce lawyer and writing in my spare time, and genuinely happy when Contemporary Books agreed to publish the book. I couldn't wait to give her the first, autographed copy.

However, Marjorie passed away on February 6, 1989.

And so with love and deep sadness, I dedicate *You're Entitled!* to her beloved memory. I'm sure she's smiling right now.

# Contents

Once you and your husband decide it's over, it's all economics • The "why's" are irrelevant • The emotional defenses • Take care of the children first • Always tell them the truth • Get help for yourself if you need it • Find one good friend for support • Begin the paper chase • Should you file first? • Do your homework • Don't sign anything your husband asks you to sign

Your husband's attorney sends you a letter • Keep your eye on the economic goals • Don't make any angry telephone calls • You don't want revenge • Why you need a *divorce* laywer . . . right away • *Henderson v. Henderson*: January 1987, Margo hires De Angelis and files for divorce

How to find the best divorce lawyer in your county—what should you look for? • Find out if he or she has a good track record • The human factor • Get a written fee agreement • Internal Revenue Service Ruling 59/60 • What you should and shouldn't expect from your attorney • You can fire your attorney and hire someone else if you have to

The variables that affect the size of your legal fees • There is no set fee • Your fee will be based on the economic issues, not on "getting a divorce" • What does your lawyer charge per hour? • You have to pay for all court costs and litigation expenses • The original retainer • Your lawyer's time records • Charges for telephone calls and correspondence • Additional retainers • You can't retain a divorce lawyer on a contingent fee • There is no flat fee either • Who pays counsel fees if your husband wants to settle? • Using a joint account or a bundle of cash for your counsel fees

January 1987 • Margo, Roger, Jennifer, and Jeffrey • You listen in as Roger meets with his lawyer, Joe Fenster, and hears the bad news • Tracey wants to marry Roger • Roger believes that Margo will break

Why your lawyer must meet with your husband's lawyer immediately • Suppose your husband won't get out of the house? • Getting a court order for exclusive possession of your home • What happens if he locks you out? • Get rid of his stuff • Get a temporary support order as soon as possible • Make sure you're covered by medical insurance • Don't let him steal your car • Nail down the furniture • Don't let him cancel the life insurance • Freeze the major assets • Going on the offensive • Now you need discovery • Watch out for the lazy lawyer • Define custody and visitation quickly • Rules for dating

# Acknowledgments

Most authors say that writing is a lonely task. I don't believe it, for I haven't been alone since that summer of '86 in Avalon, New Jersey, when I began to write *You're Entitled!*

I could clearly feel the presence of my grandfather, Meyer Sudick, the tough little carpenter who had the courage to leave Czarist Russia in the early 1900s to begin a new life with my grandmother, Ida, in the Golden Land.

Of course, my mother, Esther, has been with me all of the time. It must have been during those early years of my life as she read to me that I learned to love the printed words found in books.

But I couldn't have become a writer, or a lawyer, or even a man, without the love and guidance of my stepfather, Cesare J. De Angelis. He may not have been my biological father, but he was my Dad.

There were many others who have helped me start on this midlife change of career. Donna Jackson, the senior editor of *New Woman* magazine, who encouraged me to write; and Nancy Coffey, my publisher, who expressed faith in my abilities and joined me in a mutual admiration society.

I also cannot forget Betsy Amster, my patient editor, who taught me to make words "work" or cut them out, and Margo Korbel, who created a manuscript out of my scribblings.

Nor could I have been comfortable when it came to writing about business valuation without the generous assistance of Jay Fishman, president of Financial Research, Inc., of Ardmore, Pennsylvania.

Similar recognition is equally due Marvin Snyder, president of Pension Analysis Consultants, Inc., Merion, Pennsylvania, with regard to the subject of pension valuation. Jay and Marvin are simply the best business and pension valuation experts in the country. I must also express sincere thanks to my gifted friend, Frederick Cohen, Esquire, who read the manuscript and offered valuable suggestions.

As I faced the daily challenge of blank pages, I always sensed the loving presence of my three children. Could I let them down? Didn't I have to show them that you can be whatever you want to be? And so, with undying gratitude for their love and inspiration, I dedicate this book (the first of many) to Barbara, Michael, and Jason.

And finally, three people who have provided special inspiration and encouragement when they were sorely needed, were always with me.

First, my daughter Barbara, the author of *How to Make Love All the Time*, who took time from her busy schedule to offer helpful criticism.

Next, my dear friend Barney, who taught me that I really wanted to succeed.

And, last but not least, Priscilla, who gave unstinting love and laughter when the going got tough.

Writing is *not* a lonely task.

# Introduction

Believe it or not, there are good marriages. But there is no such thing as a good divorce. I know. I have gone through it a few thousand times. But if your marriage is over—if you've done everything possible to save your marriage without success—you have to learn all about divorce.

So this is not a book about saving marriages or how to succeed in relationships, but how to survive the legal trauma of divorce and, most important, how to *take control* of the proceedings, and get what you're entitled to.

I've practiced divorce law for over thirty years, so I know what divorce is all about—from start to finish. I'd like to tell you about it. If your marriage is breaking up, or if you've already separated and are about to become involved in a divorce, or even if you're now involved in divorce proceedings and have an attorney, you should learn something in our discussions that will help you in the difficult days and years ahead.

A few words about my practice. With few exceptions, all I've done is divorce work. I suppose that makes me a specialist. Futhermore, I've represented an almost equal number of men and women so that I have an insight into what you are going through as well as what your husband is feeling and thinking. And, of course, I know what your husband's lawyer is thinking at each stage of the divorce proceedings. So will you once you've read this book.

First let me tell you what I've learned about women who become involved in a divorce proceeding. Not all women, but most. Chances are you're angry, scared, confused, and probably hurting. And you have no idea of what on earth you're getting into.

Now it doesn't make any difference whether your husband "walked out" on you, or you did the "walking," or neither of you "walked" but the marriage just fell apart. It still hurts and you're still frightened. Unless you've gone through a divorce proceeding before, you must feel as if you're about to go paddling up the Amazon in a small canoe.

I understand all of that. After all, a divorce proceeding is the only time our society places two people in combat who were once very much in love and who may be the parents of small children who still love both of them.

Yes, I know what you're feeling. But it's my job to guide you through the perilous journey ahead, to protect you from harm, and, finally, to help you get what the law says you're entitled to. Stated simply, this book is about "getting yours!"

What does "getting yours" mean? Well, your state has a divorce law that sets forth in very dry language what you (*and your husband*) are entitled to:

- A division of all property you and he acquired during the marriage
- Child support (if you have children)
- Alimony for you (maybe)
- Your lawyer's fees and court costs (maybe)
- Plus a laundry list of additional economic protection you will need to get by
- And certainly a piece of paper that says you and your husband are divorced from each other and are free to remarry (the Decree of Divorce)

But you must realize that while the divorce code in your state may provide you with something called equitable distribution, this does not mean that you can get a shopping cart, wheel it into the courthouse, and pick out what you want.

No, it's not as easy as that. He'll say you should sell the house, split the proceeds with him, and go to work—while *you* may feel you need the house, and alimony besides, to raise the kids since you don't make as much as he does. Generally, you have to fight over every single "right" you have. Nothing comes easily in divorce.

More often than not, your husband will fight like hell to *prevent you* from getting an equitable distribution of *all* of the assets. He and his attorney will put roadblock after roadblock in your legal path to delay your receiving a fair distribution, hoping you will go broke before you ever get to the equitable distribution hearing.

His plan is that you will become discouraged with the delay, the expense, and his apparent stronger bargaining position and simply give up and accept whatever he's offering. (This is called *"I want to get it over with!"*)

Now, it doesn't have to be like that, does it? If your husband is a reasonable, considerate, and compassionate person, you and he could just sit down with two yellow legal pads and work it all out in one night right at the kitchen table. Hah! If he were that kind of a guy, you wouldn't be where you are!

Not only do I know what your emotional state is at the very beginning, I also know what questions you have—at least the first five hundred questions. That's easy.

- What am I entitled to?
- How long will the divorce take?
- What will it cost?
- Do I need an expensive lawyer?
- Can't my husband and I mediate this thing without lawyers?
- Does he have to pay all the bills during the proceedings?
- Who pays my old bills?
- Will I have to testify in court?
- What happens if . . .

This list is endless.

So with those introductory thoughts, imagine that you're coming into my office for the first time and that it's your first such experience. Come on in, sit down, and relax.

### "It's not fair!"

These three little words will be my first words to you, and we will often repeat them to each other.

You see, divorce doesn't work. At least not according to your expectations. Sure, within the first few minutes my paralegal will bring you a copy of the state's divorce code and we'll go through it together. But then I'll tell you that you can't win. You've already lost. So has your husband. The emotional and economic security you had before will never return. (Neither will the fighting, of course.)

In the typical case, your husband has more money to hire expensive lawyers, retain high-powered expert witnesses, and he can spend years and years in litigation just to wear you down. On the other hand, you have to take care of yourself, the children, the home, and learn all about a brand-new field—divorce litigation.

And I don't make it any easier for you when I tell you that you will become frustrated, drained, and sick and tired of the whole mess, while you spend money you don't have for lawyer's fees and court costs in a proceeding that doesn't work.

I can almost guarantee you that it will take longer than you think, cost more than you ever dreamed, and that there will come a time when you will hate the judicial system.

All right. If it's not fair, how can you get yours? Good question. That's why I wrote this book.

You may have heard about recent statistical and sociological studies that indicate that in divorce proceedings women and children get the short end of the stick. Or you may have read newspaper accounts of these studies that prove that women "lose" and men "win" in divorce litigation. Don't pay any attention to them.

• *You* don't have to get the short end!

- *You* are not a statistic.
- *You* don't have to end up poverty-stricken.
- *You* don't have to "lose."

Now I am not saying that this book will show you how to "win," because no one "wins" in divorce litigation. The very nature of divorce requires that both parties "lose." But at the same time, the divorce code of your state is carved in granite, and you are entitled to get exactly what the code specifies.

So I will try to teach you the economics of divorce, and I will try to tell you as much as I can about the litigation process—even though you may have never been in a courtroom before.

It is not written that you get the short end of the stick. It is written otherwise.

Of course, while I talk to you about economics, accounting, and divorce law, I can see the tears in your eyes and the almost imperceptible shaking in your hand as you write your check. I can almost feel what you're going through. But, to the best of my ability I'll show you how to take control of your anger, fear, and frustrations and to fight like hell for your economic security—and that of your children as well.

So much for why this book was written and what I hope it will do for you.

Now let me tell you what this book is *not*. First, this is not a legal textbook. It is not intended for lawyers, although some divorce lawyers may find the discussions on strategy and tactics of interest.

It is intended, rather, for women who find themselves about to become involved or who are already involved in divorce proceedings, and want to know what to expect, how long it will take, how much it will cost, and generally, what's going to happen, and when.

Second, this is not a "how-to-do-it-yourself" handbook. You cannot read this book and represent yourself. *You need an attorney*. But understanding the legal concepts described here will help you in your relationship with your attorney. Because you will have a clearer understanding of the ground rules, you will be a better client.

Third, this book will not deal at much length with the complex and often bitter issues of custody and visitation litigation. These matters are not, strictly speaking, part of divorce, and the subject is so sensitive and complicated that it requires a book in itself.

Finally, keep in mind that there is not *one* divorce law in our nation but *fifty*. Each of our states is sovereign and each has its own divorce code. And each code is different. If you live in Texas, for instance, you will need a lawyer who practices in Texas. Furthermore, legal procedure differs from county to county within each state. As a result, your lawyer will explain the local procedures as they apply to your case, as well as your state divorce law. Therefore, the book is not a compilation of fifty divorce codes from fifty different states, nor a review of legal procedures in every county in our country, but rather a general overview of what divorce litigation will mean to you and how you can manage to get through it no matter where you live.

A few general comments about our talk on divorce will be helpful before we begin.

Obviously, a divorce case involving a husband who is ill and unemployed is one thing, and one involving a husband who owns a company listed on the New York Stock Exchange is another. If you and your husband are childless, it's much less complicated than if you have three teenagers to educate.

If you have a career and are on the same or a similar economic footing, you're not going to be interested in the chapter on alimony. But if you don't know where your next mortgage payment is coming from, you'll need to know all about alimony.

If your husband has a business, property division is one thing; if he's a professional, it's quite different. The possibilities are infinite.

The point is, each case will be different. Whatever your situation, the dynamics of litigation will be the same, as will the dollars and sense of divorce. Therefore, if I tell you a story about a husband who makes $500,000 a year and your husband makes only $20,000, don't worry about the substantive difference—the principles will be the same.

To help you understand the various stages of divorce proceedings, we'll do a bit of role-playing. I will be your lawyer, you will be Margo Henderson, and your husband will be Roger. You have two children, Jennifer, twelve, and Jeffrey, ten. You have a degree in secondary education but have been a full-time homemaker since Jennifer was born. Roger is a distributor of electronic components.

Later on I'll give you more details of the economic and personal background of the Hendersons, and we'll follow *their* case throughout the book. I hope it makes it easier for you, although you may not identify directly with Margo's personal situation, such a model should be helpful.

OK, let's talk about divorce.

Everybody knows that the best things in the whole wide world
are pasta, sex, and children.
Everybody also knows that the worst things
are taxes, death, and divorce.

This is a book about divorce.

# You're Entitled!

# One

# One to Get Set and Two to Get Ready

Let's start with the obvious. I'm not a psychiatrist or a psychologist. Therefore, I can't deal with your emotions from a professional point of view. I can sympathize with your feelings and express my compassion, but I can't tell you "why" anything is happening: "Why did my husband leave?" "Why did he cancel all our charge accounts?" "Why doesn't he care if the children have a roof over their heads?" These are all good questions I can't answer.

The "why's" are irrelevant: or at least unanswerable. The point is, once you, your husband, or the two of you decide that the marriage is over, it's all economics.

But I *can*, as can any good divorce lawyer, tell you what the law says you're entitled to, how to go about getting those rights enforced, how long it will take (approximately), how much it will cost (again approximately), and generally what to expect during this strange journey you're about to begin.

I can also help you realize that the law is on your side—that no matter how tough and even ruthless your husband may seem, you will be protected and, indeed, you may have the upper hand.

At the same time, there are psychological aspects to what an experienced divorce lawyer does. For example, the lawyer has to decide whether you can withstand the rigors of divorce litigation

1

and year after year of financial uncertainty. He or she must be able to determine when your husband is "bluffing" and when he isn't: that is, to "predict" what your husband ultimately will settle for. Your attorney must have insight into your husband's fears and be a "mind reader"—at least a "legal" mind reader.

The truth is, divorce hurts. It hurts long before you ever think of lawyers and courts, and it hurts more after you become legally involved. And if you have children, it's a nightmare. You may get what you're entitled to in your divorce litigation, but the children never get what they want.

So understand that I realize the depth of your feelings and that I will try to accommodate those feelings as I prepare you for the realities of divorce litigation. I tell you all of this now because we have to talk about "nuts and bolts" from here on.

Let's talk about what you have to do at the very beginning. Once you and your husband have decided to separate but no one has gone to a lawyer yet, you are engaging in a silent war before the outbreak of open hostilities. Sure, you may be fighting continually, but nobody has shot at anybody yet. You may have agreed to a trial separation where he takes an apartment on a short-term basis and you remain in the home with the children. (In my experience, "trial separation" is merely a nicety for "the marriage is finished.") Or he might refuse to leave and asks *you* to get out. The point is, the two of you have come to the conclusion that the marriage just won't work, that it is time to live apart from each other.

## THE EMOTIONAL DEFENSES
### Take Care of the Children

If you are in this stage now (no war, no peace), the first thing you must do is take care of the children, who need a therapist. Children cannot understand the separation of their parents. They don't want you to separate; they want you to live together and be happy so that they can be happy. Their entire world consists of Mom, Dad, and Them. They can't understand how that world could be shattered.

You may not have enough emotional energy at this point to take care of yourself *and* the children. Therefore, you should find a therapist, one particularly experienced in working with children struggling through their parents' divorce.

## You Must Tell the Children the Truth

It will not be easy to tell the children what's happening, but it's got to be done, and done in a manner designed to hurt them as little as possible. How do you do this? Tell them the truth.

- You know that Dad and I are not happy with each other.
- You know that we love you very much and want you to be happy.
- Dad and I have decided to separate—he will be living in his own place and you will be visiting him there.
- You and I will stay in the house and you will go to school and see your friends, just like you do now.
- Your Dad and I think it would be helpful if you talked to Dr. _____ about your feelings.
- Yes, there probably will be a divorce.

Whatever you do, don't avoid telling them the truth, and don't try to sugarcoat it. (When I was growing up in South Philadelphia, one of my playmates told me that his father had just taken a job upstate and that, according to his mother, the job would last between five and ten years.)

*Don't hide the truth from your children.*

## Get Help for Yourself If You Need It

Whether you need a therapist to help you get through the turmoil basically is up to you. Of course, you will be meeting with the children's therapist to learn how you can help them. You may decide to consult their therapist to sort out your own feelings, or you may want one of your own.

Don't be afraid, as many women are, that "if I go to a shrink my husband will say I'm crazy and take the children from me." Not true. The courts will expect you to need some support during this very difficult period of your life. Going to a therapist, especially with the children, shows your concern for them and will not be interpreted as a sign that you are "crazy."

I usually suggest that my clients get counseling at the beginning of a divorce case, to channel their anger. I don't mean to imply that if you're mad at your stupid husband you need a therapist. What I *do* mean is that if your anger is debilitating—if you're so mad you can't think clearly—you could use some trained help in directing your anger to more productive results. If you can afford it, you should seek the support of a professional trained in emotional health care. If you can't afford it, ask the court for financial help. (See Chapter 15, "Temporary Alimony.")

It can't hurt. It can help a lot.

### Find One Good Friend

I also want you to seek out one good friend whom you can confide in, trust, and talk to. I want to meet that good friend at our next meeting so I can explain just what I'm explaining to you. As we go through the months and years of litigation, your good friend will come in with you from time to time to learn what is going on legally. This gives you the opportunity to check with your friend in the evenings and on weekends and to have someone to lean on—someone who has an understanding of what your divorce proceeding is all about, without the emotions that can cloud clear vision. ("Ethel, what in the world was he talking about today?")

### Begin the Paper Chase

The separation or trial separation may or may not lead to divorce. If it doesn't and you can work things out, then you won't need to prepare evidence for litigation (income tax returns, charge account slips, and other papers showing financial worth or income). On the other hand, if the "silent war" escalates into a shooting war and final separation, now is a good time to begin accumulating evidence of your economic situation, which will become so important later on. You will be chasing papers all day long.

This does *not* mean that you should break into your husband's office or rifle his safe but that you should begin keeping a private record (or copies) of any papers that will show a judge something about your economic situation. Let me give you some examples:

- Find any income tax returns, financial statements, or deeds—*anything* in writing that would help someone understand your husband's financial position, especially if he has a business or profession (these are worth their weight in gold).
- Locate canceled checks and bank statements for the past three years, which will show how much it cost to run the household

when things were rosy (they're absolutely necessary).
- Collect all medical, dental, or health care bills (for both you and the children).
- Copy any papers or correspondence from his employer concerning a pension or profit-sharing plan.
- Assemble any papers concerning your home—mortgage statements, improvements, building contracts, receipts, estimates for repairs, or homeowner's insurance policies. Get it all.

I can't give you a list of everything to look for. Just get me a "suitcase full of papers," even those *you* don't think are important. Let me (and the experts you'll need later on) decide whether they're important.

Now I notice you're grimacing. You don't like it. You don't want to spy. You haven't even decided to get a divorce. Sure, you and your husband are sleeping in separate bedrooms, and he has mentioned the "D" word, but do you really *have* to do this dirty work?

Of course you don't *have* to. You can wait until he leaves, taking every single canceled check, bank statement, or income tax return and the cupboard is bare—after which you can spend a few thousand dollars on something called *discovery* to get copies of the papers you need for your case (if they still exist, that is). No, don't be squeamish about getting ready. If you and your husband kiss and make up you can put all the papers back and save the copies— just in case.

As you'll see, divorce cases are won by paperwork and planning, not by fear. Fear is self-defeating; get rid of it. Go find the papers. It's one of the first steps in *taking control*.

## Find a Good Divorce Attorney in Your County

Not only will you need an attorney who practices in your *state* but one who practices in the *county* where you live (more on this later). Every divorce case, indeed every lawsuit in our state courts, is first heard in the county courthouse, and the first thing you have to do is determine in which county you live. This is important because the procedures affecting divorce litigation differ from county to county within the same state. This leads me to discuss *venue*. Let's say you and your husband live in Dade County, Florida, and that he works or operates a business there. You will have to file your divorce complaint in Dade County, which is where the venue is.

But suppose your husband works for a company with offices around the state or operates a business with branches around the country. You're now in danger of his moving and filing for divorce in, say Jacksonville, or, worse, Chicago.

You'd be fighting your divorce case in unfriendly territory; and worse, you'd need *two* lawyers, one to talk to on a day-to-day basis and one to try your case.

Can he do this? Easy. So if your husband already has moved to another county or state or is likely to do so, tell your attorney *at once*.

## Should You Fire the First Shot?

This brings us to the most difficult decision you'll have to make today. If your marriage is really over you should seriously consider filing for divorce *now*. As far as the law is concerned, it doesn't make any difference *who* files first. No longer do we have innocent or guilty parties in divorce proceedings. You don't get more property if you file first or less if he does. But *timing* is extremely important to you. Why? Let me explain.

Suppose your husband starts to tighten the financial screws. He begins to hide assets, sell off parts of his business to his brother-in-law, or create a phony paper trail suggesting that his financial condition is shaky. At the same time, he tries to lull you into inactivity. Suppose he suggests that you don't really need the big house you're living in or asks you to sign papers you don't understand.

Suppose he says:

Look, hon, let's not give up. Let's try to work this thing out amicably. We don't have to hire expensive divorce lawyers and spend a fortune for fees. OK?

It is not OK for you. First of all, when you file a divorce complaint (the paper that starts your proceedings), your lawyer will ask for temporary alimony, temporary child support, and temporary lawyer's fees and court costs, among other things. (The complaint also will ask the court to "freeze" certain assets, such as CDs or mutual funds, so they can't be dissipated or hidden.) In most states, the temporary alimony, child support, and lawyer's fees you ask for in your complaint *will be retroactive to the day on which you filed your complaint!*

So if you spend six months in meaningless negotiations while your husband is getting ready to *ambush* you, you will lose six months of support and maintenance and six months of lawyer's fees. Your inactivity may cost you thousands of dollars.

Now you say: (1) "Oh my goodness, I can't sue him for divorce yet—we're still living together." Or (2) "Look, what you say may be legally correct but I want to give the marriage another chance. Once I file, it's all over!" Or (3) "I couldn't do that—he'd kill me!"

Answers to the above:

1. Yes you can.
2. It's up to you.
3. No he won't.

Explanation:

1. Believe it or not, you don't have to be physically separated to file for divorce. In many states the court can issue a decree of divorce even in those rare cases where two people still live under the same roof, if they both have filed affidavits that their marriage is "irretrievably" broken.
2. Of course if you and your husband are still working on your marriage you shouldn't file for divorce. "Working on" includes periodic marriage counseling, sincere attempts to communicate and, most of all, your gut feeling that this is only a storm you and he will ride out. But if you know it's OVER, you should file.
3. No he won't kill you. He may rant and rave if you file first or shout that the sky is falling and *now* he'll get you, but once you

file you have the law on your side. Your lawyer will protect you from any physical harm or threats of harm. Not only that but your lawyer will use the framework of the divorce code in your state to protect your financial security.

## STORY

Helen, a new client, told me that she and her husband, Burt, were still living together. Helen was in her fifties and instantly I could see the signs of twenty-five years of domination by Burt.

Of course, the fact that Helen and Burt were still living together was Helen's conclusion. They had slept in separate bedrooms for the past eight years, hadn't talked to each other for five, and ate separately.

When I asked Helen what Burt did for a living, her answer was shocking. "I'm not sure. You see, we don't talk to each other."

Anyway, Helen had found a document she couldn't understand and handed it to me, along with an apology for "spying." The document was a statement from a national stock brokerage firm showing an account for Burton Smith and a balance for the current month in the amount of $350,000.

I told Helen that she should consider filing immediately for divorce. Moreover, she should file for an injunction freezing the $350,000 so Burt couldn't waltz away with it before the case was listed for trial. I wanted to dictate the divorce complaint and file it that same day.

Helen's eyes fluttered with real fear. "Oh my," she said, "he would kill me!"

Over the next few weeks, we talked about her fear and then, after Helen consulted a therapist I'd used in these situations, reluctantly she agreed to file a divorce complaint.

I rushed to the courthouse to get a quick hearing for the injunction. I couldn't wait to question Burt about the $350,000.

Of course you know the sad ending by now. Three weeks later, Burt took the stand at the injunction hearing and (with a straight face) told the judge:

"Well, Your Honor, my father—he's 70—is in the investment

business and he had this money and—you know—he wanted to put it in my name for a few days. I didn't even know he did it, you see."

The judge looked at Burt quizzically. "Is the $350,000 still in your account, Mr. Smith?"

Burt smiled. "Oh no, Your Honor, I gave it back to my father. It was never really mine, you know what I mean?"

Well it took three years of litigation to chase the $350,000. We finally caught up with it and although Helen was awarded 60 percent of it, it cost her a *lot* in attorney's fees just to play catch-up. So, economically speaking, filing first may be necessary. Should you file first and later decide that the marriage will work after all or that you and your husband should give it another try, it takes about fifteen minutes for your lawyer to withdraw the complaint on grounds of reconciliation.

## Do Your Homework

When you finally select a divorce lawyer (see Chapter 3, "You and Your Lawyer: Finding Mr. or Ms. Right"), he or she will be overjoyed if you bring in some written background of your life with your husband. So don't wait for an assignment; do your homework in advance.

Go to the five-and-ten and buy at least seven spiral notebooks (different colors) and begin writing these "stories":

1. *Me*: Your age, background, education, vocational history, health, ambitions, assets, debts, total financial picture;
2. *My Children*: Birth dates, health, school history, participation in religious, cultural, and athletic activities, general needs, summer camp, private lessons, special needs;
3. *My Husband*: Same as Item 1;
4. *What I Know About My Husband's Business or Practice* (if applicable): Chronological history, original investment, partners (if any), what he has told you over the years, whom he does business with, the extent to which he has paid personal expenses through the business, including your help or participation in the business or profession, and the name of his accountant, creditors, and competitors—in short, everything and

anything you can think of (include the same information if *you're* in a business or profession);

5. *My Home*: When purchased, price, down payment, improvements, present condition, future needs, mortgage balance, and monthly payments;

6. *How We Lived*: Cars, travel, vacations, restaurants, domestic help, health clubs, swimming clubs, country clubs, and luxuries (include those the children enjoy); in other words, a complete and detailed description of your standard of living for five years (or all your married years if less than five) preceding separation; and finally, if there was cash, where it was kept and how it was spent;

7. *Witnesses*: Names, addresses, and telephone numbers of everybody and anybody who can testify about any fact in notebooks one through six.

Work on these notebooks as often as possible. You might want to carry them in a briefcase when you go out in case you think of something else. You might also want to keep them in a secure place so "you-know-who" doesn't read them.

One more thing: if possible, bring along the copy of your certificate of marriage when you first meet with your lawyer.

## CHECKLIST: GETTING READY

1. Take care of the children first; get them a therapist.
2. Get help for yourself if you need it; put your anger to work for you; find a good friend who will ride shotgun for you.
3. Begin the paper chase.
4. Find a good divorce lawyer in your county.
5. File for divorce first if it's in your best economic interest.
6. Do your homework.
7. Above all, don't sign anything!

Now let's assume that for whatever reason you don't want to file first (maybe there's no $350,000 stock account floating around). Assume further that you and your husband are still "talking"—still living together and still trying to avoid the inevitable.

All the same, you may be in for a shock when you open the mail some day and find a letter from your husband's attorney telling you it's all over—just as Margo Henderson was when she opened her mail that dreary Monday morning of January 12, 1987 (see Figure 1.1).

## FIGURE 1.1
## DEAR MADAM . . .

*Fenster, Clark, & Williams*
*Attorneys At Law*
*Suite 500, Fidelity Building*
*Smithdale*

*Joseph Fenster*
*James C. Clark*
*Steward G. Williams*

January 9, 1987

Mrs. Margo Henderson
576 Oak Drive
Smithdale, _____

                Re: <u>Henderson v. Henderson</u>

Dear Madam:

    This office represents your husband, Roger, who has asked us to commence marriage dissolution proceedings, and to seek a fair and equitable property division.

    Will you kindly refer this letter to your attorney and have him contact us so that we can explore the possibilities of an amicable settlement with the thought in mind of avoiding litigation.

                Very truly yours,

                Joseph Fenster

JF:al
cc: Mr. Roger Henderson
    c/o Henderson Electronics, Inc.

# Two

# "Dear Madam": The Indians Attack

And so the first shot has been fired. Your immediate response is anger, or maybe revenge. You want to call your mother or your girlfriend—or almost anybody—and tell them what an SOB your husband is. You feel betrayed and you're mad. Then you think of the children and you become madder. You'll always think that the bombing of Pearl Harbor really happened on January 12, 1987, at about 10:30 A.M., when you opened the letter.

Now of course it may *not* happen like this, which may be a worst-case picture. As mature adults, you and your husband may decide that a divorce is inevitable, that there should be a separation the week after Easter, that you should retain an attorney and file a complaint, that he will give you money for the initial retainer, and that he will move out of the house without any argument. Yes, it *can* happen this way, and it's commendable if he is that rational.

However, in three decades of practicing divorce law, I've seen it happen that way only three or four times. So let's take the worst-case scenario.

First of all, keep your eye on your ultimate goal, a fair and just settlement of the dissolution of the marriage partnership, an equitable division of property, reasonable support for the children, alimony for you if you qualify, a contribution toward your legal fees, and so on. These are economic goals, which is what modern divorce is all about today.

What you don't want is revenge: You *don't* want him flogged in the town square. You *don't* want him exiled to Libya. You *don't* want to take out a full-page ad in your local newspaper with the words *Liar-Cheat* beneath his photograph.

More important, however, is the negative and counterproductive effect of your desire for revenge. *It distorts your perception of reality, prevents you from thinking clearly, and stands in the way of your taking control.*

Moreover, neither flogging, exile, nor bad publicity will help you. And finally, the divorce code in your state doesn't mention any of these as something you're entitled to.

## DON'T MAKE ANGRY TELEPHONE CALLS

Don't call your husband's attorney and say, "This is Margo Henderson. I just got a letter from you and I want you to know what a bastard my husband is." It will serve no purpose. You must learn to deal with your anger at this point and to *use* it to your advantage, not let it use you.

As a matter of fact, don't make *any* angry calls. There will come a day when you've been separated for a month or two and you're feeling lonely and confused and there's not enough money to buy your kid a new baseball glove, and the roof has begun to leak. You look at the telephone and think, "I'll fix the SOB!" *Don't do it.*

Here is a list of people *not* to call when you feel like this:

Your mother . . . she can't help
Your husband . . . a no-no—let your lawyer do the talking
His attorney . . . never
His partner or boss . . . your lawyer will talk to him
His banker . . . and him too
His best friend . . . what for?
His girlfriend . . . dangerous
The IRS. . . . think first

Don't call anybody. You won't feel any better, only worse. You may miss the sound of your husband's voice, even in anger, but don't call him. *You can't win anything on the telephone.*

Above all, when things get rough—and they will—don't call the IRS. Remember, calling the IRS is for reporting a federal crime, which may result in a criminal conviction where your husband is fined, imprisoned, or both. At the very least, the government can place a lien on all your husband's assets. How does that help you? I don't think it does. Eventually the IRS may catch up with your tax-cheating husband, but I would leave the matter in your attorney's hands. If he can prove your husband is a tax cheat, the judge will consider that fact when awarding you alimony, child support, and lawyer's fees.

The only call you should make is to a divorce attorney. (You've heard the old saying, "Don't get mad, get even!")

## FIND A GOOD DIVORCE LAWYER

Just as your husband has the right to an attorney in order to dissolve the marriage and protect *his* assets, you've got to get an attorney to represent you. As your respective representatives, each attorney will seek to either settle the case or go to court and fight it out (litigation).

In either event, you won't find yourself in a shouting match with your husband; there will be no name-calling contest; nor will anyone sit in judgment of who can scream the loudest. The divorce proceeding will be a lawsuit with rules of procedure just like an accident case or a legal dispute between two banks. As in any lawsuit his attorney will advance his position and your attorney will argue your side, and if there is no settlement eventually a judge will decide who gets what.

So your first thought should be "how do I get the best divorce lawyer I can afford," not "who can I call to 'get back' at him."

### Why Do You Need a Divorce Lawyer?

As you will find out, divorce law is a specialty. There are lawyers who handle nothing but maritime cases, others who litigate personal injury suits, and still others who specialize in criminal cases. What you need is a *specialist in divorce.*

It makes no difference that you have an uncle, cousin, or family friend who is a lawyer; if he or she is not a divorce lawyer with years of experience in matrimonial litigation you need to look further. Forget the good rapport with the attorney who got you a sizable settlement in that accident case years ago.

Avoid also confiding in an attorney who is a general practitioner but wants to learn more about matrimonial law using you as a guinea pig. Although I don't think many lawyers would exploit you like this, you should never give anyone the opportunity to learn at your expense. Get a *divorce* lawyer—and get one quickly.

Why quickly? First of all, if your husband's lawyer doesn't hear from an attorney within a week or so, he will have Roger file a divorce complaint, a legal document that formally seeks the termination of your marriage and a division of the marital property.

But your husband's divorce complaint won't ask for alimony for you, child support for the children, or money for your lawyer and the expert witnesses you'll need. All his complaint will seek is a divorce and the sale of your home so he can get some money from the proceeds (*his* idea of equitable distribution).

Therefore, if he files a complaint for divorce you need an attorney to file immediately what is called a counterclaim in divorce, which says, "I have been sued for divorce. OK, I want a divorce too. He says he wants the marital property divided; I want that too. But *I* want temporary alimony for myself and child support for my children. And I want that hot-shot husband of mine to start paying for my lawyer, my court costs, and the expert witnesses my lawyer tells me I have to retain. And while I'm at it, I want the judge to confirm that I should continue to have custody of my children."

Therefore, if your husband has already filed, your attorney will file a counterclaim within days after your first interview. If your husband hasn't filed yet, your attorney may suggest you file first. So don't delay in choosing an attorney. (We'll talk about finding a good divorce lawyer in Chapter 3.)

### Do You Need an Expensive Divorce Lawyer?

Now we have to stop a moment and talk about money. Some lawyers are inexpensive, some are moderate, and still others are expensive. You have to be practical. If you don't have any money and your husband has very little, or if you and your husband are on a fairly equal economic footing, you should not look for an expensive attorney just to "get even." In this case you and your husband should try to work out a settlement on an amicable basis, and then you can retain an attorney to formalize your agreement into a legal document. But you don't need a "heavy hitter."

This does not mean that you and your husband will use the same attorney; you can't. If, however, your marriage has been a relatively short one, there are no children, and there is no real estate or business assets to be divided, this way keeps the costs down.

If you don't have any money on hand but there are significant marital assets (such as your home, bank accounts, a business, stock portfolios, and pension funds), you need a top-flight divorce attorney.

If you're broke but there are valuable marital assets, contact the county bar association and ask for the number of the Lawyers Referral Service, a bar association program designed to refer qualified clients to attorneys who specialize in certain fields and charge lower hourly rates than do high-powered divorce specialists.

If you have some savings and your relatives can help (*now* you call your mother!), and you believe the assets of the marriage are worth fighting for, you need a good divorce lawyer regardless of expense.

Incidentally, if you are in the fortunate situation where the marital assets are significant (for example in the hundreds of thousands of dollars) or where your husband has a successful business or profession, you may want a super-specialist. Write the American Academy of Matrimonial Lawyers at 20 North Michigan Avenue, Suite 540, Chicago, Illinois, 60602 (or call 312/263-6477) for the names of members in your county.

## Chronology: Henderson v. Henderson, January 1987

On the morning of January 15, 1987, my secretary, Marge, ushered Margo Henderson into my office. I saw a tall, handsome woman about 38 years old, whose eyes were puffy and somewhat dazed. She was extremely nervous, and when she handed me the letter from Joe Fenster her hands shook visibly.

Over coffee she told me that, for some time now, she'd suspected Roger had been seeing another woman and that when she'd discovered it for sure on New Year's Eve she told him to leave the next day. Then she began to cry.

I waited a few minutes, then said, "Tell me about Roger." She seemed awed by him. "He'll do anything to win—he always wins," she said. "He's tough—he's ruthless. If he wants something he gets it."

"Give me an example," I said.

"Well this may seem silly, but he has big feet and he says he can only wear handmade shoes—he has them made in London. They cost $350 a pair."

We talked economics for a while and then I advised her to sign the papers for a divorce complaint that day, which she did.

We agreed that I would represent her for $150 an hour and that she would pay me an initial retainer of $2,500.

The next day, January 16, I filed the divorce complaint in the courthouse and sent a copy of it to Roger's lawyer, Joe Fenster. Figure 2.1 (see pages 18–23) shows what it looked like.

The battle had begun.

## CHECKLIST: IN CASE THE INDIANS ATTACK

1. Don't make rash telephone calls you'll regret later.
2. Find a good divorce lawyer:
   - You need a specialist. Don't hire a general practitioner.
   - If you're broke, get the number for the bar association's lawyers referral service in your county.
   - If there's a lot of money at stake you may want to write or call the American Academy of Matrimonial Lawyers.

Now, go find the best divorce lawyer you can afford. *Quickly.*

# FIGURE 2.1
# COMPLAINT IN DIVORCE

IN THE FAMILY COURT OF SMITH COUNTY_____

MARGO HENDERSON,                    :   NO. 87-1234
              Plaintiff
                                    :

     vs.
                                    :

ROGER HENDERSON,
              Defendant             :   IN DIVORCE

COMPLAINT

COUNT ONE - DIVORCE

1. Plaintiff is Margo Henderson, and she currently resides at 576 Oak Drive, Smithdale, _____.

2. Defendant is Roger Henderson. His residence address is Parklane Apartments, Central Avenue, Smithdale, _____.

3. Plaintiff and Defendant are sui juris, and both have been bona fide residents of the State of _____for a period of more than one year immediately preceding the filing of this Complaint.

4. Plaintiff and Defendant were married on June 15, 1975 at Spring Valley, _____ . A certified copy of the marriage certificate is attached hereto, made a part hereof, and marked Exhibit "A".

5. There have been no prior actions for divorce or annulment between the parties.

6. The marriage is irretrievably broken; the Plaintiff has executed an Affidavit of Consent and believes that the Defendant will likewise execute an Affidavit of Consent.

7. The Defendant has offered to the Plaintiff such indignities as to render her condition intolerable and life burdensome.

8. The Plaintiff is the injured and innocent spouse.

9. This action is not collusive as defined by Section _____ of the Divorce Code.

WHEREFORE, Plaintiff requests this Honorable Court to enter a Decree in Divorce, A.V.M., divorcing Plaintiff and Defendant, pursuant to Section _____ of the Divorce Code.

## COUNT TWO - EQUITABLE DISTRIBUTION

10. Paragraphs 1 through 4 of this Complaibt are incorporated herein by reference as though set forth in full.

11. Plaintiff and Defendant have acquired property, both real and personal, during their marriage from June 15, 1975 to the present.

12. Plaintiff and/or Defendant have acquired, prior to the marriage or subsequent thereto, "non-marital property" which has increased in value since the date of the marriage and/or subsequent to its acquisition during the marriage, which increase in value is "marital property".

13. Plaintiff and Defendant have been unable to agree as to an equitable distribution of said property.

WHEREFORE, Plaintiff requests this Honorable Court to equitably divide, distribute or assign the marital property between the parties in such proportions as the Court shall deem just, pursuant to Section _____ of the Divorce Code.

## COUNT III - ALIMONY

14. Paragraphs 1 through 4 of this Complaint are incorporated herein by reference as though set forth in full.

15. Plaintiff lacks sufficient property to provide for her reasonable needs and is unable to support herself through appropriate employment.

16. Defendant is a distributor of electronic equipment and supplies and earns in excess of $75,000 per year.

WHEREFORE, Plaintiff requests this Honorable Court to enter an award of alimony pursuant to Section _____ of the Divorce Code.

COUNT IV - ALIMONY PENDENTE LITE, COUNSEL
FEES, COSTS AND EXPENSES

17.   Paragraphs 1 through 4 of Count I, and paragraphs 15 and 16 of Count III of this Complaint are incorporated herein by reference as though set forth in full.

18.   Defendant owns or controls assets valued in excess of $250,000.

19.   Plaintiff is unable to maintain herself during the course of this litigation.

20.   Plaintiff is unable to pay for the reasonable expenses of litigation which have, and will, accrue during the course of these proceedings, in particular, for the expenses of a certified public accountant, and experts in real estate appraisal, pension fund appraisal, a general personal property appraiser, and for such other expenses for expert witnesses as become necessary.

WHEREFORE, Plaintiff requests this Honorable Court to enter an award of alimony pendente lite, interim counsel fees, costs and expenses until final hearing, and thereupon to award such additional counsel fees, costs and expenses as deemed appropriate, pursuant to Section ____ of the Divorce Code.

COUNT V - REQUEST FOR EXCLUSIVE POSSESSION
OF MARITAL PREMISES

21.   Paragraphs 1 through 4 of this Complaint are incorporated herein by reference as though set forth in full.

22.   The Plaintiff resides at 576 Oak Drive, Smithdale, _____ with her two minor children, Jennifer, age 9  and Jeffrey, age 7, all of whom have resided in the marital premises since 1980.

23.   As the result of the foregoing, the Plaintiff, for herself and on behalf of her minor children Jennifer and Jeffrey, requests this Honorable Court to grant them exclusive possession of premises 576 Oak Drive, Smithdale, _____, until such time as a final disposition of this matter can be made.

24. This request is made pursuant to Section _____ of the Divorce Code.

WHEREFORE, Plaintiff requests this Honorable Court to grant her and her two minor children interim exclusive possession of the marital premises, pending final hearing, and permanent exclusive possession of the marital premises at that time.

### COUNT VI - CHILD SUPPORT

25. Paragraphs 1 through 4, 15, 16 and 18 of this Complaint are incorporated herein by reference as though set forth in full.

26. Plaintiff is the mother of two minor children, Jennifer, age 9 and Jeffrey, age 7, both of whom reside with Plaintiff. The Defendant has neglected his duty to support, or sufficiently support, the aforementioned children.

27. No support Order has been entered prior hereto. Plaintiff is not receiving public assistance.

28. Plaintiff last received support from the Defendant in the amount of $500.00 on December 26, 1986.

WHEREFORE, Plaintiff requests this Honorable Court to grant a Support Order for the two minor children of the parties.

### COUNT VII - CUSTODY

29. Paragraphs 1 through 4 of this Complaint are incorporated herein by reference as though set forth in full.

30. Plaintiff and Defendant are the parents of Jennifer Henderson, born December 15, 1977, and Jeffrey Henderson, born July 10, 1980.

31. Plaintiff believes, and therefore avers, that it is in the best interest and welfare of these minor children that she have primary custody of the said children.

32. There have been no other custody proceedings involving these minor children. The best interest and permanent welfare of the children will be served by granting the relief requested.

WHEREFORE, Plaintiff requests this Honorable Court to issue a Decree awarding her custody of said minor children.

### Count VIII - REQUEST FOR ORDER DIRECTING DEFENDANT TO MAINTAIN LIFE INSURANCE POLICIES

33. Paragraphs 1 through 4 of this Complaint are incorporated herein by reference as though set forth in full.

34. During the marriage of the parties Defendant maintained certain life insurance policies in which the Plaintiff was the designated beneficiary.

35. The Plaintiff avers, and therefore believes, that the Defendant may cancel said beneficiary designations unless prohibited from doing so by this Honorable Court.

WHEREFORE, Plaintiff requests this Honorable Court to grant an Order directing the Defendant to maintain all existing life insurance policies and the beneficiary designations noted therein, pursuant to Section _____ of the Divorce Code.

### COUNT IX - SPECIAL RELIEF

36. Paragraphs 1 through 4 of this Complaint are incorporated herein by reference as though set forth in full.

37. Over the course of the parties' marriage, they have accumulated marital assets in which Plaintiff has a substantial interest in excess of $250,000.

38. Defendant refuses to recognize or acknowledge Plaintiff's interest in the said property and Plaintiff fears that Defendant will dispose, encumber, or alienate some or all of the marital assets without regard to Plaintiff's interest therein, in spite of Plaintiff's pending action for Equitable Distribution of same.

WHEREFORE, Plaintiff requests this Honorable Court to issue a Preliminary Decree pursuant to Section _____ of the Divorce Code, restraining Defendant from transferring, assigning, selling or encumbering any of the marital assets belonging to the parties pending final hearing on Equitable Distribution.

Sidney M. DeAngelis, Esquire

Attorney for Plaintiff, Margo Henderson

# Three

# You and Your Lawyer: Finding Mr. or Ms. Right

Margo chose me as her lawyer, but let's backtrack a moment to the choice *you* have to make.

## HOW DO YOU GO ABOUT IT?

Don't forget that you want a lawyer who is experienced in your *county*. (There are cases where you may want a nationally known expert in divorce law, but those are the rare cases where you are dealing with millions of dollars and money is no object.) In the ordinary case, you will need to know the names of the few experts in your county who practice law day in and day out and have been doing so for ten or more years. You should call the attorneys you know to find out whom they consider to be the experts in your county.

Then begin to canvass your friends, especially those who've gone through a divorce. Find out who represented them and *their husbands*, and get an honest appraisal of these attorneys.

At this point, you should begin to keep a list of the attorneys recommended to you by your friends, relatives, other attorneys, and business associates. You'll find that you get the same recommendations of divorce specialists from everyone you talk to.

24

If for any reason you can't come up with a list of three attorneys who practice divorce law in your county, you should go to the bar association of your county and ask for the name of the lawyer who is the chairperson of the Family Law Committe or Family Law Section of your local bar association. Remember that the committee chairperson is a divorce lawyer and will know who is good and who isn't. Ask for the names of three or four divorce lawyers in the county who specialize in and have been active in divorce law.

If you still can't find anyone after trying all of this, just walk into your county courthouse and ask to see the chief clerk, who is the person responsible for filing all lawsuits. Ask the clerk who the good divorce lawyers are, and you will probably get some help here.

Let's suppose you've been given the names of three divorce lawyers. They all have good reputations. They are all supposed to be fair and reasonable men or women. How do you decide among them? The best way is to interview them.

## WHAT SHOULD YOU LOOK FOR?

When you interview divorce lawyers, you should look for certain qualities. First of all, you need someone who is intelligent. You will be able to judge "smarts" by the manner in which an attorney questions you about your husband's job or business, the children, your home, the mortgage, and your economic situation.

Second, you don't want an "arm waver" or a "shouter"; life isn't TV. You want someone who is calm, cool, confident, convincing, and articulate. (It would be nice if your lawyer had a sense of humor.) Size up the candidate at the very beginning, determining whether he or she can convince a judge that your position is the correct one, that indeed you "wear the white hat."

Although many divorce cases are settled (and thus never get to court), assume that yours will *not* be settled. Therefore, you want a *trial lawyer* who specializes in divorce.

Divorce cases are almost never tried before juries. Your attorney's job is to get all of the relevant facts from you and present them in a form that will persuade a judge that you're entitled to your economic rights in the termination of the marriage. Your attorney does not *testify* on your behalf; he or she *argues* on your behalf. If your case is not settled, you will testify when the time comes after being prepared to do so by your lawyer.

Of course, your lawyer must understand divorce law. Therefore, his or her first task must be to explain it to you. Next, ask about recent decisions in your state with regard to division of property, alimony, and child support. If he can explain these to you in plain English, you're on the right track. If he can't, you need someone else.

### Determine the Candidate's Track Record

Ask for copies of any county cases in which the candidate represented one of the parties so you can read in black and white how he or she did. Also, find out if the attorney has handled many cases that were decided by the Supreme or Appeals Court in your state; if nothing else, these opinions will demonstrate appellate experience and, therefore, knowledge of what to do in case your trial judge "goes haywire." (Suppose, for example, you lose custody of your children, or get only 10 percent of the marital assets. In such a case it's essential that your lawyer have appellate experience.)

### The Human Factor

There is one other quality that will be of extreme importance to you and it is difficult to find—compassion. You will need an attorney who cares, who really gives a damn whether your kids eat roast chicken or TV dinners, whether you drive or take a bus to the supermarket. They don't teach compassion in law school; a lawyer either has it or doesn't.

Compassion is essential in a divorce lawyer who has to understand your fears and frustrations, know when you're hurting, sense when you're about to crack, and use just the right words to give you the courage you need to carry on.

Now, this shouldn't be overdone. Too much compassion and that fighting edge is lost. But if you can find a Ghengis Khan who studied accounting and then went to law school, and who deep, deep down *cares* about humanity, *that's* who you want.

## Get Your Fee Agreement in Writing

The original consultation with your lawyer will cost between $100 and $250, depending on his or her hourly rate. (Be sure to ask about hourly rates and consultation rates in advance.)

Try to confine the initial consultation to an economic history of the marriage and the facts concerning you and your children. This is no time to tell your attorney how much your heart is broken or that you hate your husband's mother.

Once you have decided to retain a particular lawyer, ask for an explanation of how he or she gets paid. Whatever you do, don't hire an attorney who says, "Well, give me a $1,000 retainer and we'll work the rest out" or "I'll take care of it later." That type of confused thinking leads to difficulties in the future. Your attorney must be crystal clear about his charges and court expenses so that you know exactly what you're getting yourself into.

This attorney must also be willing to put it into writing. If he or she is not or says, "I'll take care of it later," you should smile and leave.

---

### TIP: ASK FOR A COPY OF IRS 59/60

If your husband has a business or you are in business with your husband, ask your attorney-candidate at the first interview for a copy of *Internal Revenue Service Ruling 59/60 (IRS 59/60)*. If the response is a confused look or "I don't have one," thank him or her for the time, pay for the consultation, and leave.

If your husband operates his own business, or is a professional—doctor, lawyer, accountant, psychologist, etc.—you'll have to prove the value of his business or practice. IRS 59/60 deals with the methods of valuation of closely held corporations. It's vital to your case. Therefore, if the attorney you're interviewing doesn't know about IRS 59/60, you're in the wrong place.

---

Before paying a retainer, request a written fee agreement setting forth complete and specific details of (1) all fees you have to pay, (2) when you have to pay them, and (3) all the court costs and expenses you will incur. If you don't get this document within one week, something is wrong and you should see someone else. Ask for it at the first meeting and make sure you get it *before* you give the lawyer any retainer.

After you hire an attorney and have paid the retainer, immediately go to a stationer and buy a box of legal-sized manila folders and tabs. You will need a complete filing system for all the documents and letters he or she will send your way.

### What You Should Expect from Your Attorney

1. Copies of everything in your case that comes across his or her desk: memoranda of every conversation held with your husband's lawyer or with the judge in your absence.
2. A clear explanation of what your rights are and how the attorney will go about securing those rights for you.
3. The maintenance of proper time records and monthly bills (see the next chapter).
4. An explanation of court costs, expert witness fees, and a clear description of all the expenses you will be expected to pay.
5. A promise to use his or her best efforts to settle the case without going to court or, if it can't be settled, to prepare you for litigation.
6. A promise to return your telephone calls as soon as possible.
7. The assurance that you will be kept up to date on settlement negotiations.

### What You Should Not Expect from Your Attorney

1. *Emotional Help*: Although you can call your attorney any time, you should not call for solace or comfort. He is not your therapist or your husband and cannot answer the "why's."
2. *House Repairs*: Remember what your lawyer's job is—that of a trained and skilled professional who will secure the best possible settlement or court verdict for you with regard to the dissolution of the economic partnership you and your husband have created. However, he is not a roofer.

## *Telephone Conversation, Monday, 6:00 A.M.*

Client: Sidney, I'm sorry to call you at home this early, but you should see this place—it's a mess. I've got water all over the place and it'll cost a fortune to replace the furniture. That bastard husband of mine never had the money to fix the roof—he only had money for his women. What'll I do?

Me: Call a roofer. Please.

3. Predictions of the Future: Your lawyer is not a fortune teller and does not "know" how long it will take for your case to be settled, when your husband will offer to settle the case on your terms, or how long it will take for a judge to decide the case once the final hearing is over. He or she has general ideas which, of course, will be shared with you, but he cannot predict exactly what will happen in your case.

4. A Personal Relationship: Some women see their male attorneys as attractive gentlemen who seem to have their interests at heart, perhaps much more so than did their husband or other men in their past. I assure you that his interest is professional. He will be polite and of course will show interest in your problems. He will do his best to solve those problems for you, but you should not take this attention to be "personal." If you find your interest becoming other than professional or if *he* is flirting with *you*, stop it immediately, as it can only interfere with the prosecution of your case. If it gets out of hand, get another attorney at once. Forget "L.A. Law." No flirting! No exceptions!

## You Can Fire Your Attorney If Necessary

If you're not getting along, you can fire your attorney at any time; you don't need a reason. I don't want to suggest that you fire him because he didn't return a telephone call or because you saw him laughing while talking to your husband's lawyer. However, if there is a major disagreement that cannot be resolved, you're better off finding someone else. All you have to do is write a simple letter explaining that you no longer wish to be represented by him. (Keep a copy of the letter for your files.)

Upon termination, you will owe for legal services up to the date of discharge, but the contract between the two of you will have ended. You see, although your fee agreement with your attorney is a contract, it is not a lifetime contract. Of course, firing your attorney may cause you additional problems you don't need. He may refuse to turn over your file to your *new* attorney; or you and he may become involved in a fee dispute; or your divorce proceeding may be held up.

But these are short-term difficulties. In the long run, it's more important for you to be represented by an attorney with whom you can get along.

## CHECKLIST: FINDING THE RIGHT LAWYER

1. Look for the lawyer who is persuasive, cool, and can explain complicated legal and economic concepts in simple, understandable terms. Get someone who is tough but caring.
2. Inquire about his or her track record.
3. Ask for an explanation of fees and a sample fee agreement.
4. If you or your husband have a business or are professionals, ask for a copy of IRS 59/60.
5. Never get personal with your lawyer. Keep your relationship on a professional basis.
6. If the two of you are incompatible, get someone else.

However, selecting a smart, tough, and persuasive divorce lawyer isn't enough. Now ask the most important question of all: *how much will it cost?*

# Four

# Counsel Fees: How Long Is a Piece of String?

As you will see when we get into the economic nuts and bolts of divorce litigation, the extent of your counsel fees will depend on certain variables:

- Will you and your husband settle the dispute quickly, or will there be lengthy litigation?
- If there are children will you fight over custody, support, college tuition, and other matters affecting them?
- Do you and/or your husband have a business or a profession that must be valued as a marital asset?
- Are there pension funds or profit-sharing plans in the marital pot?
- Will your husband willingly cooperate with your attorney and financial experts in allowing them to examine all of his tax returns, canceled checks, books and records, and every piece of paper your team wants to look at?

The more complex these issues are and the more roadblocks your husband sets up to avoid financial discovery, the longer the proceedings will take and the more it will cost.

31

Even so, you have a right to know how your fees will be computed.

## THERE IS NO SET FEE FOR DIVORCE

Bear in mind from the very beginning that the divorce itself is the *least* important part of a divorce proceeding. You have not gone to your lawyer merely to dissolve a marriage but to retain the financial security you enjoyed during the marriage; that is, to secure a division of property, support for the children, alimony, maintenance of life and health insurance, use of an automobile, college education for the children, and all of the components that form the economic basis of marriage.

Therefore, when a client asks me how much her divorce will cost, I ask her how long is a piece of string. Obviously she can't answer my question and, just as obviously, I can't answer hers.

The point is, what you want is not merely a divorce—you want a divorce *plus economic security*.

### Now It's All Economics

The real job you've given your lawyer is the necessity imposed on you by the law that *you* identify and prove the value of the assets you and your husband accumulated during your marriage. These are called *marital assets*, and include anything of value that came into your possession, either individually or jointly, from the moment you were married—real estate, bank accounts, CDs, stocks, bonds, mutual funds, *your husband's business or profession* (not his *job*, however), profit-sharing and pension funds, money people owe you, cars, furniture, jewelry, antiques, anything that has value.

What you're really in court for is to determine how much of that economic partnership you will be awarded, not merely to "get a divorce." That's why you can't tell how much it will cost or how long it will take. It depends.

### What Does Your Lawyer Charge per Hour?

To start with, counsel fees depend on your attorney's hourly rate. If your attorney does not have an hourly rate but suggests billing you from time to time depending on the case, walk out. You're entitled to know what the hourly rate is and to have this in writing. In general, hourly rates among divorce specialists range from $100 to $250, depending on the experience of the attorney and the geographic area in which he or she practices. Don't let this frighten you. You need a good divorce attorney and the money you will pay him or her for counsel fees will be well worth it. (Chances are, you'll get a better settlement or a bigger court verdict.) Divorce litigation today is more like complicated commercial litigation where one oil company sues another for interference with a contract. You need a good, *experienced* lawyer, and good lawyers are expensive.

### You Have to Pay for All Court Costs and Litigation Expenses

Your obligation to pay your divorce attorney will not stop at the hourly rate but will include an agreement that, in the event you can't settle with your husband, you pay for all costs incurred in the divorce action. These costs will include expert witnesses, depositions, subpoenas, occasional travel to other locations for proceedings in other courts, stenographic transcripts of court proceedings, and sometimes even the services of other attorneys. The list of expenses in divorce litigation is endless. Later on, we'll discuss the specific nature of these additional costs and when they may be necessary. For the present, however, you must understand that, in addition to your attorney's fees, you will have to pay for *all* costs.

### The Original Retainer

Once you and your attorney agree on an hourly rate—let's assume $100—your attorney will ask you to pay him a retainer of anywhere from $1,000 to $15,000 or $20,000, depending on his view of the complexity of your case. Therefore, a $1,000 retainer (ten hours in advance at an hourly rate of $100) might be requested if your case is perceived as fairly simple, i.e., no fights over children or relatively few assets. On the other hand, if your husband has a business or profession to be valued, there are real estate and pension holdings to fight over and myriad complicated accounting and valuation issues, your attorney could ask for a $10,000 retainer (one hundred hours in advance). Retainers are routine—

you wouldn't want your attorney to stop work at the end of every hour in order to bill you.

### Your Attorney Must Keep Accurate Time Records

After you have agreed on the initial retainer, you should ask how your attorney keeps track of the time spent on your behalf. (After all, it's *your* money.)

Your attorney should maintain at all times a record in which the time spent for each client is documented. Although these records vary in format, their purpose is constant: to allow your attorney to note just what was done on which date for your case. These time records are kept contemporaneously with the work, and a secretary or paralegal accumulates all of them for each client at the end of the week. In this manner, at any point in the case your attorney can determine how much time has been spent on your behalf and therefore the total of your legal fees up to that point. Figure 4.1 shows a sample time slip (the hourly rate is $150).

## FIGURE 4.1
### SAMPLE ATTORNEY'S TIME SLIP

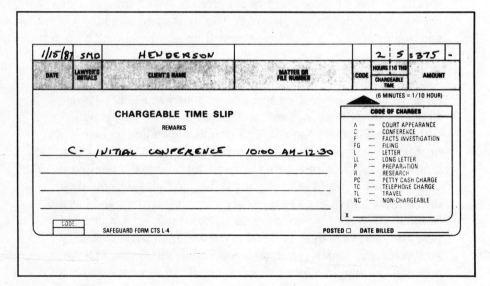

Your attorney's promise to keep accurate time records does not necessarily preclude fee problems. You must also insist on receiving monthly bills so you can check the records against your own recollection in order to prevent disputes about time. (You don't want to get into arguments over a charge for a three-hour conference you thought took only a half hour.)

Furthermore, insist that you be permitted to examine these time records on a weekly or monthly basis so you can compare the time sheets with your own recollection of how often you have seen your attorney, how long each visit took, how many meetings he or she had with opposing counsel, how many times you went to court, how long your attorney was in court, and so forth.

Don't be bashful. If you think something's wrong, bring it up. Communicate! Your lawyer will still represent you.

### Charging for Telephone Calls and Letters
Another problem to resolve is what to do about the thirty-second telephone call and the letter that takes fifteen seconds to read. The most common practice is to agree on a fixed fee, such as one-tenth of an hour. At $100 per hour this would translate into $10 to place or take a call or to dictate or read a letter.

Ten dollars for a telephone call may sound like a lot of money, but it is not unreasonable to select a fixed charge for telephone calls and correspondence in order to avoid disputes. Consider how impractical it would be if your attorney were forced to "clock" telephone calls, the reading of a letter, or the dictation of a pleading on a per-second basis. It is far better to arrive at a fixed charge for such services so that there will be no fee dispute about them later on.

### Additional Retainers
Let's suppose that you have hired an attorney at $100 per hour and have paid a $1,000 retainer. Within a week more than ten hours have been incurred on your behalf, and by the end of the month a total of thirty hours have been expended on your case. You receive a bill for $3,000 giving you credit for $1,000 paid on account. You now owe $2,000. As your case goes on, unless you are independently wealthy you will soon be broke.

Therefore, at the initial interview you should clearly determine what happens when the initial retainer has been used up. If you don't have savings set aside or can't borrow the necessary funds, your attorney may agree to wait until the conclusion of the case for the balance of his or her fees.

Most attorneys are amenable to this procedure, provided they are paid a substantial enough retainer (say, $2,500 or more) at the outset and provided they believe there will be sufficient funds in the case to cover their professional services. For example, if you and your husband have managed to accumulate mutual funds of $10,000 or $20,000 (remember, it doesn't make any difference whose name is on the fund), then your attorney can take the chance of putting in one hundred or so hours for you and getting paid when the marital estate is distributed.

On the other hand, if no such marital funds exist and you can't come up with the requested retainer, you may not be able to retain the attorney of your choice.

There is another possibility you should explore. Let's suppose the attorney you've selected will not agree to accept a retainer and then wait until the end of the case to be paid. But let's also assume that you can manage to acquire additional funds up to a certain point—$7,500 or $10,000, for example.

Ask whether your attorney would be willing to agree in writing that your obligation to pay retainers will be limited to a fixed sum, say $7,500, and that additional retainers will be due quarterly or semiannually in the amount of $1,000 or $1,500. In that case, the lawyer's "waiting period" begins after receipt of the $7,500.

It's a matter of economics, negotiation, and common sense, but get it done in the beginning. *And get it in writing.*

### You Can't Retain a Divorce Lawyer on a Contingency Fee Basis

At this point you may want to know whether you can retain a divorce attorney on a contingency fee basis, similar to a personal injury attorney who takes an accident case for, say, 25 percent or 30 percent of the settlement. The answer is no. In the first place, contingency fee agreements for domestic relations lawyers are usually prohibited by the state canons of professional ethics.

Second, it would be impossible to compute a contingency fee because of the uniqueness of divorce law. For instance, should the contingency fee take into account child support payments, private school tuition, and orthodontia payments for your children? Should a contingency fee percentage be taken out of your weekly alimony payments?

Obviously, it just wouldn't work. In any event, it's not permitted, so you should just forget it.

## Your Attorney May Ask You to Pay a Final Fee

At the same time, you should know that many experienced divorce lawyers may insist that you pay an additional or "final" fee (over and above the hourly rate) when your case is over, either by way of settlement or court verdict. This will usually occur in cases where the marital assets are in the hundreds of thousands or millions. But your lawyer too may insert this clause in his standard fee agreement. See Figure 4.2 (page 38) for an example of this standard clause.

Well, you'll ask, didn't you just say that divorce lawyers can't charge contingency fees—that most states just don't permit them?

Yes, I did. But most states will permit an additional or final fee based upon the *results obtained* by your lawyer as consequence of his ability and experience. Confused? Sure you are, but there is a slight difference and you should understand it.

You can't hire a divorce attorney on a straight contingency fee. Most state codes of professional responsibility don't permit it. However, most states *will* permit your lawyer to charge an additional fee upon the conclusion of your case, over and above the hourly rate you've been charged, *if you've agreed to this final fee in your fee agreement.* Let's see how it works.

Suppose you and your husband separate, and you have acquired a million dollars of real estate during the marriage. (As you'll see later on, it doesn't make any difference whose name it's in or even if it's all in the name of a corporation owned by your husband.)

Let's suppose your husband doesn't believe in equitable distribution. So he "hangs tough," makes no reasonable offers, and waits for you to "crack." You don't "crack." Instead, you hire an experienced matrimonial attorney who asks you to agree to a final

# FIGURE 4.2
## STANDARD FEE AGREEMENT CLAUSE

1.  In addition to the foregoing, WIFE shall pay to ATTORNEY a Final Fee upon termination of the Marital dispute, either by way of an amicable Agreement or by way of a Court Order following litigation.  This Final Fee shall be based upon the factors set forth in Rules of Professional Conduct 1.5:

RULES OF PROFESSIONAL CONDUCT
RULE 1.5 FEES

(1)  Whether the fee is fixed or contingent;

(2)  The time and labor required, the novelty and difficulty of the questions involved, and the skill requisite to perform the legal service properly;

(3)  The likelihood, if apparent to the client, that the acceptance of the particular employment will preclude other employment by the lawyer;

(4)  The fee customarily charged in the locality for similar legal services;

(5)  The amount involved and the results obtained;

(6)  The time limitations imposed by the client or by the circumstances;

(7)  The nature and length of the professional relationship with the client; and

(8)  The experience, reputation, and ability of the lawyer or lawyers performing the services.

2.  The foregoing Final Fee shall be the subject of negotiation by and between ATTORNEY and WIFE as the marital dispute reaches its conclusion.

3.  ATTORNEY and WIFE shall submit their dispute to binding arbitration to the Domestic Relations Section of the County Bar Association, both parties agreeing to be bound by said decision and neither party to have any right of appeal whatsoever.  In the event that said Arbitrator selected by the Domestic Relations Section is to be compensated, said compensation shall be paid by the parties in such amount and such proportion as the Arbitrator shall determine.

fee clause in your retainer agreement. The agreement will provide that the final fee will be based upon the "results achieved," and will be agreed upon by you and him at the conclusion of the case, or will be the subject of arbitration in the case of a dispute.

Two years of trench-warfare litigation follow. Your attorney locates hidden assets, gets top appraisals for the real estate and scares the hell out of your husband, who slowly but surely begins to believe in equitable distribution.

Up to now, there have been no offers at all. But suddenly, your husband offers you a settlement of $450,000. You are overjoyed and accept the settlement. Let's say you've paid your attorney $15,000 and owe him another $20,000—or total fee of $35,000 based upon his hourly rate.

He then suggests a final fee of $25,000 over and above the $35,000, or a total fee of $60,000. If you agree, his total fee is $60,000. If you don't agree, your dispute will be decided by a board of arbitrators, usually three matrimonial attorneys selected by the County Bar Association.

Final fees are always sticky to deal with. They're not fun and sometimes present horrendous problems between you and your attorney. But they exist and you should know about them.

### No Flat Fee Either

Nor can your attorney quote you a flat fee such as he would for the preparation of a will or the drafting of a contract. He has no idea how complex the case will be and, therefore, how long it will take. So it is impossible for him to calculate in advance just how many hours will be required for your case. There are no fixed fees in divorce cases.

Question:   How much will it cost?
 Answer:   How long is a piece of string?

## Who Pays Counsel Fees if There Is a Settlement?
### Chronology: Henderson v. Henderson, January 1987

Margo:   Sidney, I don't think Roger will ever agree to settle this case amicably—he's too stubborn, and he believes that the longer he bargains the more likely I'll give in. But what happens about my fees if he does want to settle?

  Me:   Well Margo, it's a little early to talk about settlement because, as you know, we don't have any economic facts yet. We don't know what the business is worth, for one thing, or how much he has in the profit-sharing plan, but I can answer the question in general terms.

Let's suppose you and I and your experts agree on a suggested settlement. Now, putting the numbers aside, let's suppose you think the proposed settlement is just dandy, and you authorize me to submit it to Fenster.

Now I dictate a letter to Fenster indicating what you'll take to settle the case (and the letter contains a paragraph that prevents Fenster from showing it to a judge if we ever get to court). Anyhow, the letter also tells Fenster what my fees are up to that date, what you've spent for court costs, expert witnesses—everything it's cost you so far.

So I say, "Fenster, this is what Margo wants in order to settle the case—$X$ dollars. If Roger agrees to it we won't go to court. But Margo also owes me $Y$ dollars and she wants Roger to pay that too. And finally, Margo has spent $Z$ dollars for court costs and expert witnesses, and she insists he reimburse her for those as well."

Margo: OK, but suppose my stubborn husband won't go for it?

Me: Then we go ahead with the litigation. But we never stop negotiating, either. Actually, we litigate by day and negotiate by night.

Margo: Does he have to agree to pay your fees if we settle?

Me: Absolutely not. He can say, "OK, De Angelis, I'll go along with her settlement—it's fair—but I won't give you one thin dime. *You* have made my life miserable."

Margo: What then?

Me: Well, you have two choices. You can take the settlement he has agreed to pay and pay me out of the proceeds. Say he agrees to give you the house, the furniture, your car, and $25,000, and you owe me $7,500. You just take it out of the $25,000.

Or you can tell him (through me, of course) to go fly a kite—that you want your settlement *plus* all fees and expenses, or there's no deal. After all, when we get to a final hearing, the judge will decide how much of your fees Roger will pay.

Margo: I understand—but doesn't it make sense for him to settle soon so your fees don't run up?

Me: Sure it does. But when was the last time he acted sensibly?

## Don't Rely on Your Husband to Pay Your Lawyer

In most states you cannot go to an attorney and say, "I'll pay you anything you want, now go to court and get it from my husband." As you will see later on, most judges are very reluctant to make your husband pay for your attorney fees in general, and in most cases will not make him pay for the initial retainer. Your lawyer will be able to apply for counsel fees as your case proceeds through the courts, but you can't rely on the outcome.

If the case is not settled and goes to trial, your attorney will ask the judge to award him or her a sum of money for counsel fees, to be paid by your husband. But that usually will take place at the *end* of your case (see Chapter 13, "Does Your Husband Have to Pay for Your Lawyer and for Litigation Expenses?").

## Can You Use a Joint Account for Counsel Fees?

What do you do when you have virtually no money in your own account but you and your husband have, say, $7,000 in a joint savings account and you need a retainer of $2,500?

Let's refine the problem a bit and make the answer more difficult. Suppose you and your husband are still living together and are engaged in a continuing discussion on whether you should separate. Let us suppose that he is paying all of the bills, as he has in the past, that you have the use of your charge accounts, and that everything is going along on a more or less normal basis, at least economically if not emotionally. Now you find yourself sitting across from an attorney you have decided is the one for you if divorce becomes inevitable, and he's just informed you that you need $2,500 as the original retainer. You have about $50 in your own checking account, but you know there's approximately $7,000 in the joint savings account. Again, what do you do?

When my clients confront me with this thorny problem, I tell them that I can't answer the question for them. If they believe that their marriage may work and that divorce is *not* inevitable, I tell them to leave the savings account alone and take their chances. On the other hand, if they believe that divorce is inevitable and that their husband may make things difficult for them once the matter gets into the courts, I tell them that they can remove one-half the savings from the account. In this case:

Don't take the whole $7,000, just $3,500. It's not illegal or im-moral—half of the savings account may be yours, and you need the money for a lawyer and court costs. But remember, you're firing the first shot.

If you decide to make this withdrawal should you tell your husband about it? Absolutely. It will go like this:

### *Your Living Room, Tuesday, 9:00 P.M.*

---

Roger, I went to an attorney yesterday and asked what would happen in the event that we separated and got involved in a divorce proceeding. I just wanted to find out what my rights were.

We had a talk, and he then told me that I would need a retainer of $2,500. I told him that I was not ready to proceed but, on the other hand, I was concerned that I would not have a retainer for him in the event that you and I could not work things out.

So I want you to know that I took $3,500 out of our joint account and put it in my own account with the understanding that if you and I work everything out, I would put the money back. I hope you understand.

It's not easy to say these words, but it's necessary.

Will the court think unkindly of you when your husband testifies that you did this? Not really. Courts expect that joint accounts will be divided up by separating couples on an informal basis and as long as you did not take all of the money, you will not be "penalized" for taking the amount you needed for a retainer.

## Suppose There's a Bundle of Cash

Now suppose that you find yourself with no funds, needing money for an initial retainer, and the only money you know of is a pile of cash in a jointly owned safe deposit box or in a cigar box in your husband's bedroom closet. Now what? Well grit your teeth and do the following, step by step:

1. Take the money. All of it.
2. Have it photographed. (Yes, call a commercial photographer to come to your home or apartment or the bank if it's in a joint safe deposit box. Open the box and have a picture taken of the bills.)
3. Take the money to your bank and ask a bank officer to count it for you, deposit it into your personal account, and give you a duplicate deposit receipt.

4. Tell your attorney when you have done this and he or she will write a letter to your husband's attorney that will look like Figure 4.3.

## FIGURE 4.3

## NOTIFICATION OF DISPOSITION OF
## CASH FOUND ON MARITAL PREMISES

---

**SIDNEY M. DeANGELIS**
Attorney At Law
Main Street Professional Building
Smithdale

January 23, 1987

Joseph Fenster, Esquire
Fenster, Clark & Williams
Suite 500
Fidelity Building
Smithdale, _____

Re: <u>Henderson v. Henderson</u>

Dear Joe:

    As you know, I represent Mrs. Margo Henderson, who has filed a Complaint in Divorce against your client, Roger Henderson.

    When Mrs. Henderson came in for her initial conference she advised me that she had discovered a cigar box containing $10,400 in $50 and $100 bills, in Mr. Henderson's closet in the master bedroom on the second floor.

    You are hereby advised that Mrs. Henderson has removed $2,500 from the box and paid it to me as her initial retainer. She has deposited the remaining $7,900 in her personal account at Smithdale National Bank.

    In any event, we agree to treat the entire $10,400 as a marital asset, and will so stipulate at the time of final hearing.

Sincerely yours,

SIDNEY M. DE ANGELIS

SMD:e
cc: Mrs. Margo Henderson

---

Now, you will ask, why take only *half* of a joint savings account but *all* of the hidden cash?

Well, taking some of the joint savings account is merely anticipating that sooner or later, the court will divide that account on something close to a fifty–fifty basis.

However, family court judges look upon hidden cash as "poisoned fruit," and the mere fact that the cash exists suggests income tax evasion, unscrupulous business dealings, or a lack of credibility on the part of your husband. Even if your husband should prove that you knew about the existence of the cash it is more likely that the judge will look at *him* with a jaundiced eye when it comes time to decide who is telling the truth. Anyhow, the judge will not be offended if you take all of the cash. Furthermore, anything you take goes into the marital pot and will be divided officially by the judge.

At the same time, you will have to account for the cash you took, and that is why I insist that my clients deposit the cash into their checking or savings account. This way, they will always have a record of what they used the money for.

Let's take the case of a woman whose husband leaves her on January 1, 1989, and then refuses to pay her anything for temporary child support or alimony, knowing full well that the court will not hear her support case until April or May. She can then withdraw, say, two or three hundred dollars a week for living expenses, pay the mortgage, and explain to the court later on that she used the cash for reasonable and necessary living expenses. No one will complain except her husband, who wanted to "starve her out."

## CHECKLIST: COUNSEL FEES

1. The more complex your case the more it will cost, unless you can settle with your husband.
2. You and your attorney have to agree on an hourly rate.
3. You must require that he or she keep accurate time records.
4. You will be expected to give your attorney an original retainer for $X$ hours in advance.

5. You will be obligated for additional retainers. Agree at the beginning on when and how much. You will also be obligated to pay all court costs and litigation expenses.
6. You can't get representation on a contingency or flat-fee basis.
7. Whatever the arrangement, get a *written* fee agreement or get another lawyer.
8. In most cases your husband will not have to pay your original retainer.
9. You can take your retainer from joint funds or from hidden cash.

Now that you've got a lawyer, let's eavesdrop on Roger and his lawyer. It should be interesting.

Five

# *Henderson v. Henderson:*
# Hiding in His Lawyer's Closet

To help you through the complicated sections of this book on equitable distribution, temporary alimony, permanent alimony, temporary counsel fees, and the rest of what you're entitled to, a little role-playing would be useful. Here's what we'll do.

I will be me. Easy (except that I practice in *your* state). You will be Margo Henderson—thirty-eight, bright (naturally) but confused, and worse, scared to death about your financial future. You have been married to Roger for almost fourteen years.

On New Year's Eve, you picked up the phone to call a friend. That's when you heard Roger tell Tracey—from the bedroom phone—that he missed her and loved her. The morning after, January 1, he walked out.

Roger, now forty-two, was exciting before you married him, attentive for the first few years of marriage, increasingly difficult after the children were born, and frequently out of town for the past five years. You'll never know what kept him out of the house— Tracey, the approach of midlife crisis, or the need to make money. You tried hard to get Roger to family therapy before he left but he refused. "You need a shrink not me," he growled. Anyhow, it doesn't matter anymore. On that miserable Monday morning in January, you heard from Mr. Joseph Fenster, Esquire.

46

Although you're a college graduate, you haven't worked since Jennifer was born. You're sophisticated, worldly, and well-read, but to you divorce has always been something that happened to someone else. Even when Roger's secretary began those Friday afternoon calls ("Roger has to attend a sales conference in Chicago this weekend—he'll call you on Saturday morning"), you never connected them with divorce. It seems so strange, so frightening [*my God, why me?*].

Jennifer and Jeff don't like it. They seem disoriented, to say the least. Your mother, of course, reminds you that she *never* trusted him, and here you have just filed a divorce complaint. Wonderful. You've never been in a courtroom in your life.

For the first time in a long time, you balance your own checkbook. It's OK; you have a balance of $340. And then you remember the joint savings account [*was it $6,000 or $6,500?*], but you can't find the passbook. So you go to the bank, sign a lost passbook affidavit, then walk quickly to the teller's window. The mortgage payment ($687) is due on February 1. [*Uh-Oh. Account closed January 9, 1987. Bastard!*]

You don't know any lawyers (you've never even been to a lawyer's office), and you don't think you can retain a lawyer for $340.

So you feel scared, lonely, and very, very vulnerable. It doesn't make sense. And yes, you miss Roger—the Roger who stayed up all night once when three-year-old Jen had a fever . . . the Roger who made love to you on the living room floor after your birthday party. . . .

But you don't have the time or energy to think of *that* Roger anymore. The mortgage is due in two weeks, the $2,000 heating bill is still due, and your car—[*Oh, shit, the car is owned by the company!*] The company—Henderson Electronics, Inc. (Hooray for HEI!), the little company that Roger and you played around with a long, long time ago after he got his electrical engineering degree.

Don't mess around teaching history to pimply faced kids, Margo. C'mon into the office and do the billing, the inventory records, you know—the paperwork. Hell, we can't afford hired help yet, but this company will grow, I promise. All kinds of companies will be using electronic components, you'll see.

So HEI was born, and, just like Roger promised, it grew. Eventually, Roger had ten people working for him, and there was money for anything you or the kids needed.

Well, what happens if he picks up the car? How do the kids get to karate classes or the dentist? There's no public transportation in Smithdale.

And the mortgage. Who pays for your beautiful, four-bedroom suburban ranch you've lived in for seven years? Whose is it? Will it have to be sold?

So you begin to make calls. A neighbor's friend tells you that there is something in your state called *equitable distribution*. Sure, that's what Roger wants, a divorce and a fair and equitable property division. Then your neighbor's friend, who is a divorce maven because she went through it six years ago, tells you that right away you have to make up a list of the marital assets. *What are marital assets?*

Well, for one thing, you *both* own the house.

[*The mutual funds—whose name are they in, anyhow? Oh, he has that big profit-sharing plan that's in stocks.*

*OK, I've seen some Merrill Lynch statements—where* are *they?*

*Why didn't I insist on knowing what we had—why didn't I ask more questions?*

*This is too much for me to handle. What I need is a tough divorce lawyer.*]

### Chronology: Henderson v. Henderson, January 1987

At the very same time, a few miles away, your go-get-'em, Type A, very successful husband is sitting in Joseph Fenster's waiting room. Fenster, who was recommended by Roger's company lawyer, has practiced divorce or matrimonial law for fifteen years. Roger wanted somebody feisty, tough, and mean to women and children. That's exactly Fenster's reputation.

Roger is not nearly as worried as you are. After all, for him it's just another business deal.

[*How soon can I get a divorce? How much will it cost? How often can I see the kids? And if I marry Tracey, will she sign a prenuptial agreement?*

*Christ, how long do I have to wait here?*]

(And now, Margo, by the magic of intuitive electronics you will be transported to a closet in Joseph Fenster's private office where you will be able to hear every word that Roger and his lawyer speak. It is early January 1987, and Fenster has just written to you. You haven't met me yet. Shhh! Listen!)

Fenster:   Glad to see you again, Roger.

Roger:   I got you all the papers you asked for, and I guess my accountant has been in touch with you?

Fenster:   Yeah, Picker came in last week and gave me all the statements I needed, and we've spent about a half day going over your financial situation.

Roger:   How does it look?

Fenster:   Not so good. Let me tell you about your exposure.

Roger:   What do you mean—exposure?

Fenster:   Well, you know we have equitable distribution in this state, and the new divorce code gives your wife the right to ask for a *helluva lot*. So I guess it's time for me to give you the bad news, which is that there's no good news.

Roger:   Shoot!

Fenster:   What the courts do now is make up a list of every asset you and your wife have accumulated from the day you were married until—let's see, you separated on New Year's Day of this year, right?

Roger:   Right.

Fenster:   OK. So if you keep in mind that it doesn't make any difference whose name or title these things are in, you've got one big list of assets. Let me show you the bad news on my blackboard here. First, Roger, we'll start with your house. What do you think it would sell for now?

Roger:   I guess about 175 or 200. But there's a mortgage of, say, 50.

Fenster:   OK. Let's take the 175 figure and we'll subtract $50,000 for the mortgage and put 125 over here on the right-hand side. Now we have to talk about HEI.

Roger:     Why do we have to talk about it—it's *my* business isn't it?

Fenster:   Listen to me, will ya? It's a marital asset, something you and
           your wife acquired during the marriage so it has to be valued
           just like the house and the furniture.

Roger:     But it's a corporation, damn it. I own all of the stock.

Fenster:   I know it's a corporation, but it doesn't make any difference.
           It's an asset, it has value, and it came into the marriage
           partnership. OK.?

Roger:     What partnership?

Fenster:   That's more bad news, Roger. The law looks at marriage now
           as an economic partnership, which in your case was started
           twelve years ago and ended temporarily in January 1987, so
           that everything that came into this partnership has to be
           divided.

Roger:     Well, she's not going to get part of my business, is she?

Fenster:   No, she won't get part of it, but unless we can settle this case
           beforehand, the judge will make a list of all the assets, total
           their value, and then give her a percentage of the total. What
           we've got to do now is come up with a ballpark value of the
           marital pot. So far, we've got 125 for the house. Now we've
           got to come up with a value for the business and every other
           asset.

Roger:     Well, you have the last balance sheet. The net worth doesn't
           show any more than 20 or 30—

Fenster:   (interrupting) Hey, it's not the book value, Roger. It's the *fair
           market value*. Margo can get a business valuation expert to
           come into court and say that the business is worth $600,000 or
           $700,000.

Roger:     No way! The business isn't worth anywhere near that. Who
           wants to buy my business anyhow?

Fenster:   That's not the point. Your business has a theoretical fair
           market value, and the divorce code lets your wife get a
           business valuation expert and have him testify to what he
           thinks it's worth. So what I'm gonna do for now is put an
           estimate down here of $400,000.

Roger:     Where do you get that bullshit figure?

Fenster:   Hey, look—I've been through this before. I've been doing this for fifteen years. What I think the experts will do is take your last five years' adjusted net earnings, that is, not the earnings you reported but the earnings Margo's accountant believes you should have reported, and multiply it by somewhere between, let's say, five and eight, and that's how I get to the ballpark figure of $400,000.

Roger: What accountant? She doesn't have an accountant.

Fenster: She will, Roger. Your wife has the right to hire an accountant to help her in analyzing your business. He will go through all your books and records—

Roger: Like hell he will!

Fenster: Like hell he won't! The court will permit him to look at every single record you've kept in the last five or ten years, make copies and then testify in court that you've been paying for your Mercedes, some vacations, some things you've fixed up around the house, and a lot of personal crap through the business. And then the judge will come up with $400,000 for the business—if you're lucky.

Roger: But my business isn't worth $400,000! I couldn't sell it if I wanted to.

Fenster: C'mon, it doesn't matter whether you could actually sell it; it's a theoretical sale. OK, now the accountant tells me you've got $80,000 in a profit-sharing plan.

Roger: Yeah, that's mine too. She didn't do anything to build that up. I've been working my ass off for fifteeen years for this company. Where does she come to share in that?

Fenster: You're missin' the point. She doesn't share in it; in other words the court doesn't divide up each particular asset. What the judge does is figure out what's in the total pot, come up with her percentage, and then give her the house. The difference to bring her up to her share will come from you in cash.

Roger: But you can see from the statement that we're cash poor.

Fenster: The judge could care less. If you don't have the cash, the court can make you sell some assets or put a lien on your assets and make you pay it over the years. Wait a minute—I'm still not through. Your accountant tells me the company gave your father $35,000 for consulting fees over the past five years.

Roger: Sure, that came out of money we didn't need in the business and that I put into mutual funds. But that's all in my father's name.

Fenster: No way. It doesn't make any difference whose name it's in. If it came into the marital partnership, it's part of the marital pot and a marital asset. Let me keep on going. She'll hire an accountant to go over your canceled checks and business records. She'll hire a pension and profit-sharing plan expert—

Roger: (interrupting) Joe, before you go on any longer with this legal bullshit, do you realize that Margo doesn't have a dime? I cleaned out the savings account after I left, and she doesn't have enough money to pay next month's mortgage. Where is she going to get the money to hire a lawyer and all these experts to come to court?

Fenster: Well . . . more bad news. Not only will the court give her this equitable distribution we're talking about but the court can also award her money for every kind of expert she needs—an accountant, valuation experts, real estate appraisers, and whatever else she needs for expert testimony.

Roger: You mean I may have to pay for these experts who are out to get me?

Fenster: You might. I'm not sayin' you're gonna have to pay for them right away, but you may have to pay sooner or later. Anyhow, we're not finished. We also throw into this marital pot your checking account, any savings you have, the cars—

Roger: No way! The Mercedes and her Cutlass are owned by the corporation.

Fenster: Pay attention, pal. It doesn't make any difference if they're owned by the Salvation Army. Remember, title don't count now. The cars get appraised and thrown into the marital pot. Sure you'll keep your Mercedes. But if it's worth $20,000 now and her car is worth $6,000, just on that transaction alone you'll owe her $6,000 or $7,000.

Roger: What else?

Fenster: Well, I'm not finished with the bad news—it gets worse. She's also got the right to come into court and say she needs temporary alimony because she can't support herself.

| | |
|---|---|
| Roger: | Wait a minute! Margo is a certified high school teacher. When we first got married she was making $12,000 or $13,000 a year. Hell, she can make $20,000 or $22,000 now. |
| Fenster: | When was the last time she taught school? |
| Roger: | I don't know, maybe ten years ago. I don't remember. |
| Fenster: | Then she's going to get temporary alimony, and you're going to have to pay child support. |
| Roger: | Oh for crissake, I take care of the kids. I buy them whatever clothes they need. I take them out to dinner. I'm going to take them on an Easter vacation. |
| Fenster: | I don't mean buying them clothes or takin' them out to dinner or even vacations, Roger. You're gonna have to come up with a couple of hundred dollars a week for their support, and Margo will spend it any way she wants. |
| Roger: | Does it get any worse? |
| Fenster: | Absolutely. If she gets a smart lawyer, someone who knows divorce law, he'll make you continue paying the life insurance policies, Blue Cross & Blue Shield or whatever medical coverage you have. He'll make you pay the mortgage so they don't get foreclosed on, and he'll come up with all kinds of other things that will only cost you money. |
| | And remember, while he's doing all this—and depending on who she gets—it can cost you $100 to $200 an hour. |
| Roger: | You mean I may have to pay for the son-of-a-bitch? |
| Fenster: | Hey, that's what I've been trying to tell you all morning. |
| Roger: | Tell me how that works. |
| Fenster: | Well, let's say her lawyer charges $150 an hour. He keeps time records; every time he talks to her, to me, to the CPA, and any other experts . . . every letter he writes, every document he files in court, even *waiting* time, he sends her a bill, and if she can't pay it he asks the judge to make *you* pay it. |
| Roger: | What do the judges usually do with these things? |
| Fenster: | It depends. Say he runs up fifty hours in the next month—that's $7,500. |
| Roger: | Fifty hours! Are you kidding? |
| Fenster: | C'mon Roger, it'll be closer to two, maybe three hundred hours before we can wind this thing up. |

Roger:      I won't pay for her lawyer—I'll tell you that right now!

Fenster:    You'll pay it, pal, one way or the other.

Roger:      (thinking) Wait a minute, Joe. Don't they have to get a lot of information from my business records before they can do any of this? I mean they can't just go into court and say I can afford all this. After all, I only draw $25,000 a year.

Fenster:    Sure they go through your business records, Roger. They go through your canceled checks, your American Express and VISA receipts. They look at all your business files; they dig and dig and dig.

Roger:      Suppose we don't let them dig. Suppose we tell them I don't want my competitors to know about my business. Can't you stop this?

Fenster:    Look, we don't have compulsory disclosure in this state—it's up to the judge. I can delay it, but I can't stop it. No matter what I say—invasion of privacy or competitors—it's only a delaying tactic because judges usually let the wife's accountant go through your records with a magnifying glass. And the more they find, the more they'll use it to hurt you.

Roger:      And I have to pay for this?

Fenster:    You got it.

Roger gets up, walks around the room, looks out the window, and comes back to Fenster's desk.

Roger:      How much will it cost to get me out of this, Joe?

Fenster picks up a yellow pad and begins to do some marital arithmetic.

Fenster:    You better sit down, Rog. Just adding up what we got so far, I get close to $800,000. I forgot to ask you, who owns the warehouse?

Roger:      The corporation. You already valued the business.

Fenster:    I'm afraid not, Roger. If you've got the warehouse in at book value and you've depreciated it, and I'm sure you have, Margo and her smart divorce lawyer will get a real estate appraiser to put in the current fair market value, so let's throw in another

$50,000 for that. You're looking at $850,000 as a total marital pot.

Roger:     So what will it cost to get out of it? Give me a number. Bottom line.

Fenster:   I can give you a round number. If the court finds the total marital assets are $850,000, and if the court decides to give her 50 percent, which is 425, and if the house is appraised at 125 net, you're lookin' at a $300,000 price tag plus the house plus alimony plus child support plus counsel fees and expert witness fees.

Roger:     Joe, I see these numbers and I appreciate what you're saying, and I'm sure you know your business, but there's one thing you don't know. Margo will never be able to take this. She's nervous, she's scared, and she'll just never stand up to me in a courtroom. I guarantee you that. Let's offer her the house and $25,000 and get the damn case over with.

Fenster:   If she gets a good divorce lawyer, Roger, it won't work.

Roger:     It will work, Joe. You don't realize she's scared to death. I went over to pick up the kids last week and her eyes were red and her hands were shaking. You know, she's been seeing a shrink for five or six years.

Fenster:   Well you may be right, but I don't think so. I think this is going to take a long, long time before it's over.

Roger:     Whaddya mean a long time? Hey, Joe, wait'll you meet Tracey—she's only 29, has the longest legs in town, and she wants to get married by June.

Fenster:   June 1990?

Roger:     Ya gotta be kiddin'!

Fenster:   This case will take three, maybe four years, Rog.

Roger:     Margo will break, Joe. I'm telling you, she'll break. She always gives in to me. Always.

Fenster:   Well she may, Roger, but it's going to cost you a hell of a lot of money in counsel fees.

Roger:     Listen to me. I want out as soon as possible. I don't care what it costs.

And so you, Margo Henderson; me, your lawyer; your husband, Roger; and Joe Fenster become locked in a modern American tragedy: divorce litigation. Involve one broken heart (yours); two frightened children; one tough-guy husband; and two smart, aggressive lawyers bound by professional duty to do the best they can for their respective clients.

Although these are the major players, there are dozens of minor players in the cast—accountants, business valuation experts, real estate appraisers, CPAs, child psychologists, vocational consultants, maybe even custody specialists, home repair contractors, doctors, and dentists. The list is endless.

Finally, and most important, there is another character—a now nameless, faceless judge who some day will sit in judgment on your case and decide the future life-style of you and your children. Will your kids have a rich father and a poor mother? Will you have to sell your home? What if Tracey wants to have children with Roger?

Well, you're in it, and certain realities must be faced. You're in a war, and you've got to win. How? And what happens first?

# Six

# Batten Down the Hatches: The Preliminaries

Soon after you and your husband have retained attorneys, the two lawyers will schedule an informal meeting to discuss the overall aspects of the case, such as total assets and respective incomes. They will also deal with any particular problems that exist. But don't expect this first meeting to lead to an early settlement. Neither attorney, especially yours, knows enough about the facts of the case to engage in realistic settlement discussions.

The first meeting, however, is extremely important to you because it provides your attorney with an opportunity to "batten down the hatches." After all, you don't want to worry about not having a roof over your head or having your car disappear.

Let's go down the list of those agreements your attorney must try to secure *within the first week* after the divorce complaint is filed.

## IF YOUR HUSBAND WON'T LEAVE

Suppose your husband is very stubborn and says, "I'm not leaving, you leave." Can your attorney do anything to get him out? The answer is yes. Almost every divorce code provides that either spouse can petition the court for *exclusive possession* of the marital residence. A petition is a document an attorney prepares and files in court that sets forth (in this case) why you want to live in the house without your husband and asks the court to direct him to leave. The petition has nothing to do with who ultimately gets the marital residence; it simply addresses who lives there while the case is being tried. (By the way, it makes no difference whose name is on the deed/lease, but rather who the court believes should live in the home or apartment pending a final decision.)

The question of who is entitled to exclusive temporary possession of the marital residence is not as simple as it would appear. First of all, the courts do not throw every husband out on his ear just because his wife says, "I'm going through a divorce and I don't want to live with the bastard anymore."

Second, the presence of children further complicates the question. For example, if the judge gives a wife exclusive possession of the marital home, what happens to the children? If the children are very young (say three and five), then a judge might be inclined to suggest to your husband that he would be better off finding separate quarters and seeing the children on a defined visitation schedule. If the children are old enough to make choices, it's a different story. In my experience, I have rarely seen children who express a desire that either parent leave the marital residence. Whether they're six or sixteen, they want "Mommy" and "Daddy" to live together, and that's what they tell the judge.

Some judges dodge this issue, saying they will not throw anybody out of the house merely because the parties are not getting along. Other judges avoid the problem by maintaining that they first have to decide child custody before throwing either parent out. On the other hand, if the situation has caused emotional damage to a wife and she is seeing a therapist, the courts are more inclined to toss hubby out. (If you live in New York City you know this doesn't apply; the judge may order your husband to build a partition through the apartment and live on his side, but he won't throw him out!)

Of course if there is evidence of abuse (even verbal), threats of abuse, or violent confrontations over the divorce itself, judges will usually ask the husband to leave.

Keep in mind that petitions for exclusive possession of a marital residence are distinct from protection from abuse proceedings, or wife beating. For exclusive possession, you don't have to prove that your husband beat you or threatened to hurt you. You merely assert in your petition that living with your husband in the midst of divorce proceedings is impossible, and that it has a deleterious effect on your health and, more important, on your children's health.

The husband who stubbornly refuses to leave always argues that it's his home too—"I don't have to leave, make her leave." Some of these husbands are well-intentioned men who want to avoid for as long as possible the unhappy existence of a weekend father. On the other hand, there are those who are "sticking it" to their wives, realizing that their very presence in the home creates unbearable pressure.

Remember that upon his first visit to an attorney, your husband will hear about his financial exposure under the divorce law of your state. At that point, many men make an irrational decision, which is: "Well, I'll stay in the house until she gets sick and tired of me, and then in order to get me out she'll have to give up on her financial demands."

Now this rarely, if ever, works. But if he won't go, continue asking him to leave while at the same time suggesting that there will be no fighting over visitation and that it will be harmful for the children if he stays. If he doesn't see the light, file a petition to get him out. Immediately.

Therefore, if your husband is still in the house, at the very first meeting your attorney should request exclusive possession of the house and tell his attorney that your husband should leave within so many days. In *most* cases your husband's attorney will agree and merely ask for a reasonable amount of time for his client to find an apartment.

Even if your husband has left the home you still want a court order *keeping him out* in case he tries, for any reason, to move back into the house—say, after a bad day in court or when he finds out that you're dating.

If your husband agrees to move, your attorney should immediately have his attorney sign a *stipulation*; that is, a written agreement between the two attorneys indicating your husband's agreement to move out by a certain date and not to return until the court decides who gets the property or apartment. After being signed by both attorneys, you, and your husband, this stipulation is then signed by a judge, at which time it becomes an order of court. Figure 6.1 shows a stipulation for exclusive possession.

## FIGURE 6.1
## STIPULATION OF COUNSEL
## (EXCLUSIVE POSSESSION OF MARITAL RESIDENCE)

```
          In the Family Court of Smith County,_____

Margo Henderson                         No. 87-1234
              Plaintiff
     vs.

Roger Henderson                         In Divorce
              Defendant



              Stipulation of Counsel

     And now this 20th day of January, 1987, it is hereby
agreed and stipulated by and between Sidney M. DeAngelis,
Esquire, counsel for the Plaintiff, Margo Henderson, and
Joseph Fenster, Esquire, counsel for the Defendant, Roger
Henderson, that the Plaintiff and the minor children of the
parties, Jeffrey and Jennifer, shall have exclusive
possession of premises 576 Oak Drive, Smithdale,_____,
and this order shall take effect by no later than
January 30, 1987, and shall be binding upon the parties until
further Order of the Court.

     This Order shall be without prejudice to the rights of
either party under the Divorce Code of this State.



_____      _____
Margo Henderson               Roger Henderson



_____      _____
Attorney for Margo Henderson  Attorney for Roger Henderson


     And now, this 23rd day of January, 1987, the foregoing
stipulation is approved and made an order of this Court.



                    By the Court:



                    _____
                    Thomas J. White, J.
```

Let's suppose that your husband has agreed to leave the house within ten days. Obviously this will be a difficult time for both of you and, insofar as possible, you should avoid discussing the divorce, the merits of your respective attorneys, how much you expect to get, etc. This will accomplish nothing except to create unnecessary tension. All you can do is be polite and grit your teeth. (*You* may need orthodontia before your divorce case is finally over!)

## SUPPOSE HE LOCKS YOU OUT

Now what about the real wise-guy husband who decides to play King of the Hill and locks you out while you're shopping? What do you do?

Well, you don't bang on the door or break windows or go to a phone for a knock-down, drag-out telephone fight. I wouldn't even bother to call the police. In most cases, they'll stay out of it.

Simply call your lawyer and arrange to stay somewhere for the night. The next morning, you'll be in front of an emergency family court judge who will, in ninety-nine out of a hundred cases, order Mr. Crazy out and further order him to stay away from you for the duration.

This kind of tactic will accomplish nothing for your husband. Sure, you'll be upset for awhile, but remember, he can do it only once. Moreover, from then on the court will consider him some kind of nut. Just stay cool, and let your lawyer do the work.

### Get Rid of His Stuff

When your husband leaves, make sure he takes all of his personal property with him. You don't want him visiting the house to retrieve clothing, golf clubs, tennis rackets, tools, or books. You don't want him using the bathroom, taking a shower, opening up the refrigerator, or sitting in his favorite chair. This is no good for him, it's no good for you, and it's devastating for the children. Therefore, get his stuff out, *all of it*, and make sure he understands the rules. *It's your turf!*

Suppose you have a stubborn husband who wants to give you a hard time and perceives the divorce litigation as an opportunity to "get back" at you for his transgressions (only a psychiatrist can explain what I mean). This kind of husband will say, "It's my house and I can come there anytime I want. After all, my wrenches are in the garage and I can come and look at them any damn time I want to."

Here is what you do:

1. Your lawyer makes *one* telephone call to his lawyer: "Get his stuff out in twenty-four hours or we're going to ship it to him UPS collect";
2. Your lawyer waits twenty-four hours and then writes *one* letter to his lawyer confirming the telephone request and giving Mr. Wise Guy another twenty-four hours to pick up his wrenches, golf clubs, whatever;
3. If the telephone call and the letter do not work, you wait twenty-four hours and pack all of his belongings, call a delivery service, and ship them to him *collect*.

That's it—he'll get the message. And he will learn that you're not going to "wimp" through the divorce proceedings.

Once you've gotten him and his stuff out, the most important consideration is food and shelter. You need a temporary support order.

## GET A TEMPORARY SUPPORT ORDER AS SOON AS POSSIBLE

Assume that up until this point your husband has been giving you $200 a week for food and incidental household expenses and has been paying all of the remaining bills, including the mortgage payments. Assume also you're a homemaker and have no independent income.

Now you and your husband have decided to separate or the court has asked him to leave. What happens if he leaves and then you find that all the charge accounts have been canceled, that the mortgage has not been paid, and all you get in the mail are bills?

*Telephone Conversation, Monday, 9:30 A.M.,*
*Between You and Your Not So Aggressive Lawyer*

| | |
|---|---|
| You: | (screaming) That SOB is trying to starve us. He won't send any money. He stopped the charges. Take him to court! |
| Your N.S.A. Lawyer: | Calm down. I'll call his lawyer and get back to you. |

Ten minutes later:

| | |
|---|---|
| Your N.S.A. Lawyer: | Fenster says Roger can't pay any support. He says Roger had to rent an apartment, pay him a retainer, and business is bad. He says, "Take him to court." |
| You: | (screaming louder) But we need money right now! |
| Your N.S.A. Lawyer: | I know, but it will take several months to get to court. . . . |

Can this be avoided? Well, the aggressive attorney will anticipate this situation. Therefore, at the first meeting between the two attorneys your attorney should seek a stipulation for a *temporary support order*, which means that your husband will agree to pay you a set amount of money to cover the expenses of food, mortgage, utilities, telephone, medical bills, clothing, car expenses, and other necessities until such time as the court makes a permanent order in that regard. Your husband's attorney does not have to agree to this, knowing that it will take you months to get a permanent order. However, your attorney should press hard to get a *temporary* support order at the outset, so that you don't have to worry about basic necessities.

If your husband's attorney is reasonable and if your husband doesn't want to overly antagonize you at the outset of the case, your attorney can probably get such a stipulation, which is signed by the court. Figure 6.2 (see page 64) shows what the temporary support order will look like.

The words *without prejudice* mean that the temporary order will

## FIGURE 6.2

## STIPULATION OF COUNSEL
## (TEMPORARY SUPPORT ORDER)

---

In the Family Court of Smith County, _____

Margo Henderson                 Support Case - No. 87-1059
            Plaintiff
    vs.

Roger Henderson                 Domestic Relations Division
            Defendant

### Stipulation of Counsel

    And now this 20th day of January, 1987, it is hereby
agreed and stipulated by and between Sidney M. De Angelis,
Esquire, counsel for the Plaintiff, Margo Henderson, and
Joseph Fenster, Esquire, counsel for the Defendant, Roger
Henderson, that the Defendant shall forthwith pay the
Plaintiff the weekly sum of Two Hundred Dollars ($200) as
temporary support to be paid, effective this day, through
the Domestic Relations Office of this County.

    In addition, the Defendant shall pay the mortgage
payment, taxes, and homeowners insurance premiums on
premises 576 Oak Drive, Smithdale, all utilities, including
telephone at such premises, all unreimbursed medical and
dental expenses for the Plaintiff, and the two minor
children, Jeffrey and Jennifer, and further the Defendant
agrees to permit the Plaintiff to utilize his Exxon gasoline
credit card.

    This order is without prejudice to the rights of the
parties, and shall continue until further Order of this Court.


_____         _____
Margo Henderson                 Roger Henderson


_____         _____
Attorney for Margo Henderson    Attorney for Roger Henderson


    And now, this 23rd day of January, 1987, the foregoing
Stipulation is approved and made an Order of this Court.


                                By the Court,


                                _____
                                Thomas J. White, J.

not bind the judge who determines at the final alimony and support hearing what you and the children really need. That order can be for more or less than $200, depending on what the judge believes your husband can afford.

But what happens if Fenster will not agree to a temporary order of support and maintenance? Your attorney must *immediately* file a petition for temporary alimony for you and child support for the children. The domestic relations office must be "badgered" for a prompt preliminary hearing to impose a temporary order on your husband so that you literally don't starve.

If your husband still refuses to agree to a temporary voluntary order, the domestic relations officer will set up an emergency hearing before a family court judge (that day or within the next few days) to explain the circumstances. You will then have temporary support. This temporary order will not be what you need to live on for the next few years, but will merely provide you with money for the basic necessities, such as food, medical and dental expenses, and mortgage and utilities, until you can get to court for a full hearing on your actual needs. It requires a great deal of running around on the part of your attorney, who must convince judges and courthouse employees to take you out of turn. However, it can be done.

Not only does this petition for temporary alimony (called alimony *pendente lite*—Latin for "pending the proceedings") and child support get some food on the table and pay the bills, but it sets a date for the first court encounter with your husband—say in two or three months.

Now your husband realizes that he must appear in court with his books and records and explain to a family court judge why the kids shouldn't eat or have new clothing.

Furthermore, he begins to realize that it's not as easy as he thought; you are fighting back. What's more, *the law is on your side!*

(Of course, if you're making $50,000 a year or your husband is on his deathbed, naturally you won't be pressing for temporary support. But if you don't have the money to properly maintain yourself and the children, go get him. Do it now!)

---

## TIP: WATCH OUT FOR THE
## NONAGGRESSIVE LAWYER!

If your lawyer drags his feet, he's actually representing your husband. Insist that he file at once for a court hearing for temporary alimony and child support.

---

As soon as you get a court date, have your attorney subpoena your husband's business (or employment) records, canceled checks, bank records, income tax returns, and anything else your lawyer feels will be helpful.

Meanwhile, *don't* plead with your husband for money for food or bills; *don't* ask him "why" he is doing this to you and the children (come on, you know why he's doing it); in fact, *don't* even talk to him. Again, if he won't agree to a temporary order, fight for one.

We'll talk more about temporary alimony and child support proceedings later on. (Incidentally, as used in this book, the words *alimony* and *support* are interchangeable.)

## MAKE SURE YOU'RE COVERED BY
## MEDICAL INSURANCE

You will also need a stipulation and a court order requiring your husband to continue medical and dental insurance coverage. If he works for a company that provides this coverage as part of his employment, there will be nothing he can do to terminate it.

If your husband is self-employed, however, and he's particularly bitter about the divorce and impending legal proceedings that may require him to pay you a great deal of money, he may go off the deep end and remove you and/or the children from his company policy. Your attorney should anticipate this "scorched-earth" strategy and request a stipulation and court order *right away*. If necessary, he or she will file a petition for temporary medical coverage, right? (You're beginning to understand!)

## MAKE SURE HE DOESN'T CANCEL THE LIFE INSURANCE

Suppose during the marriage that Roger had $100,000 of life insurance, naming you as beneficiary. Now you have to get a stipulation that:

1. He will maintain the insurance at least until the court issues a divorce decree;
2. He will pay the premiums when due and notify your attorney that he has done so (by providing a copy of the canceled check);
3. He will not change the beneficiary designation until the court rules otherwise; and
4. He will not borrow against the policy's cash surrender value pending a final court ruling.

If he won't agree to this stipulation, take him to court. *If he dies during the divorce proceedings and you're not the beneficiary, even though you're still his wife you don't get a dime of life insurance!*

## MAKE SURE YOU HAVE A CAR

Suppose you have a car, but it's not in your name. It's either owned jointly by you and your husband or owned or leased by your husband's company. (As you will see, it makes no difference at the final hearing whose name is on the title.) What you've got to do now, however, is to get a stipulation from his attorney that your husband will not interfere with your use of that car pending the final court hearing. You want some written assurance signed by a judge and filed with the court that you will not go out to your car one morning and find it gone. (Most husbands will not engage in this sort of dirty play, but some do.) You now have your third court order.

Of course you know what to do if he won't agree to the automobile stipulation. Take him to court. If he wants to play hardball, play hardball (see Figure 6.3, page 68).

## FIGURE 6.3

## STIPULATION OF COUNSEL
## (EXCLUSIVE POSSESSION OF AUTOMOBILE)

```
In the Family Court of Smith County, _____

Margo Henderson                        No. 87-1234
            Plaintiff
   vs.

Roger Henderson                        In Divorce
            Defendant

            Stipulation of Counsel

    And now this 20th day of January, 1987, it is hereby
agreed and stipulated by and between Sidney M. De Angelis,
Esquire, counsel for the Plaintiff, Margo Henderson, and
Joseph Fenster, Esquire, counsel for the Defendant, Roger
Henderson, that the Plaintiff, Margo Henderson, shall have
exclusive possession of a certain 1985 Oldsmobile, motor
registration no. 1234567, that the Defendant, Roger
Henderson, will forthwith provide her with the motor vehicle
registration card, and shall also maintain the presently
existing automobile liability and collision policy #6789
issued by Universal Casualty Insurance Co., pending final
Order of this court.

    This order is without prejudice to the rights of the
parties under the Divorce Code, and shall continue until
further order of the Court.


_____        _____
Margo Henderson                 Roger Henderson


_____        _____
Attorney for Margo Henderson    Attorney for Roger Henderson


    And now, this 23rd of January, 1987, the foregoing
Stipulation is approved and made an Order of this Court.


                        By the Court,


                        _____
                        Thomas J. White, J.
```

## NAIL THE FURNITURE DOWN

At the final hearing you and your husband may fight over the TV, the stereo, the furniture, and other personal property he and you have acquired during the marriage. What you should avoid, however, is fighting over these things at the beginning of the case.

Therefore at the very first meeting, your attorney should secure a stipulation from your husband's attorney, without prejudice as to who gets what at the end of the case, that your husband will not interfere with your use of all furnishings, appliances, rugs and carpeting, etc. located in your home until such time as the court makes a final decision. Again, a written stipulation and a court order will allow you to breathe easier in this regard. You won't have to worry that you'll come home from shopping or work some day to an empty house.

## FREEZE THE MAJOR ASSETS

Finally, if your husband has a large number of investments or other assets titled in his name or if he has a business, your attorney will want to get a *temporary freeze order* tying these assets up to prevent them from "disappearing."

If you and your husband own real estate jointly, he won't be able to sell it without your signature. But if he owns real estate in his own name or in the name of a partnership or corporation, you'll have to "freeze" that property to prevent him from selling it off— for example, to his brother for half its value.

This order should also include a prohibition against each of you from selling or concealing any assets, thus making it impossible for the court to eventually distribute all marital assets. The order should apply to your husband's business insofar as it relates to the sale of his company or any part of it, without restricting his right to conduct ordinary day-to-day business.

By the way, be sure to keep a diary of any threats your husband makes in this regard:

Don't try to fight me—I'll run the business into the ground before you get anything!

I don't give a damn who your lawyer is—I'll move everything I can to Alaska and burn the rest!

I'll declare bankruptcy before I give you a cent, baby!

Make a careful note of these "goodies"—date, time, and where you were when he said them. If you have to go to court to freeze assets, you've got some ammunition.

Once again, if your husband's attorney agrees to this stipulation, it should be filed as an additional court order. If he does not agree to it, your attorney should go to court *immediately* and seek a hearing for the freeze order.

It's far better to identify the assets at the beginning and to know where the proceeds are going if they are sold, than to play hide-and-seek at the end of the case. If your attorney doesn't insist on this strategy up front, read this chapter to him or her.

## TAKE THE OFFENSIVE! (NOW YOU NEED DISCOVERY)

Once you've got the status quo—groceries, mortgage payment, utilities, medical insurance, your car, etc.—it's time for your attorney to take the offensive. A letter requesting discovery, such as the one shown in Figure 6.4, *must* be sent to your husband's attorney as soon as the preliminaries are taken care of.

### FIGURE 6.4
### REQUEST FOR DISCOVERY

**SIDNEY M. DeANGELIS**
Attorney At Law
Main Street Professional Building
Smithdale

January 26, 1987

Joseph Fenster, Esquire
Suite 500
Fidelity Building
Smithdale, _____

Re: <u>Henderson v. Henderson</u>

Dear Joe:

In order for my client to effectively pursue her rights under the Divorce Code, she must be able to examine certain books and records relative to your client's earning capacity and net worth.

I am attaching hereto a <u>partial</u> list of documents which our accountant and I would like to review and copy. Please let me know if we can do this within the next seven days.

        If, for any reason, your client will not agree to
this discovery, let me know and I will file a Discovery
Petition with the Court seeking an Order directing him
to cooperate.

        Your client's cooperation will be productive in
permitting settlement discussions to commence at an early
stage and further to avoid large bills for counsel fees.
In this connection, you might want to advise him that my
hourly rate is $150.

                        Sincerely,

                        SIDNEY M. DE ANGELIS

SMD:e
cc: Mrs. Margo Henderson


Personal Income Tax Returns (Form 1040) for the past five
years;

Corporate Income Tax Returns (Form 1120) for the past
five years;

All tax returns for any partnership in which he has an
interest (Form 1065) for the past five years;

All financial statements prepared for Henderson Electronics,
Inc., by the company's accounting firm for the past five
years;

Your client's personal cancelled checks, bank statements,
and checkbook stubs for the past five years;

Cancelled checks, bank statements, and checkbook stubs for
Henderson Electronics, Inc., for the past five years;

The cash receipts and cash disbursements ledgers of
Henderson Electronics, Inc., for the past five years;

All of your client's life and casualty insurance policies;

The general ledger for Henderson Electronics, Inc., for
the past five years;

Copies of all American Express and Visa or other credit
card bills and individual vouchers for credit cards in
the name of HEI or your client individually for the past
five years.

When you get a copy of this letter you will be very pleased to
have spent $15 for this one-tenth hour of professional services.
When your husband gets a copy of it he will realize again that you
may not "break" after all.

And you will begin to take control.

(By the way, some states have adopted mandatory disclosure,

where the defendant spouse has to produce the documents the plaintiff lawyer wants to examine. Other states exercise discretionary disclosure—the court can order it or deny it. For purposes of this discussion, assume that the *Henderson* case takes place in a state where discovery is discretionary.)

By now you may be asking whether your husband will be angry at you over the various stipulations and court orders your attorney is insisting on (freezing the assets, making sure he doesn't take the car away, continuing insurance coverage, asking for discovery). Answer: Oh boy, will he get angry! The better your attorney is the angrier your husband will be. He may become livid enough to call and threaten you with oblivion if you insist on "harassing" him in this awful manner. But you're not Chicken Little, and the sky isn't falling. You know it, and he knows you know it. *Your husband's feelings don't count anymore.* What counts is the underlying financial security of your family. What counts is your taking control of your own financial destiny.


## GET A CUSTODY AND VISITATION AGREEMENT
The other thing you should do at the outset is define with your husband what visitation rights he will have during the divorce proceedings.

Your attorney will tell you that while it may take years for all property and alimony rights to be decided it will take just a few months for the court to rule on your husband's request for custody or visitation, in the event you and he can't reach agreement about the children.

Therefore, the very first thing you and your husband must do is attempt to *avoid custody and visitation litigation* by working out reasonable and liberal visitation for him.

Your attorney must get a stipulation that you will have *primary custody* of the children, at least until the court rules otherwise. This means that the kids live with you. This stipulation must also include the specific visitation schedule your husband will have until the final hearing. The first part, primary custody, is vitally important to you. It avoids, at least for the present, the nightmare of a custody fight. The second part, a visitation schedule, is vital to your husband. If he doesn't get a fair visitation schedule at the outset, he may go berserk and begin a custody battle.

It has been my experience that the shock of a breakup encourages men to "strike back" at their wives by demanding custody of the children, when what they really want is more liberal visitation than their wives have agreed to.

Think what it's like for your husband to pack up his clothes and leave the home in which his children live. I assure you that it is devastating and many men never get over it. Therefore, sit down with your husband, preferably *before* separation, and hold out the olive branch:

> Roger, I know how difficult it's going to be for you with regard to the children. I know that you love them and they love you. I want you to know that I will not interfere with that. I mean that sincerely. I promise you that I will do everything in my power to foster that relationship.
>
> As soon as you find an apartment, I think we should sit down and tell the children that they will be visiting you and that they will see almost as much of you as they have in the past.
>
> Of course it won't be easy for them to understand this, but I am going to do everything I can to help them get through this very difficult period. Roger, we may fight over the money from now until kingdom come, but I will never fight you in your attempts to see and love the children.

Working out a temporary stipulation for visitation is as important to him as food and shelter are to you. If, for whatever reason, you give him a hard time on visitation you will find yourself fighting in the courts for years in a bloodbath you will regret.

---

### TIP
Never use denial of visitation as a weapon, or the granting of visitation as a reward.

---

Your husband has as much right to see the children as you do, and the mere fact that you may be their primary custodian and live in the same house with them does not give you the moral or legal right to make it difficult for him to do so.

At the same time, you don't want to be sitting down at dinner with the kids one night and see Roger coming up the driveway. *You need a visitation schedule as much as he does.*

So resolve the visitation issue right away with a *temporary schedule of visitation* (see Figure 6.5), which is usually approved by the courts. (For our purposes, I'm assuming that your husband and you will be living in the same community and that the children are under twelve years old.)

## FIGURE 6.5
### STIPULATION OF COUNSEL
### (SCHEDULE OF VISITATION)

```
In the Family Court of Smith County, _____


Margo Henderson                    Custody Case - 87-756
            Plaintiff
     vs.

Roger Henderson
            Defendant

              Stipulation of Counsel

     AND NOW, this 23rd day of January, 1987, it is hereby
agreed and stipulated by and between Sidney M. De Angelis,
Esquire, counsel for the Plaintiff, Margo Henderson, and
Joseph Fenster, Esquire, counsel for the Defendant, Roger
Henderson, that the primary custody of the minor children,
Jeffrey and Jennifer Henderson, will be in the Plaintiff,
Margo Henderson, and the the Defendant, Roger Henderson,
shall have the following rights of visitation:

a.   Commencing every Friday at 5 p.m. and ending every
     Sunday at 6 p.m. for three successive weekends.

b.   On the fourth weekend, the children shall remain in
     the custody of their mother and on the fifth weekend
     the foregoing visitation will resume.

c.   The defendant shall have the additional right, during
     the fourth weekend, to visit with his children from
     12 until 5 p.m. on each Saturday.

d.   The defendant shall have the right to uninterrupted
     telephone communication with his children, so long as
     it does not interfere with their sleeping hours or
     school work.
```

e. The plaintiff shall consult with the defendant with regard to any school problem which may affect the children, and shall keep the defendant advised of any medical, dental, or psychiatric treatment they may need.

f. The parties agree to divide all holidays between them.

g. The defendant shall have additional visitation with his children on his birthday and on Father's Day.

h. In addition thereto, the defendant shall enjoy such further visitation as the parties may mutually agree upon.

This order is without prejudice to the rights of either party with respect to final custody or with respect to a final visitation order, and shall remain in effect until changed by written order of this court.

_____          _____
Margo Henderson                      Roger Henderson

_____          _____
Attorney for Margo Henderson         Attorney for Roger Henderson

And now, this 23rd day of January, 1987, the foregoing stipulation is approved and made an Order of this Court.

By the Court:

_____
Thomas, J. White, J.

## DATING

Another reason you have to know when your husband is expected has to do with dating. What happens if some night you're watching a movie with your date, there's a knock on the door, and He-e-e-e-e-re's Roger?

Legally, you can date from the moment you separate. Some states, however, may consider your dating "misconduct" in deciding alimony and property division, but even those states refer to "misconduct" while you live with your husband, not to post-separation misconduct.

But never mind what the law says—here's the De Angelis Law of Dating:

1. Don't start dating seven minutes after he leaves. Otherwise, his lawyer will try to prove you knew the guy *before* the separation. He won't be able to do it, but you don't need the aggravation in court.
2. Don't let the dating get "splashy." Ostentatious gifts and big parties with strolling violinists are no-nos. (If you meet a guy like this, you may not care how much you get in your divorce case).
3. Don't let the guy sleep over—not even in the guest room. This is for the children's sake, but even if you don't have children, wait till your case is over before choosing a new roommate.
4. Don't walk into the courtroom with a suntan. You'll be shocked to see your vacation pal sitting in the front row under *subpoena* (trying to hide *his* suntan).
5. A general rule about your dating: Shhhh!

## HE CAN DATE ALL HE WANTS; YOU SHOULDN'T

The law says that either party can have their own personal life once they're separated. Don't you believe it!

*You* have to be careful, but he doesn't. *You* can't do anything glitzy or showy, but he can. You have to be quiet about your dating; he can have a harem and show off his women in public.

Remember those three little words?

*It's not fair!*

Whether you like it or not, whether it's fair or not, watch out for the double standard. It hasn't died yet.

For all of these reasons, therefore, get right to the visitation problem. Sit down with your attorney and come up with a *temporary* schedule of visitation.

### Chronology: Henderson v. Henderson, January 1987

I've known Joe Fenster for fifteen years, and we've had a lot of cases together. I know all of his moves, and he knows most of mine. As soon as I filed Margo's divorce complaint I called to tell him that I was in the case. He gave me his usual opening.

Fenster:  I thought you didn't take these five-and-dime cases, De Angelis.

Me: OK Joe, it's a nothing case, but let's get together early next week to lay some ground rules—possession, support, visitation, the preliminaries.

Fenster: Support? No way! You must be kidding! Henderson is practically bankrupt! You know she threw him out.

Me: Sure Joe. Is Tuesday at 9:00 OK? I'll bring the bagels—you get the coffee.

Fenster: The guy's broke—how you gonna get paid, huh?

Me: Tuesday at 9:00, Joe. Have a good weekend.

Our meeting went as I expected. For forty-five minutes Fenster told me how bad the business was, how Margo could make $30,000 a year as a school teacher, and how poor Roger's heart was broken and he would have to see a psychiatrist. Then we got down to business. He agreed to the following stipulations:

1. Roger would stay away from the house.
2. Roger would get all of his personal belongings out in five days.
3. Roger would pay $200 a week plus all of the bills as temporary support until we got to court (for the final order).
4. Roger would maintain the medical and dental coverage until we got to court.
5. Roger would let Margo drive the "company" Cutlass without interference until we got to court.
6. Roger would carry her automobile insurance until we got to court.
7. Roger would continue the life insurance and not borrow against it.
8. Roger (and Margo) would accept a mutual freeze of the major assets.

In fact, Fenster was very affable ("Look, Sid, we don't want her to get so scared and mad that she won't settle—hey, he's a real down-to-earth guy. He doesn't want to hurt her, you know, he wants to settle real soon.")

But when I asked for discovery, Fenster turned mean, and he wasn't acting.

Fenster: No way, De Angelis, no way! This isn't a big case and we don't want you to run up big fees while you look for something that isn't there. We'll send you the tax returns, but that's it. I don't give a damn what you file!

Me: (smiling) OK Joe, I'll have the stipulations here for your signature at 10:00 tomorrow.

Fenster: Why don't we settle the case now, Sid? No use in running up big fees.

Me: (still smiling) As soon as I get discovery, Joe.

We shook hands and I left. I stopped in his reception room and called my office:

Marge, type up all the stipulations with the exception of discovery. And the amount for support is $200. Everything else is the same as I dictated yesterday. And we'll file the petition for discovery later today. I'll be back in fifteen minutes.

---

## CHECKLIST: THE PRELIMINARIES
---

1. Make sure your husband leaves, takes all of his belongings and agrees to stay away from the house (except for visitation).
2. Get a temporary alimony and support order as soon as possible; if he won't agree to one, go to court.
3. Make sure you and the children are covered by medical insurance.
4. Make sure your car doesn't get "stolen."
5. Nail the household items down.
6. Make sure you're covered by his life insurance policies.
7. Go after immediate discovery.
8. Arrange for him to have *liberal* visitation. Avoid a fight over how often he sees the children.

Now let's see if your case can't be settled before you get into litigation.

Seven

# Why Can't My Case Be Settled Right Away?

By this point you will want to know why you and your husband can't settle your divorce case at once, without litigation and thousands of dollars in lawyer's fees. After all, there is nothing to stop you from arriving at an agreement on all major issues, and both of you are fearful of a long, acrimonious, and expensive court battle. So why can't you do it *now*? The answer is, simply, "It can't be settled now." Here's why.

### *Chronology: Henderson v. Henderson, Telephone Conversation, Monday, 10:30 A.M.*

Joe: How ya doin', De Angelis?

Me: Good, Joe. Still mad at me?

Joe: No-o-o-o way, Sid. Look, I got good news for you! Roger wants to settle the whole damn case—he says Margo wants it over with. He wants the four of us to meet. He thinks you'll realize what a nice guy he is once you meet him.

Me: (looking at my book) How about next Wednesday at 11:00?

Joe: See ya, pal.

## *Telephone Conversation, fifteen minutes later*

Me:    Margo, this is Sidney. How are you?

Margo:    Fine, Sidney. What's up?

Me:    Well, Fenster called. We filed a petition for discovery, and all of a sudden Fenster says Roger wants to settle—he doesn't want a long fight.

Margo:    Oh Sidney, I can't believe it! I'm so happy! You mean it's all over so soon!

Me:    Margo, calm down. All it means is that Fenster and Roger want a four-way meeting with us on Wednesday at 11:00—at Joe's office. It's not over by any means, so don't get your hopes up. And don't call Roger.

Margo:    Sidney, that's *wonderful* news—I'm thrilled!

Me:    Margo, if I were you I wouldn't be so thrilled. Anyhow, be here at 10:30 on Wednesday and we'll go to Fenster's office together.

We didn't wait long in Fenster's waiting room before the secretary told us to go right into Joe's conference room. Margo was bright-eyed and bushy-tailed, and I felt like I was about to enter a Turkish bazaar—for the fiftieth time.

I didn't like Roger when I saw him, and he didn't like me. He was a big guy—well over six feet tall and must have weighed 260–280. He was smoking a fat cigar and looked as arrogant as a storm trooper. I didn't like him, his bushy mustache, or his practiced machismo at all. And I hated his ugly wing tips. Fenster was all smiles and greeted Margo like the maitre'd at a fancy restaurant. Margo was all smiles too—she looked like a child about to open up her Christmas presents.

Fenster:    Hello, Mrs. Henderson. I'm Joe Fenster.

Me:    And I'm Sidney De Angelis, Roger. (Roger glares at me, says nothing.)

Fenster:    I'm glad you came over today. It's important that we try to avoid costly litigation here and see if we can't settle the case. I take it there's no possibility of reconciliation? (Roger glares again, Margo looks up at the ceiling.)

Fenster:  OK. Well Roger and I have spent some time preparing a settlement proposal I consider fair and reasonable. (At this point, I become bored.)

Me:  Sure Joe, what do you have in mind?

Fenster handed out copies of a typewritten proposal, smiling like an undertaker at a funeral. This is what was on the paper:

## FIGURE 7.1
## SETTLEMENT PROPOSAL

*Fenster, Clark, & Williams*
*Attorneys At Law*
*Suite 500, Fidelity Building*
*Smithdale*

*Joseph Fenster*
*James C. Clark*
*Steward G. Williams*

HENDERSON v. HENDERSON

Settlement proposal submitted without prejudice on February 11, 1987.

1. Mrs. Henderson to get house and contents on Oak Drive;

2. Mr. Henderson to pay mortgage payment for six months;

3. Mr. Henderson to pay child support of $200 per week until children go off to college, or are emancipated; support to be reduced by one-third as each child leaves;

4. Each party to keep bank accounts and other assets in their own name;

5. Parties to share college tuition and other expenses 50-50;

6. Mrs. Henderson to get title to Cutlass;

7. Each party to pay their own legal fees and costs of litigation.

8. Divorce to be issued within 30 days.

I looked at Margo: her face had turned ashen. Then I winked.

|        |                                                                                                                                                                                                                                                             |
|--------|---|
| Me:    | Well Joe, this is certainly a very reasonable offer and both Mrs. Henderson and I are eager to settle this case, but what about the business? What's it worth, would you say? (Roger really glares at me.)                                                    |
| Fenster: | It's worth nothin', Sid. The book value shows maybe 20 or 25, but who wants to buy a wholesale electronic components business these days? There are no buyers, you know that.                                                                               |
| Me:    | Yeah I know, but I think we ought to put settlement talk on the back burner until we get some appraisals.                                                                                                                                                    |
| Fenster: | (snapping at me—for Roger's benefit) I thought this was a negotiating session.                                                                                                                                                                             |
| Me:    | It is, but we have to postpone meaningful negotiations until our business valuation expert, Jay Fisher, concludes his appraisal of HEI. And until we get a list of all the assets in this case, regardless of title, and some serious appraisals.             |
| Roger: | (who has finally lost his temper) Look, De Angelis, if you want a fight you've got it. I don't care if it takes ten years, but if you want to settle, OK, let's settle. (Roger walks over to Margo) Don't you want to settle, Margo?                          |
| Margo: | (remembering what I told her to say) Only when Sidney has all the facts, Roger.                                                                                                                                                                              |
| Me:    | (getting up) Look Joe, get me a list of every asset and put down what you think each one is worth. Then I'll have Fisher's people go through the company tax returns, books and records, visit the warehouse, talk to Roger, and come up with a business valuation. In the meantime, let's keep in touch. (Margo and I smile at them and walk out. Who says you can't take control?) |

You are probably wondering now whether Roger and his lawyer expected us to say, "OK, it's a deal." Well, Fenster didn't expect it; he and I have had that conversation ten times in the last five years. (I call it the "Divorce Minuet"; we dance a bit but we don't really touch.) Actually, Joe is a bright lawyer, but he has a cramped brain.

On the other hand, Roger expected Margo to jump for joy when she saw his offer. Like most businessmen who find themselves involved in divorce litigation, Roger didn't believe that his business would be part of the marital pot. Sure he can read the divorce code, but he develops temporary blindness when he sees the words ". . . and the Court shall equitably divide the marital property." And as far as paying alimony after the divorce, that's against his religion. What most husbands believe is that by deeding their wives the marital home they are giving up 50 percent of its value to their wives who should grab it as a complete and *total* settlement.

So your husband has no intention of *settling* the case at the first four-way meeting—unless he can *settle on his terms*. Therefore he will make a ridiculous offer to see whether you grab it. Part of it is playacting; he wants to appear generous and conciliatory. Then if you turn it down he can always say, "She doesn't want to settle." Does every husband play this game? Not every husband—just most.

Let's stop for a minute and analyze the average businessman faced with divorce negotiations. First of all, he approaches the negotiations almost devoid of emotion. At most, he will be a little anxious but no more so than if he was in the plumbing supply business and bidding on a carload of toilets.

Why? Within the first few months of the litigation process, he's in no hurry. He's probably paying less in temporary alimony and child support than it cost him to run the household when the family lived together.

So your husband will try to make you feel it's your fault if the case isn't settled at the first meeting. This is how it will go:

### *Telephone Conversation, Tuesday, 6:30 A.M.*

Roger:   Margo, I've been thinking all night. I couldn't sleep. Look, your lawyer wants to run up big fees—that's clear, isn't it?

Margo:   I—uh—don't know, Roger.

Roger:   Sure it is. Fenster wants to talk settlement, and all De Angelis wants to do is run up bills for experts—who's gonna pay for them, anyhow?

Margo:   I don't know, Roger.

Roger:   Well, don't let him push you around. He'll eat up your settlement in unnecessary fees and expenses. Call him and tell him you want it settled right away.

Now, that sounds reasonable doesn't it? And it is, except it won't work. In the first few months following separation, your attorney has *no idea* how to settle your case, for there simply is no knowledge of what the marital assets are or what they're worth. (In a later chapter, you will see how much time your attorney has to spend on *discovery* in order to find out what your case is worth.) Obviously if you and your husband have been fully communicative with regard to marital assets, or you know that all there is is the house and $100,000 in a CD, then you and your attorney certainly can discuss settlement at an early stage of the game. But if, as in most cases, you have no idea what the assets are worth, or indeed *what* the assets are, the first meeting will be nothing more than a gathering to schedule other meetings.

And yet, that's important.

In a divorce case you can sit back and shoot at each other for years and years until a judge finally holds a final hearing and decides who gets what. Everyone knows that there is not too much lawyers can do to speed up the process of litigation. Everyone knows this, but the only way to ease this long, agonizing process is to have a complete and full exchange of financial information at the very outset. You can't bid your hand unless you can see your cards.

## WHAT YOUR HUSBAND CAN DO TO EXPEDITE AN EARLY SETTLEMENT

If your husband really wants to get it over with quickly, he should:

1. Have his accountant provide your accountant with *all* of his books and records, tax returns, financial statements, canceled checks; that is, every single piece of paper he has accumulated in the past five years of his business or profession; and
2. Submit himself to depositions (a series of questions your attorney will present to him under oath before a court reporter); these questions and answers form the basis of the discovery process.

If your husband does all this and your attorney, accountant, and business valuation expert are satisfied that they have all the information they need, certainly you have a foundation for early settlement negotiations. This type of cooperation, however, is rare. Instead, most husbands I'm afraid, will sit back and play "Defense," saying, "OK, we've got to settle this case, right? OK. I'll give you the house and that's it. Isn't that fair?" The answer is, of course, it might or might not be fair; you can't know until you have all of the financial information you need.

If you turn down his initial offer—which you should—your husband will say, "She's a greedy bitch!" Most husbands will make it impossible for you to come up with the numbers you need for a fair settlement. They will conspire with their attorneys to drag you through months and months and years of the discovery process, hoping you will surrender. They will urge their attorneys not to cooperate and they will hide or destroy records. In these cases, you can't settle anything. Despite this, you must keep the lines of communication open, and your lawyer must keep asking for the records.

Now let's consider whether you and your husband can avoid a long and costly divorce fight through *mediation*.

## WHAT IS DIVORCE MEDIATION?

In many major cities, divorce mediation clinics have been established to assist couples involved in bitter marital property disputes. The purpose of such clinics is to save the unhappy couple untold emotional damage and excessive attorney's fees. The mediator, then, represents the *couple* rather than either party, working to bring about a fair and quick settlement.

Usually mediators have been trained in the social sciences—psychology, family therapy, or social work—and they sincerely believe that mediation is better than litigation. Of course it is, however, while I applaud their good intentions and sincere efforts, such practitioners simply do not have the requisite knowledge of divorce law, pension law, accounting, real estate, business valuation, or any of the legal and economic concepts underlying equitable distribution and community property.

Suppose, for example, you and your husband own a home, a few bank accounts, and nothing else. A mediator can say, "Look, let's avoid the bloodbath. Let's sell the house and divide the proceeds 50–50." You don't need a mediator to do that.

But what if there's a business to be valued along with a pension plan and you can't make it without alimony for at least five years? How can a mediator value the husband's business and then negotiate equitable distribution based on its fair market value as well as the present value of the pension plan? How can a mediator determine alimony needs? If the marital assets are substantial and your husband is a "tough guy" you believe is dishonest about what he owns, mediation helps *him,* not you.

### Does Divorce Mediation Work?

Divorce mediation is a nice idea, but it doesn't work. First, you and your husband generally do not have *equal bargaining power.* Second, the divorce code and its interpretation require professionally trained and experienced divorce lawyers. Third, it is usually not in your best interest to have nonspecialists venture into the areas of equitable distribution, business valuation, and alimony.

### What About Arbitration?

Would it be sensible for you and your husband to *arbitrate* your marital dispute? After all, the arbitrators, professional "dispute settlers," will be fair and independent, and it won't take years and cost thousands of dollars.

Sure it's sensible, but ordinarily arbitration won't work for divorce litigation. In the first place, you need a trained and experienced advocate to present evidence; that means a divorce attorney. Second, you need a trained and experienced authority to evaluate the evidence and apply the divorce code to the facts of your case; that means a judge.

The American Arbitration Association, excellent at solving commercial and construction disputes, has a large pool of independent lawyers, engineers, and other specialists available to solve almost any legal dispute—except in the area of divorce. You get the picture. I'm afraid arbitration won't work.

## CAN YOU AND YOUR HUSBAND AGREE TO CUT DOWN ON LITIGATION COSTS?

Sure. Let's call it *cooperative litigation*. If you and your husband conclude that each of you requires a divorce lawyer and various expert witnesses, you can cut down the time and cost of litigation by agreeing to:

1. A *complete* exchange of all financial information, *without any exceptions*
2. The use of only one expert (*one* real estate appraiser to value your home, *one* pension expert, *one* business valuation expert, etc.)

With cooperative litigation, there's no agreement on how much money is in the pot, simply an agreement to limit expenses. It doesn't happen often. That hard-headed businessman husband of yours doesn't care how much he spends for *his* business valuation expert (after all, he wants a low valuation).

This approach rarely works unless both parties are very, very reasonable.

---

## CHECKLIST: EARLY SETTLEMENT

---

1. A four-way meeting without full and complete prior discovery is a waste of time. It's nothing more than a social event.
2. Mediation doesn't work unless you and your husband are on the same economic and emotional footing.
3. If your husband wants an early settlement, he has to open up his books and records—putting *everything* on the table.

Now let's discuss what to do when your husband wants to talk directly with *you* about settlement. What should you do?

## Eight

# Dealing with the Enemy: How to Treat Him

Your husband would rather negotiate with *you* than with your lawyer. You don't know divorce law; he doesn't have to pay $150 to $200 an hour to talk to you; and he believes that in the end he can make you do what he wants. This short but important chapter focuses on how to deal with your husband during divorce litigation.

Contact with him is inevitable and can occur at any time or place: over the telephone, at child visitation "pickup and delivery," in the courthouse corridors, or at four-way settlement meetings— almost anytime *he* wants to have contact.

I usually suggest that if they can afford it my clients get a private unlisted phone number for themselves, leaving the old number intact so their husband can call the children. That way, clients won't be bothered.

### NO FRATERNIZATION!
Whether or not you get a private line, the rules are simple: don't talk to him and don't fraternize!

Consider this situation, in my experience a typical one. Your husband is a self-made man who has worked up to his present position after years of hard work. He is used to giving orders and getting his way. If he's a Type A behavior personality on top of this, he's not even used to negotiating.

He now finds himself in a situation where the woman he has dominated for fifteen years has suddenly turned into a tigress. She's hired a smart, tenacious attorney, and it appears—to him at least—that the divorce law favors women. He's faced with conditions he can't control, and he doesn't like it. He doesn't like you or your lawyer. The few times he has seen your lawyer, he has sensed that he is on to him and will not be bulldozed. He feels not only that he is being "taken," but that he is being left out of the ring while the two lawyers box. He misses pushing you around and arguing with you. The only way he can get any contact with you now is by coming around to talk to you, which he will do in the guise of sincerity: "Let's settle this, hon. I don't want to hurt you." Most likely all he wants is to get into an argument: "You haven't changed. I don't know why I bother to talk to you!" Then he'll walk out and slam the door.

So you find yourself in a second or third four-way meeting where once again your lawyer repeats your demands for settlement, which haven't changed since the first four-way meeting. Your husband and his lawyer continue to protest that he just can't afford to pay what you demand, and the meeting ends in frustration on both sides.

That same night he calls to "talk to the children," after which he gets you on the phone:

Roger:  Look, Margo, that farce the lawyers are playing out is costing us a lot of money. Money which should go to the children. I think they're just building up fees. Why can't you and I settle this case?

It sounds reasonable to you and you *are* concerned about your lawyer's fees, so you go "into the thicket" with him:

You:  Well, Roger, we've told you time and time again what I need and what the children need and you always say you can't afford it when you and I know you can. So it's really up to you.

Roger:   Well, why don't I come over tonight or why don't you meet me
         for a drink, we'll see if we can settle it. I really don't hate you,
         and I want to see you and the children happy and I want to get it
         over with. Let's meet for a drink.

So off you go. Two hours later you're back home, furious at him,
furious at yourself for going to see him, and more confused than
ever. In good faith you tried to settle your case directly with your
husband, even though you're at a terrible disadvantage in negotiating with him face to face. It's something you've always had
difficulty doing, and now that you're dealing with the economic
complexities of divorce law, you can't possible represent yourself.
What was accomplished? You got your feelings hurt by talking to
him, but worse than that, *your husband has driven a wedge
between you and your lawyer*, negotiating by day and manipulat-
ing by night.

    Let us suppose you and your husband are fighting specifically
over how long you can live in the house with the children until it's
time to sell. Your youngest child is three years old, and you want at
least fifteen years before you have to sell the house. Your husband
wants the house sold now and will get, let's say, 40 percent of the
proceeds, which he needs for his business. At a negotiating session,
his lawyer has offered you five years, but you stick to fifteen. It
goes on and on, with your lawyer arguing that the children should
not be uprooted for fifteen years and his lawyer arguing that you
can't sit on a valuable asset and deprive his client of money. That
meeting goes nowhere, and everyone realizes that the issue won't
be decided by the court for at least three more years. Nothing is
settled.

    Later that evening, sitting across from you, Roger looks you
straight in the eye:

Look, Margo, you know my business is cash poor. I want to take
care of you, I really do, but after all, I've got a life to lead too. I
think the kids will be all right to move when they're about eight or
ten years old. So why don't we settle this thing and sell the house
when Jeff is ten years old. You'll probably be remarried then and

supported by your husband, and I'll be able to get some money for my business. Come on, hon, let's settle the case.

You feel weak, vulnerable, and confused. You realize you shouldn't make any agreement without your attorney, so in order to stop the conversation without his feeling rebuffed, you say, "Well, let me think about it." *Those few words, "let me think about it," are a signal to your husband that he can disregard what your lawyer says during the day and get to you at night.* At that moment, he may as well tell his attorney, "Don't even bother anymore with negotiating sessions with her attorney, I can take care of her." And he will. He will call you, take you out to dinner, ply you with wine, and keep talking about five years versus fifteen years until finally you will say, "OK, let's make it seven." Of course that doesn't settle anything because then he'll start on the amount of child support because he now knows:

1. He is eroding your confidence in your attorney.
2. He is wearing you down.
3. He can get you to agree to things your attorney would not let you agree to if he were present.
4. You're going to act as your own attorney from now on.

---

## TIP
Don't talk to your husband about the case. Never act as your own attorney.

---

You can talk to him about the children—their health, school, athletic activities, and the nice things they say about him. Or you can ask about his family. *Never* should you discuss the litigation— equitable distribution, alimony, or whether your lawyer is better than his.

Here are some more "don'ts" to remember when dealing with your husband:

1. *Don't* talk to him about your dating. "Roger, I'm on my way to Acapulco with Herb, I can't talk to you." Bad. It doesn't add anything to the settlement discussions. It is hostile and you should avoid this kind of "nya-nya" talk.
2. *Don't* date him. In 90 percent of the cases, his dating you during litigation is a malicious attempt to undermine your confidence in your legal position.
3. *Don't* fall for the "Let's-take-the-children-to-dinner" or "Let's-take-the-children-to-the-amusement-park" routine. It will hurt you, him, and, worst of all, the children.
4. *Don't* call his friends, relatives, business associates, accountants, or anyone to complain that he is not being reasonable in the negotiations. This does no one any good. (If you can't resist the temptation, the judge may issue a restraining order to stop you from doing it again.)

Here is a list of "do's," and all of them concern the children.

1. If it's Father's Day, his birthday, or a religious holiday, have the children sign and mail a greeting card to their father.
2. Make sure that when they get report cards or papers from school they call their father to share the news. (You should mail him xeroxed copies.)
3. Have copies of significant medical reports on the children sent to him immediately.
4. Make sure that he gets a ticket—two in case he is dating—so that he can share in the joy of the children's activities. (He doesn't have to sit next to you, you know.)
5. Always speak to the children in a pleasant, friendly tone about their father no matter how you may really feel about him. Do not carry the slings and arrows of litigation into your home. Always remember that although you and your husband are fighting in court over money, the children and their father are not litigants. No matter how you feel about him, don't allow these feelings to color the way in which the children see their father.
6. If he is dating or living with someone, include that person in your conversations with the children. ("Jennifer, it was very

nice of Tracey to buy that blouse for you last weekend. Don't you think you should write her a little note and thank her for it?")

Remember, you've got to get through this divorce with integrity and self-esteem. Hurting the children or enlisting them as fellow combatants will not accomplish this. *Their father will not always be your husband, but he will always be their father.* Teach this to your children as diligently as you can; it will be worth it in the long run.

But once you've discussed the children or his mother's health, you have nothing else to talk about. *Do not discuss your divorce case.*

If you and Roger could sit down and intelligently talk about legal issues, you wouldn't be in divorce litigation. You wouldn't need two attorneys.

After you hire an attorney, put your trust in him. He represents you and your children. Your husband is not looking out for your best interests. He is the enemy. Sorry, but it's true. SO DON'T TALK TO HIM.

Now let's talk about your rights. What *are* you entitled to?

# Nine

# "Sidney, What Are My Rights?"

### Chronology: Henderson v. Henderson, Late February 1987

Margo: Sidney, now that we've gone through the charade of settlement, what's next?

Me: Well, I think it's time to answer the question you asked when you first came in. Remember, "What are my rights?"

Margo: You said the question was premature.

Me: It was then, but now we've got the temporary orders you need so you can think clearly. We're on our way to discovery, and we're getting a court date for a temporary alimony and child support order. So although we're still in the fact-gathering stage I can begin to answer your question.

    1. You (and Roger) are entitled to a fair distribution of the marital assets—it's called equitable distribution in this state.

    2. You're entitled to child support for Jeffrey and Jennifer until they are "emancipated," that is, marry, leave for college, or go to work.

    3. You're entitled to temporary alimony going back to the date of your complaint for divorce and continuing until you get your divorce decree.

    4. I've filed a petition for interim counsel fees and we're

waiting for a court date. We'll ask the court to give you a temporary award of attorney's fees for me and for the expense of hiring the CPA and the business valuation expert.

5. As you know, you're entitled to ask for discovery so the experts and I can look through and copy Roger's canceled checks, tax returns, every paper we feel is important; we've filed for that, too.

6. If we can't settle this case before trial, we'll eventually litigate before a judge. At that hearing, the judge will divide the assets and may award you permanent alimony for a fixed number of years after divorce.

7. There will also be a final award of counsel fees, expert witness expenses, court costs, and all miscellaneous costs you've incurred from Day One.

8. Roger may also be ordered to retain you as the beneficiary of his life insurance policies for a certain period of years.

9. The judge will decide who pays all the unpaid marital bills and loans you and Roger ran up *before* the separation.

10. And right before banging the gavel, the court will issue a divorce decree so you and Roger will be free to remarry. As you know, judges in this county will not issue a divorce decree until the economic case is decided. So you can't be divorced until that happens and neither, of course, can Roger. The two of you could agree to an earlier decree, but there's no sense in that, so the last thing the judge will do is divorce you.

Margo: OK. I understand all of that. But will I get everything on that list?

Me: It depends. The first thing you must understand is that there is no law book or legal chart that tells us what you'll actually receive. It's all a matter of interpretation of the divorce code based on the facts of your case.

Margo: But aren't there cases that will give us an idea of what I will get?

Me: Not really, Margo. The possible factual situations are infinite. Cases already decided only give us guidelines of what a judge did in a particular situation.

Margo:   Well then, how does the judge know what property to give me?

Me:   Good question, long answer. Property division is a three-part process, *IVD.*

Margo:   *IVD?*

Me:   Yes. *I*dentification, *V*aluation, and *D*istribution or allocation. First, we have to identify or list all assets you believe to be in the marital pot. They are the components of the economic partnership you and Roger created from the day you were married to the day you separated.

By the way, this identification process is your responsibility. If Roger is hiding gold bars in Tanzania it's your responsibility to find and appraise them. The judge doesn't put Roger on the rack and tighten the screws until he tells us where he's hidden his assets. That's why we need discovery. And that may be why Roger is resisting it.

Margo:   Is equitable distribution the same as community property?

Me:   No. Some states say that all property that comes into the marriage is owned as community property and upon divorce is divided on a 50–50 basis.

In our state the law says all property acquired after marriage and up to the date of separation (except some gifts and inheritances) is *marital property and will be distributed on an equitable basis.* That includes HEI, his profit-sharing plan, *everything* he has. You could get 50 percent, more, or less.

Margo:   What do you mean, "except some gifts"?

Me:   Well, in our state gifts between you and Roger count as marital assets. They are identified, valued, and distributed. Gifts from others, your parents for instance, are *nonmarital* assets; they're yours and are not distributed.

Margo:   How does the court divide? What does it consider?

Me:   Margo, think "distribute," not "divide." The court doesn't divide each asset in half or thirds—it distributes the assets.

Margo:   What do you mean?

Me:   Well, the law doesn't say that everything you and Roger own must be divided—you don't have to sell your home and furniture and split the proceeds with Roger. You don't get a percentage of his business or of each investment.

What the court does is compute the marital pot and give you

a percentage of the *total* amount by awarding you specific assets and making up any difference in cash. Here, I'll put it on the blackboard for you.

| | |
|---|---:|
| *If* your home is worth $150,000 and the mortgage balance is, say, $50,000, we have a net equity of, | $100,000 |
| *If* his business is valued at $100,000 by our business valuation expert and the court accepts it, | 100,000 |
| *If* the furniture is valued at no more than | 10,000 |
| *If* you can prove there was a cigar box with $10,400 in cash | 10,400 |
| *If* you and Roger had bank accounts worth $7,500 on January 1, 1987 | 7,500 |
| *If* we can prove that Roger's company car, the Mercedes, is used by him for personal purposes, and if we get a valuation of | $20,000 |
| *If* your Cutlass is valued at | 5,000 |
| And, *if* we ever get into his books and records and find that he's got a profit-sharing plan worth | 35,000 |

Is there anything else that you know of?

Margo: No, I can't think of anything.

Me: Then we've got a marital pot that looks like this:

| | |
|---|---:|
| House (net) | $100,000 |
| HEI | 100,000 |
| Furniture | 10,000 |
| Cash in cigar box | 10,400 |
| Bank accounts | 7,500 |
| Mercedes | 20,000 |
| Cutlass | 5,000 |
| Profit-sharing plan | 35,000 |
| Estimate of total marital assets | $287,900 |
| | or |
| | $288,000 |

The judge now has to calculate the marital liabilities. We've already counted the mortgage on your home. What else did you and Roger owe before you separated?

Margo: Well, we fixed up the rec room and we owe about $10,000 on that.

Me: OK, Margo. The marital pot is down to $278,000. Any other liabilities, that is, debts?

Margo: Just what HEI owes to the banks.

Me: Which banks? What for?

Margo: Well, I remember Roger had me sign some papers for Citizens Bank a few years ago. They were buying a bunch of components—

Me: No, that's a business debt; it'll be reflected in the business valuation.

Margo: Oh yes, some credit card bills—I don't know how much because he gets the bills at the office—but they get paid pretty promptly—

Me: Well, we'll assume we're talking about $278,000. Now, let's assume the judge decides you should get 55 percent of the pot.

Margo: How does he get 55 percent?

Me: Later, Margo. Let's understand identification and valuation first. We'll talk about distribution later.

All right, now let's take 55 percent of $278,000; that's $152,900, say $153,000. Here's one way the judge can give you $153,000.

## Margo's Award

| | |
|---|---:|
| House | $100,000 |
| Furniture | 10,000 |
| Cutlass | 5,000 |
| Bank Accounts | 7,500 |
| | $122,500 |

*Plus:* $30,500 in three annual installments of $10,166, beginning one year after the court's adjudication.

So you see Margo, the bigger the marital pot, the more distribution you get. And remember, these figures are based on assumptions. His business may be worth much more than $100,000. We don't know at this point.

Margo: I understand, Sidney, but how would I pay the mortgage, assuming I got the house—that's $687 a month. And what about utilities—I mean, how do we eat?

Me:  Margo, that's what alimony and child support is all about. All I've shown you is the first part of your divorce, property division.

After the judge decides how much property and cash you get by way of equitable distribution, he'll turn to alimony. You'll have to testify about your needs, your employability, your health, and so on; then the judge will consider how you stack up on the seventeen so-called alimony factors.

After deciding whether you get alimony and if so for how long, the judge will decide how much Roger will have to contribute to my fees and the litigation expenses you will have incurred.

We'll go through the details later on, but that's basically what you're entitled to.

Margo walked over to the blackboard, studied the figures, walked around for a few seconds, and then studied the blackboard again. She pointed at the figure of $100,000 next to HEI.

Margo:  That's it, isn't it? That's the whole case, right there.

Me:  (grinning) Welcome to the American Academy of Matrimonial Lawyers, Margo!

Margo:  Look Sidney, when you say that marital assets are "assets acquired during the marriage" I don't understand—we're still married, aren't we?

Me:  Of course. You haven't been divorced yet. But since for purposes of identification the law defines marital assets as those acquired while you lived together—after the marriage *until separation*—anything acquired after the separation is nonmarital as long as it wasn't acquired with marital money.

Margo:  What about the grandfather clock I had before I married Roger? I bought it for my room at college.

Me:  That's not a marital asset, Margo. It wasn't acquired *during* the marriage. It's a *nonmarital*, or separate, asset just the same as the furniture you bought for Jeffrey's room last week.

Margo:  Do nonmarital assets count?

Me:     Sure, but they're not distributed. They were your separate
        property when you acquired them and they remain your
        separate property after the divorce. They're the same as a gift
        from your parents or an inheritance. But—and it's a *big* but—
        they count.

Margo:  How?

Me:     Well, let me give you an extreme example. Suppose you and
        Roger acquired only a VW and two sets of skis during the
        marriage, that you had no children, and that you both had
        good jobs. Now you're in a divorce and the court must divide
        up the property if you and Roger can't agree on an amicable
        solution.

        Ordinarily, the judge would value the assets—let's say in this
        example that the VW is worth $2,000—then award each of
        you one set of skis, give the car to Roger, and award you
        $1,000, or the other way around. A 50–50 split, more or less.

        But suppose before you get to court you inherit a million
        dollars or win the lottery for a million. It doesn't change the
        *I*—the identification—or the *V*—the valuation of your assets,
        but it certainly changes the *D*—the distribution. Now the
        judge would give Roger *all* of the assets. He'd get the car and
        both sets of skis. You'd keep your million. That would be an
        equitable distribution under those facts.

        Anyway, I'd like you to get started on a net worth statement.
        Fill it in as best you can, and when I see you next week we'll
        go over it. We have to file it soon.

Margo:  What do I put down for the value of his business? I don't know
        what it's worth.

Me:     Put a question mark there and I'll type in the words "subject to
        appraisal." That's why you need a business valuation expert.
        We'll talk about expert witnesses later.

Margo:  Does Roger have to file one, too?

Me:     Yes he does. But he'll stall—he'll never file one unless we force
        him to do it. If you have any questions on it, call me.

        By the way, Margo, have you told me *everything* you know
        about the assets or possible assets? I'll get to ask Roger about
        assets you may not know of, but he'll probably lie.

Margo:  I don't think there's anything else. I guess I don't really know.

Me:     OK. We'll find out later.

Two weeks later, Margo gave me a rough draft of what she considered to be her net worth statement. I dictated some changes, had it prepared, and filed it with the court on March 1, 1987 (see Figure 9.1).

## FIGURE 9.1
## MARGO'S NET WORTH STATEMENT

```
In the Family Court of Smith County, _____

Margo Henderson                                    87-1234
            Plaintiff
    vs.

Roger Henderson                         In Divorce
            Defendant

            Plaintiff's Net Worth Statement

                    Marital Assets
1.  Single family residence at 576 Oak Drive, Smithdale    $150,000

2.  Corporate stock of Henderson Electronics, Inc.
    (100% owned by Defendant)*                             _____

3.  Various furniture at 576 Oak Drive*                    _____

4.  Various bank accounts (in possession of Defendant)       7,500

5.  1986 Mercedes (in possession of Defendant)              20,000

6.  1985 Cutlass (in possession of Plaintiff)                5,000

7.  Profit-sharing plan (in possession of Defendant)*      _____

8.  Cash in cigar box (in possession of Plaintiff)          10,400

                    Marital Liabilities
1.  First mortgage on 576 Oak Drive, Smithdale             $ 50,000

2.  Home Improvement Loan                                     9,500

    Separate (non-marital) Property Belonging to Plaintiff
1.  Various items of jewelry received as gifts from parents
    throughout marriage.*

2.  Grandfather's clock purchased before marriage.*

3.  Various items of children's furniture purchased after separation.*

*   These items are subject to appraisal so that this statement will
    be amended to include appraisal figures.  In addition, the Defendant
    has not made a full disclosure of his assets and Plaintiff
    reserves the right to further amend this statement after discovery
    is completed.
```

Now, because equitable distribution is one of the most important rights you're entitled to, and I want you to understand it thoroughly, I want to spend some time on the details.

# Ten

# Equitable Distribution: Division of Marital Property

## MARRIAGE IS NOW AN ECONOMIC CONTRACT

In America, marriage has always been considered a legal contract. Each state had laws governing marriage before there was divorce legislation. In the past two decades, however, marriage has also come to be recognized as *an economic contract* or, more specifically, a partnership. Gradually, state legislatures began adding words to the marriage vows that held certain implications:

> I take you as my lawful wedded wife.
> I take you as my lawful wedded husband.

> *From this moment on we will have an economic partnership. Everything we buy or acquire will be owned by the two of us as partners. It makes no difference in whose name we buy or acquire these items, or who put up the purchase money—it will belong to the partnership, regardless of title, . . .*

> . . . in sickness and in health, for better or worse, until death [*or divorce*] do us part.

Of course these words are not written out as such, but are implied by virtue of the equitable distribution or community property statutes that, with the exception of Mississippi, are now law in every state.

Therefore when a husband and wife conclude that their emotional contract is broken and that they should also terminate their legal contract, the law steps in and says, "OK, but what about your *economic contract*? If that's broken, who gets what?" So divorce is about the dissolution of the marriage partnership, not merely the breaking of the marriage contract. In fact, every divorce action is a two-stage proceeding: the *minor* part is dissolving the marriage, which means you're free to remarry; the *major* part has to do with economics—that is, a division of the partnership assets and income.

To understand the distinction between the legal and economic termination of marriage, let's talk about what is popularly referred to as *no-fault divorce*. Almost everyone has heard the term, and many people believe that modern divorce litigation does not concern itself with "fault" or misconduct.

In those states where divorce is granted when an affidavit of consent is filed, the divorce part of the proceeding is truly "no fault." You file an affidavit, your husband files an affidavit, and eventually you get a divorce without anyone having to prove fault or misconduct.

But in many states, this no-fault procedure has nothing to do with economic relief. It merely applies to the termination of your marriage.

As you'll see later, many states still permit evidence of fault or misconduct in the economic stage of the case—even though they ignore fault in the divorce stage.

## THE EQUITABLE DISTRIBUTION LAWS

Forty-two states and the District of Columbia now have equitable distribution divorce laws, and seven states have community property laws (Mississippi has neither). Each of these states treats marriage as an economic partnership, and when a husband and wife divorce, state mandate requires that the marital assets be divided.

In the seven community property states, property division is basically a 50–50 proposition, although some may be your separate property, or your husband's. Therefore, you and your lawyer must identify the assets and have them valued. Division is more complex in equitable distribution states where you can get more (or less) than 50 percent, but the principles of identification and valuation still apply.

### Equitable Distribution States
### (including the District of Columbia)

| | | |
|---|---|---|
| Alabama | Kentucky | Ohio |
| Alaska | Maine | Oklahoma |
| Arizona | Maryland | Oregon |
| Colorado | Massachusetts | Pennsylvania |
| Connecticut | Michigan | Rhode Island |
| Delaware | Minnesota | South Carolina |
| District of Columbia | Missouri | South Dakota |
| Florida | Montana | Tennessee |
| Georgia | Nebraska | Utah |
| Hawaii | Nevada | Vermont |
| Illinois | New Hampshire | Virginia |
| Indiana | New Jersey | Washington |
| Iowa | New York | West Virginia |
| Kansas | North Dakota | Wisconsin |
| | | Wyoming |

### Community Property States

| | |
|---|---|
| Arkansas | New Mexico |
| California | North Carolina |
| Idaho | Texas |
| Louisiana | |

Remember, this is not a legal textbook so consult your attorney to confirm the property division laws of the state where *you* live. Furthermore, the law is constantly changing. For example, until 1982, when the Mississippi Supreme Court held that a wife's contributions to the marriage could be compensated, title to property was all that counted in that state.

By now your husband must realize that the old days of "what's mine is mine" are gone, but whether he realizes (likes or accepts) it or not, divorce statutes have undergone a revolution.

The Pennsylvania code, similar to most equitable distribution statutes, has this to say about equitable distribution:

> In a proceeding for divorce or annulment, the court shall, upon request of either party, equitably divide, distribute or assign the marital property between the parties without regard to marital misconduct in such proportions as the court deems just after considering all relevant factors. . . .

Note, however, that nowhere in the statute do the legislators tell the courts what *equitable* means. Although equitable distribution may seem self-explanatory it is quite the contrary. Consequently, it has become one of the most complex fields of litigation in the United States today. It has changed domestic relations law and matrimonial practice into an area requiring the skills of highly specialized attorneys and other experts.

## What You Should Know About the
## General Principles of Equitable Distribution

1. Title doesn't count. If your husband owns property in a partnership or corporate name, or even in someone else's name, it's still marital property.
2. It's up to you to prove your husband's interest in the asset. You can't get on the witness stand and say, "I think my husband owns some land in Montana, Your Honor." You need proof.
3. The law holds that every asset acquired after marriage up to the date of separation is presumed to be a marital asset. If you or your husband believes an asset is nonmarital or separate property, you have to prove it.
4. Marital property includes your husband's business or profession but not his job. Moreover, his earning power is not a marital asset. (It is, however, a basis for alimony.)
5. You and your husband must file a net worth statement, usually within 60 or 90 days after the complaint is filed. The statement must list all assets, marital and nonmarital, and all liabilities.

- If you feel your husband is hiding an asset, list it in your net worth statement. Don't be bashful!
- All unpaid bills *as of the date of separation* have to be listed.
- If your parents gave you $10,000 to help buy your home, it's not a debt owed to them unless they had you and your husband sign a note and make periodic payments. Without such proof, the court will determine that the money was a *gift* and will not order that they be repaid.

6. Once you or your husband files a complaint in divorce, your husband cannot prevent you from getting equitable distribution.

### STORY

Albert, a successful businessman, decides to trade in his wife after twenty-five years of marriage. He has found a younger, healthier model and is planning a new life with her. He's heard about no-fault divorce and he wants one.

But he's going to be "fair." He doesn't want to hurt his wife; after all, she's been a good mother to his three children. So he'll give her the house (with the mortgage), the old furniture, and she can keep her 1982 Dodge. And he'll throw in $100 a week child support.

He tells his business lawyer to file a divorce complaint. No nine counts. Just one:

*"Count One—Divorce: The Plaintiff requests a decree of divorce from the Defendant on the basis of a no-fault, consensual divorce."*

His business lawyer doesn't realize it but he has just put "Big-Hearted" Al onto the chopping block of the equitable distribution guillotine.

His wife's divorce attorney will promptly file a counterclaim to his divorce complaint and throw in *nine* other counts in addition to Count One—Divorce:

Equitable distribution;

Temporary alimony;

Child support;

Temporary counsel fees and litigation expenses;

Exclusive possession of the marital residence;

Permanent custody of the children;

The maintenance of existing life insurance policies, naming the
   wife as irrevocable beneficiary;

Permanent alimony, final counsel fees, and litigation expenses;

A "freeze" on marital assets.

Big-hearted Al is impaled on his own lust. Sure he'll get a
divorce, and sure he'll be able to remarry. But before he walks out
of the courtroom on the fifth floor on his way to the marriage
license bureau on the first floor, the family court judge will
distribute the family assets, including the value of Al's business.
Albert can't stop it. Nor could he have stopped it if his wife filed for
divorce first—all ten counts.

7. On the other hand, you can't get equitable distribution unless
   you or your husband have filed divorce proceedings.
8. Almost every divorce code provides that its basic goal is the
   attainment of "economic justice" for the parties.
9. *You can't prevent your husband from getting a divorce.* Even if
   you refuse to sign an affidavit of consent to a no-fault divorce,
   your husband can simply wait eighteen months, two years, or
   whatever the state divorce law says, and get his freedom. In
   some states he can still get a divorce on the old fault grounds,
   such as adultery, cruelty, or desertion.

Does this mean he can keep you chained to a hot stove for twenty-
five years, then run off with a floozie and get a divorce, whether
you like it or not?

That's exactly what it means.

(But *you* get equitable distribution—whether *he* likes it or not.)

## The Equitable Distribution Formula

In all of the equitable distribution states (and the District of Columbia), family court judges apply the *IVD* formula of dividing
marital property discussed in Chapter 9. (Remember, $I$ = identification; $V$ = valuation; and $D$ = distribution.)

You should understand the three components of the formula so
you'll be a completely informed client. Sure your divorce attorney
will know the formula by heart, but I want *you* to know it almost

as well as he does. After all, it's your case, your future, and your children's future at stake. So let's take it slowly over the next few chapters and learn it. We'll talk about Identification first.

## IDENTIFICATION OF MARITAL ASSETS

1. *The marital assets are the assets that were acquired during the marriage and that existed on the day of separation.* If you and your husband had a savings account several years ago but used it up for family purposes, it's not a marital asset. It didn't exist on the day of separation. The same is true of a used car traded in on a new model some time ago or furniture given to charity.

2. *But assets your husband dissipated, or has hidden, are counted.* Let's say he cleaned out a $2,000 savings account and lost it at the track. The $2,000 is a marital asset—he'll be awarded the $2,000, and you'll get a credit for $2,000. Or he cashed in $5,000 of U.S. Savings Bonds and invested it in his brother's pet rock business. The $5,000 is a marital asset—he gets an award of the $5,000, and you get a $5,000 credit. Say he got mad and removed an expensive silver set from the house and gave it to his sister. You can prove the silver was worth $2,500 on the day of separation. The $2,500 is a marital asset. He is awarded the silver set, and you get a credit for $2,500.

3. *It's your obligation to prove the existence of marital assets.* The judge won't do it for you. Your husband may try to hide marital assets from you. But assets leave paper trails. Your attorney and accountant will be able to trace assets which have been "deep-sixed" by following the trail.

4. *List all nonmarital assets.* Anything you acquired before your marriage or after the separation is a *nonmarital asset.* Gifts from others are usually nonmarital (in some states gifts from your husband are nonmarital—check with your attorney). Inheritances, regardless of when you got them, are usually nonmarital. Nonmarital assets are listed and valued but not distributed. However, the judge will consider them in distributing the marital assets.

(Now here comes the tricky part.)

5. If a nonmarital asset has increased in value from the date of the marriage to the date of separation, *that increase in value is a marital asset and gets distributed.*

Let's take an inheritance as an example. You were married in June 1975. In 1977 Uncle Ned died and left you $15,000 in stocks (or in cash, which you promptly invested in stocks, in your own name). You and your husband separated in June 1987. At that time, the stocks had increased in value to $30,000. The stocks themselves are a *nonmarital asset.* They're yours and don't get distributed. *But the increase in value from 1977 to 1987—$15,000—is a marital asset* and gets distributed.

6. *It doesn't make any difference who paid for the asset as far as identification is concerned.* If you and your husband bought a car during the marriage and still own it on the date of separation, the car is a marital asset, regardless of who contributed what to the purchase price. (The judge may consider who paid what when he *distributes* the car.)

Here's a story about following the paper trail.

## STORY

My client, Laura, knew nothing about her husband Kenneth's investments. She knew he made "a lot of money" but not much more than that.

Ken was a manufacturer of specialty medical equipment and apparently spent as much time investing his profits as he did in earning them.

When Ken left he took all of his papers with him—no paper trail. Ken's net worth statement listed the marital home, a stock portfolio, a few small bank accounts, and a nominal value for his business. But Ken was a wheeler-dealer, and both Laura and I smelled other assets.

It took a few months to get his most recent federal individual tax return, and Laura's accountant and I immediately noticed a substantial loss from a partnership called "Jade East Associates."

"What is Jade East?" we asked Laura.

"I don't have the slightest idea," she said.

I finally got court permission a few months later to ask Ken what Jade East was. He seemed unruffled by my question.

Ken: It's a tax shelter, De Angelis. I made an investment in a partnership, and the $27,000 that shows on my return is my share of the loss for last year. It's perfectly legitimate. The accounting firm that prepared the Jade East Partnership return is a nationally known and reputable firm. It's all very proper.

Me: I'm sure the accounting is correct, sir, but I don't know what this $27,000 loss represents. What did Jade East do to lose so much money?

Ken: They invested funds and the investment lost money. It's all in accordance with IRS regulations.

Me: We're going in a circle, sir. In what did Jade East invest?

Ken: (playing dumb) I don't understand what you mean.

Me: Sure you do. Did they invest in a Chinese take-out, a Taiwanese baseball team, or an expedition to find the lost jade mines of Hunan Province in China? *What is the underlying asset?* You know exactly what I mean.

Ken: Oh, well, the partnership owns an apartment house in town, but I own only 17 percent of the total. I'm only a limited partner; my partners own 83 percent.

Me: Do you get any income from the apartment house?

Ken: No—it's a loss, it's on the income tax return.

Me: (turning to Ken's attorney) Will you kindly get me copies of the partnership returns for Jade East (Form 1065) since the inception of the partnership; the canceled checks and bank statements for Jade East for the same period; the original partnership agreement for Jade East and any amendments; the name and address of the general partner; and the cash disbursements ledger of Jade East for the past five years?

After a few months of stalling we got the documents. What did we find?

1. Ken owned 17 percent of an apartment house that had been purchased during the marriage for $1,500,000 subject to a mortgage of $1,300,000.

2. We had the apartment house appraised and found that the fair market value of the apartment house was now $2,100,000.
3. Furthermore, the mortgage had been paid down to $1,100,000, so Ken owned 17 percent of a $1,000,000 ($2,100,000 less $1,100,000) interest in an apartment house, or an asset worth $170,000.
4. But over and above this little goodie, we found that each month the limited partners received $2,000 as a "return of capital." Therefore, Ken pocketed $24,000 each year of additional income *he didn't have to report.*

Moral: Husbands can't hide assets forever, but it's up to you and your experienced divorce attorney to prove the *I* part of the formula—*Identification.* Follow the paper trail!

So much for *I*, identification of marital assets. Your net worth statement lists what you think the assets are, while your husband's represents his view. The equitable distribution judge hears all the testimony on this point at the beginning of your case and then decides *what's* in the pot.

## Your Net Worth Statement Must Also Include Your Liabilities

If you, your husband, or the two of you owed any money on the day of separation, you must list it. The court not only orders equitable distribution of marital property but of *marital liabilities* as well.

What are marital liabilities?
- The mortgage balance on your home;
- Any debts you owe to banks, savings and loan associations, or any lending institutions;
- Car loans, school loans, home improvement loans, any money you borrowed during the marriage and have not paid back in full (remember, it doesn't make any difference who signed the loan papers);
- Loans payable to relatives or friends;
- Unpaid bills at the time of the hearing (department stores, credit cards, doctors, dentists, etc.).

What usually happens is that your husband's lawyer will tell him not to pay any more bills after the separation. These bills will be listed as marital liabilities and will be considered by the court at the final equitable distribution hearing. At that time the judge will decide not only who gets what but who pays what, including the unpaid bills that have piled up since the separation. (And until that time your lawyer will have to work like hell to keep the unpaid creditors away from your door! He does this by writing letters to your creditors pleading with them to wait for equitable distribution. They usually will.)

---

## CHECKLIST: HOW TO DETERMINE WHETHER AN ASSET IS A MARITAL OR NONMARITAL ASSET

1. *Time of Acquisition:* Was the asset acquired during the marriage, that is, from the date of marriage to the date of separation? If the answer is yes, it's a marital asset.
2. *Manner of Acquisition:* Was the asset acquired as an inheritance or gift? If the answer is yes, it's a nonmarital asset. (Check with your lawyer about gifts from your husband.)
3. *Increase in Value:* Even if the asset is a nonmarital asset, has there been an increase in value from the date of marriage to the date of separation? If so, the increase in value is a marital asset, but not the asset itself.

Next, we determine what the pot is worth—Let's go on to *V, Valuation.*

# Eleven

# Valuation: Putting a Price Tag on the Marital Assets

After the intricacies of identification, valuation is fairly simple. It's mostly practical stuff but at the same time it's very important because you're now fighting over the price tag, the amount in the marital pot.

The general rule is that the more there is in the marital pot the more you get. But keep in mind that your husband will submit high appraisals for the assets you will be awarded and light appraisals for the assets he'll probably get. Here's an example:

| Item | Your Value | His Value |
|---|---|---|
| 1. Home | $140,000 | $175,000 |
| 2. Furniture | 3,000 | 10,000 |
| 3. Your old Ford | 1,000 | 2,000 |
| 4. His new Nissan | 18,000 | 12,000 |
| 5. His partnership interest | (to be appraised) | -0- |
| 6. His pension | (to be appraised) | (to be appraised) |
| 7. The two bank accounts | 6,000 | 6,000 |

## ANALYSIS

It's obvious that the only valuation you and he agree on is the amount of money in the bank accounts. It's also obvious that he values the home, the furniture, and your car—the assets you'll certainly be awarded—at a heck of a lot more than they're worth (his value for these three items, $187,000; your value, $144,000).

So we start with a battle just on these three items. If his values are adopted, you lose part of $43,000. If your values are adopted, you get a substantially higher award.

There's also a $6,000 battle over his new car. He says it's eight months old and is therefore a used car. You say it's still worth $18,000 (he paid $20,000).

But don't worry about his inflated values. Your lawyer will know how to cross-examine his so-called experts. The real battles, of course, will be over his pension and the value of his partnership interest. That's where the real money is.

---

## TIP

Keep your eye on the money. Don't fight over "things." If he has a pension and/or a business, that's where you stand and fight.

---

Now let's talk about valuation in general.

## GENERAL PRINCIPLES OF VALUATION

*Rule One*:   Nobody does it for you. You have to prove the value of each asset and each liability.

*Rule Two*:   You have to retain an expert where required. No expert, no value.

*Rule Three*:   You must retain the best pension and business valuation experts your lawyer can find, *no matter how much it costs*.

## Example: Importance of Pension and Valuation Experts
### Marital Assets

| | |
|---|---|
| 1. Home (net of mortgage) | $80,000 |
| 2. Furniture | 5,000 |
| 3. Bank accounts | 10,000 |
| 4. IRA accounts | 6,000 |
| 5. Your car | 8,000 |
| 6. His car | 12,000 |
| 7. Antique clock | 1,000 |
| 8. His business | ? |
| 9. His pension | ? |

The total of the first seven assets in our example is $122,000. Now suppose that a qualified pension expert would come in with $150,000 as the *present-day* value of his pension. Let's further suppose that a qualified business valuation expert would testify that his business could be sold for $250,000.

So the house, furniture, clock, etc. are worth $122,000, and his pension and business are worth $400,000. In other words, you could theoretically give him the first seven assets outright, take *half* of the last two, and come out ahead! As you'll see, you'll be working on valuation long before your case is ever heard by the equitable distribution judge. Let's see how it works with specific categories of marital assets.

## Residential Real Estate

This is one of the easy ones. Retain a residential real estate appraiser who will go through your home and compare it with other similar homes that have been sold in the same neighborhood or general area. This appraisal will have to be updated as your hearing date approaches, so that the court will have a current value of the property.

Of course, before the appraiser begins you'll point out any repair problems. In fact, you should have on hand a typewritten list of necessary repairs when you first meet the appraiser, pointing out any defects that might diminish the value of the property, for example:

• Your street turns into a freeway at 8 A.M. and again at 5 P.M.

- Every summer there's a terrible odor from a nearby factory.
- The neighborhood public school will close after this term.

In other words, tell him everything he has to know in order to come up with a realistic appraisal.

Don't hire your good friend Dotte to appraise your property simply because she sold you the house and sells a lot of properties in the area. If she isn't a *real estate appraiser* (as opposed to a real estate *broker*), don't hire her. *Probable cost of a residential real estate appraisal: $200 for the appraisal; $250 to testify in court.*

### Household Furniture

Don't bother with an appraisal unless you own antiques, oriental carpets, or fine art. Your husband's net worth statement will show your furniture is worth $15,000, but you can safely ignore his inflated valuation unless you have to go to court. If that's the case, at the last minute you can retain a used furniture dealer to estimate what your second-hand furniture would sell for (*not what it cost* or what it would cost to replace). *Probable cost of used furniture appraisal: $100 for the appraisal; $150 to testify in court.*

### Antiques and Fine Art

Let's assume you're living in the marital residence and realistically expect to be awarded the home as part of equitable distribution. Let's also assume that there is a valuable antique or painting in the house, *which you want.*

Of course your husband will argue that the painting is a rare work of art worth $10,000. He knows you want it, and he's willing to give it to you for a $10,000 credit.

Therefore, when you study his net worth statement, keep in mind that the value of the painting is going to be a battle in court.

Ask at the gallery where the painting was purchased for the name of an appraiser of fine art. If you don't appraise the painting, your husband may show up in court with a "ringer" who will swear that the painting is worth $10,000. Don't take the chance of getting caught unprepared. *Probable cost of a fine arts expert: $150 for the appraisal; $250 to testify in court.*

## Bank Accounts, Money Market Funds, Stocks and Bonds, etc.

Write to all banks, brokers, or any depository requesting statements as of the date of separation. (You'll also need day-of-trial statements.)

## Automobiles

Unless your husband is in the fine-car field, don't waste any money on used-car appraisers. In most cases the two attorneys will stipulate the automobile values.

---

### TIP

If you drive a car on which you still owe money, don't forget to write for a statement of the balance. Your car may be worth $7,500, but if you owe $6,000 on it, its net value is only $1,500.

---

## Jewelry

Let's suppose that until he met Tracey your husband was a generous guy and bought you jewelry for birthdays and anniversaries. Let's also suppose your parents gave you gifts of jewelry or that you inherited some from family members.

You've never bothered to appraise it, although you've insured it for what you guess is its replacement value. But you don't know how much it would *sell for*, and neither does your husband. Furthermore, your attorney tells you that most of your jewelry is a nonmarital asset and will not be distributed. So you can forget it, right?

Wrong. Your husband will insert a little item in his net worth statement to the effect: "Jewelry in wife's possession, $25,000." Actually, the jewelry cost a few thousand dollars when it was purchased or at the time the gift was made. By inflating its value, your husband hopes the difference—the "increase" in value—will go into the marital pot.

Go to a jeweler and get it appraised.

## Tax Shelters

Remember "Cagey Ken" who in the previous chapter listed a $27,000 partnership loss in Jade East on his personal income tax return because it *saved* him money, but forgot to list his interest in the partnership real estate in his statement of net worth because it would *cost* him money?

Internal Revenue is slowly phasing out these tax shelter goodies, but there still are some around, and you should be aware of how they work. In addition, your husband may have an old tax shelter that pops up on his income tax return.

---

### TIP

Where there's a tax shelter, there's an asset. Have it valued.

---

Let's suppose your husband invested $20,000 in a real estate partnership for a 1 percent partnership interest and he's obligated to invest $20,000 a year for the next three years, for a total investment of $80,000.

Now let's suppose that this particular real estate deal loses money for the first seven years (because of depreciation). There are two things for your attorney and accountant to look for:

1. Is your husband getting checks called "return of capital" that are not reportable?
2. Is the underlying asset—the office building or apartment house—worth more now than it was when he made his investment?

    Even if the answer to both questions is no, your accountant may suggest you try to get an award of half the tax shelter, particularly where *you* have substantial income. *If the tax shelter legitimately saves taxes, you can use it too.* You're entitled!

## Your Husband's Pension Plan

Before equitable distribution, your husband's pension plan was his. Whether he created a private pension plan from his own business or profession or was employed for thirty years and then retired on his pension of $750 or $1,000 a month, it was all his. If you didn't have a pension, tough. He did.

Now it's different. "His" pension is "our" pension, and you're entitled to share in it in one of three ways:

1. *You can wait for his pension to start and share in the monthly payments.* For example, your husband, now 45, will receive $1,000 a month when he's 59. You don't have any retirement fund. Your attorney can ask for an order giving you 50 percent (or whatever percentage the court thinks you're entitled to) of the pension payments when they begin.
2. *You can allow your husband to keep all of his pension rights at the time of retirement but ask the court to give you an amount of cash or property now, in an amount equal to your share of the present value of the pension plan.* The present value of a pension is a marital asset. To compute the present worth of your husband's pension rights you will need a pension expert (usually an actuary) who will base his calculations on certain assumptions concerning interest rates and mortality tables. If the present value of your husband's pension rights is $50,000, then he keeps his pension, and $50,000 is added to the marital pot. On a 50 percent award, you'd get an additional $25,000.
3. *You can ask for a negotiated settlement or court order for a payment of cash from his pension plan before he retires.* The court would sign a document called a Qualified Domestic Relations Order (QDRO), which would order the trustees of the pension plan to make the payments to you. QDROs are tricky, so make sure your pension expert is the very best. They're invaluable not only because they provide you with a piece of your husband's pension but also because they guarantee that you'll get what your husband promises.

### Using a QDRO as Collateral Security

Say you and your husband negotiate an end to your marital dispute—he agrees to give you the house and pay off the $35,000 mortgage by assuming the monthly payments.

As part of your deal he'll keep his private pension, the only other major asset, present value $50,000. How do you make certain that your ex-husband will make these mortgage payments as promised? If he doesn't, you lose your home. One way is to have your pension expert prepare a QDRO in the form of a $35,000 claim against his pension. The QDRO is signed by the judge as a court order and filed with the trustees of the pension plan. If your ex "forgets" to pay the mortgage or his new wife convinces him there are better ways to spend his money, you call your lawyer and he uses the QDRO to get you $35,000.

A QDRO is very important as an enforcement tool. Not only can it be used to guarantee that you receive that part of your husband's pension the court has awarded you (or that you've negotiated for), but it can be used to make sure your husband honors the settlement provisions (alimony and children's education, for example). If he has a private pension plan with a significant present cash value, you need a QDRO to make sure he does what he's ordered to. And you need a trained pension expert to prepare a QDRO for you. Your attorney shouldn't try to do it. (If your husband's pension is provided by his employer, you can't use a QDRO like this.)

### Your Husband's Business or Practice Is Not His Own

The biggest Husband Myth in divorce litigation is: "My business (or practice) is mine." Just like "his" pension, it's "ours." Even if he began (or inherited) his business *before* he married you, its increase in value from the date of your marriage to the date of separation is a marital asset.

It's one thing to say his business is a marital asset and another to determine its valuation. Business (or profession) valuation is the most difficult valuation problem and takes the most time. (It also involves the most money.)

---

### CHECKLIST: VALUING YOUR HUSBAND'S BUSINESS (PRACTICE)

1. Get the best expert you can afford—*before* He-Who-Buys-Everybody-Off does.

2. Disclose *everything* you know about the business or practice to the expert.

3. *Never* settle your case unless your expert first tells you what the business or practice is worth (unless you get a lump sum you're happy with).

4. Your contribution to your husband's successful business does not have to be based on your working on his assembly line or driving one of his trucks.

5. Your husband's business or practice is as much a marital asset as is your home or the furniture. Just because you can't "see" it doesn't mean it isn't there.

Before the *Henderson* case goes to trial we'll talk about the specifics of business or practice valuation. But now let's talk about the bottom line—how a judge distributes the marital assets. How much of the pot do *you* get?

# Twelve

# How Much of the Pot Do You Get?

In community property states, property division is generally a two-stage procedure: I and V, then 50-50. (But note that distribution in community property states is not as simplistic as it might appear. You don't just walk into the courthouse and say, "I want my half.")

In equitable distribution states, however, the distribution of marital property is entirely up to the judge—he can award you anywhere from nothing to 100% of the marital assets. In making his decision, the judge will listen to the *entire* history of your marriage, and carefully examine and value the marital assets. Then he'll apply certain factors from your state divorce law (called *the equitable distribution factors* or *EDFs*) to determine how much of the marriage partnership you're entitled to.

Among the EDFs considered are your age, education, health, financial status, the length of the marriage, and the number of children. *Everything counts*, including anything and everything you did to help your husband and family in the early years of your marriage. Therefore, you'll have to know your state's EDFs by heart.

Because your ED testimony will help the judge appraise or value your contribution to the successful business or job that your husband now has, you should spend hours rehearsing your ED testimony with your attorney before taking the witness stand at the final hearing.

---

## TIP

Get a copy of your divorce code and begin writing another notebook called *Divorce Factors, Equitable Distribution*, using each section heading listed in your statute. This way, you can talk intelligently with your attorney about the 401(d)(5) factor or the 401(d)(7) factor (or whatever the section number is in your state). Thus you will be prepared for court if and when the case goes to trial.

---

## THE EQUITABLE DISTRIBUTION FACTORS

To give yourself a head start, let's look at Pennsylvania's eleven EDFs (see Table 12.1, pages 124–27). Although these factors are representative of EDFs in other states, you should check with your attorney to make sure *your* state doesn't have a unique factor not listed here.

The comments to the right of each EDF indicate whether you'll get a judicial plus or minus in a particular factual situation. Keep in mind, however, that none of the divorce codes gives the EDF any numerical weight or ranks them in order of importance. That is, you don't get so many percentage points for a plus or lose a set number for a minus. *Equitable distribution is not a mathematical process but a subjective one.* Your attorney knows from appellate decisions which factors count. The monthly appellate reports keep him apprised of the *weight* of each EDF, particularly the weight of the "homemaker" contribution, 401(d)(7).

### Do Your EDF Homework

Long before you begin your final preparation for trial you'll have to do your EDF homework. Have your attorney explain each factor to you in detail, then begin writing a narrative for your attorney on each section and subsection of the EDT.

### WHAT TO COVER IN YOUR EDF NARRATIVE
*401(d)(3)(b)—Health*

Go into a chapter-and-verse description of any physical or emotional health problem. List the names of every doctor, hospital, and

# TABLE 12.1
## ANALYSIS OF EQUITABLE DISTRIBUTION FACTORS
### (Using the Pennsylvania Divorce Code as a Guide)

| Section 401(d) | Nature of Factor | Comment |
|---|---|---|
| 1. | Length of marriage | If you've been married for 15 to 20 years, you get a plus. If you've been married for 6 to 7 years or less, you get a minus. |
| 2. | Prior marriages | Two to four prior marriages constitutes a minus. |
| 3. | General data | |
| | a. Age | The older you are, the more you get and vice-versa. |
| | b. Health | If you're an arthritic and he's a marathoner, you get a big plus. |
| | c. Station | Your economic bracket. You should get an award that enables you to continue the life-style you enjoyed while living with your husband. |
| | d. Income | If your husband is an investment banker and earns $150,000 annually and you're a part-timer earning $60 a week, you get a *big* plus. |

124

| Section 401(d) | Nature of Factor | Comment |
|---|---|---|
| 3. | e. Vocational skills | Can you support yourself on your present skills? Can you increase your income after retraining? Have you ever worked during the marriage? If not, you get a big plus. |
| | f. Employability | If you have to stay at home and take care of young children, you get a big plus. If you have no career skills, you get a plus. |
| | g. Estate | This refers to the nonmarital assets you own as compared to your husband's. Chances are, you'll get a plus here. |
| | h. Liabilities | Lawyer's fees, school loans, money you borrowed from relatives, everyday bills. Usually another plus for you. |
| | i. Your needs | Very important that you and your attorney prepare for this factor. How much property do you need? How much *income-producing* property? |
| 4. | Contribution to your husband's increased earning power or education | Did you help your husband through school? Did you help him get promotions in his job? Did you help him develop his business or profession? If you did, you get a plus. |

| Section 401(d) | Nature of Factor | Comment |
|---|---|---|
| 5. | Opportunity of each party to acquire assets and income in the future | If you're a homemaker and he's a businessman, you get a big plus. His opportunity is almost unlimited, and yours is zilch. Possibility of inheritance also applies here. Your parents may have to supply information about the size of their estate. If they have none, you get a plus. |
| 6. | Sources of income including medical, retirement, insurance, or other benefits | If he has a pension, profit-sharing plan, life insurance, and/or disability insurance and you don't you get a *big* plus. |
| 7. | What each party has done to acquire, preserve, dissipate, or appreciate marital property, *including the contribution as a homemaker* | As far as you're concerned, your contribution as a homemaker *may be the most important section of your divorce code.* |
| 8. | Value of property set apart to each party | The equitable distribution judge must balance how much property you'll get and how much your husband will get. |
| 9. | Your standard of living | This factor is extremely important, since it directs the judge to consider how you lived before the separation. Don't leave anything out. If you and your husband enjoyed the good life, tell the judge about it. You'll get a plus. |

| Section 401(d) | Nature of Factor | Comment |
|---|---|---|
| 10. | Your economic circumstances, including tax ramifications, as of the date of hearing | Suppose you separated in 1982 but your case isn't heard till 1989. The marital asset selection "freezes" as of 1982, but your economic situation in 1989 is highly relevant. If he shelters his income and pays little or no taxes, and you can't do that, you get a big plus. |
| 11. | Will you have to take care of young children? | If you're a mother of three or four children under 16 and they'll be living with you, you get a big plus. You'll need a lot of equitable distribution. |

127

128     YOU'RE ENTITLED!

period of treatment. Include every diagnosis, course of treatment, and prognosis. Get help on this from your doctors.

### 401(d)(3)(e)—Vocational Skills
Describe in detail your vocational skills, prior training, employment history and income, *or the lack thereof.* List all past employment dates and salaries. And don't forget the application here of 401(d)(11), taking care of young children, if appropriate.

### 401(d)(3)(g)(h)—Estate and Liabilities
This is not another term for your net worth statement but a day-of-trial balance sheet, i.e., "This is what I *own* and this is what I *owe.*" Have your attorney type up a list of every debt you have, including his unpaid attorney's fees as of the trial date.

### 401(d)(4)—Contribution to Your Husband's Increased Earning Power or Education
Think about it. He didn't get where he is today without your help. Did you keep the kids quiet while he studied or did paperwork? Did you shelter him from household problems while he was working on his career? Did you give parties for his customers or clients? Did you attend trade shows with him and smile at his boring customers? Write it all down.

### 401(d)(5)—Opportunity to Acquire Future Capital and Income
In the ordinary case, his is unlimited and yours is zero, unless you have your own business or practice. This is especially true where he is a businessman or professional and you have a job or are the homemaker.

### 401(d)(6)—Medical, Retirement, and Pension Benefits
If he has complete medical/dental coverage, a pension plan and/or a profit-sharing plan, an IRA and/or a Keogh plan, disability insurance and/or a life insurance program with an ever-increasing cash value, *and you don't*, you score big points.

### 401(d)(7)—Your Contribution as a Homemaker
(Because this ED Factor is so important in your case, we'll skip it now and talk about it last.)

### 401(d)(8)—Value of Property Set Apart for Each Party
Directed at the judge, this factor helps balance how much property you get in relation to your needs and does the same for your husband. There's little you can do to prepare for it; your attorney will argue this section for you.

### 401(d)(9)—Prior Standard of Living
Here you go all out. If you and your husband enjoyed a luxurious life-style, write it all down in painstaking detail. If, on the other hand, you and your husband were just "comfortable," spell that out. Describe how you lived.

(This factor is extremely important if your husband is rich, used cash, has hidden assets, or is understating his income.)

### 401(d)(10)—Your Economic Circumstances at the Time of Equitable Distribution Hearing
You must be prepared to tell the equitable distribution judge exactly how much money or assets you have when you take the stand at the final hearing. You must also be prepared to describe your current net income and to project your expected net income for the next few years. Your attorney will prepare a balance sheet and your CPA will prepare a *pro forma* (estimated) tax return for the coming year, so the judge can see what your future *net* income will be.

### 401(d)(7)—Your Contribution as a Homemaker
If your husband makes a great deal more money than you do, and if you are the principal homemaker, your contribution as a home-maker is probably the most important part of your case. Let's look at 401(d)(7). This section addresses two separate and independent questions:

1. What has each party done to acquire, preserve, dissipate, or appreciate marital property?

2. What was each party's contribution as a homemaker?

The first part has to do with the way your husband handled the family money. Did he throw money away on drugs, fancy clothes, gambling, or women? Did he make stupid investments that are now worthless?

Now we get to the second part—your contribution as a homemaker. Let's assume you worked for a few years after your marriage, had children, and never resumed working. During the next ten or fifteen years your husband worked hard building his business or career, but "all you did" was take care of your husband, the children, and the home. You never worked at his place of business. What was your contribution?

Your Husband's Lawyer:  Nothing, Your Honor. She never contributed anything to the business. She never worked for her husband or helped him out. *She just stayed home*!

But you know better, and you'll write a book about your homemaking contribution so you'll be prepared to testify that:

- You raised the children, which means that you were doctor and nurse; teacher and tutor; cook, seamstress, and domestic engineer; and chauffeur.
- You took care of your husband through sickness and discouragement; relieved him of all the child-raising obligations; and allowed him to concentrate on his business, profession, or job.
- You took care of home maintenance (lawn, appliance repair, and so forth) and day-by-day operations that afforded him the opportunity to build his business or develop his practice. Accordingly, you *both* contributed to that asset.

Before leaving the EDF, let's look at a case decided by the Superior Court of Pennsylvania in 1987, *Johnson v. Johnson*, to gain some legal insight into the particular significance of the homemaking factor.

David and Pamela were married in 1966 and separated in 1983. David operated a flour and animal feed business in rural Pennsylvania, but Pamela did not participate in his business. David worked hard and his business prospered. At the divorce hearing, the court valued it at close to $600,000.

Pamela was an elementary school teacher and earned $23,000 annually. During the early years of their marriage, Pamela's earnings helped support David.

The equitable distribution judge awarded Pamela 55 percent of the marital property and $5,000 for counsel fees. David appealed, his lawyer arguing that the trial judge did not give enough weight to the fact that he, and he alone, built up the business.

The Superior Court of Pennsylvania agreed in part with David, ruling that Pamela had received sufficient assets through equitable distribution and did not need contribution for counsel fees. However, the court affirmed the 55 percent equitable distribution award, stating that the trial judge had correctly determined the relative contributions of each partner to the accumulation of marital assets.

There were three judges on the superior court panel that decided this case. Each judge has the right to agree or dissent. Each judge also has the right to express a *concurring opinion*, which agrees with the majority opinion but states a different line of reasoning.

The Honorable Phyllis W. Beck of the Pennsylvania Superior Court wrote a concurring opinion, a portion of which follows.

*The court, in balancing each party's contribution to the marriage, concluded they were equal, and therefore offset each other. The fact that the husband concentrated his efforts on building the business and that the wife concentrated hers on maintaining the home does not entitle the husband to a greater share of the value of the business than the court awarded him.*

*Each party to a marriage contributes to that enterprise in accordance with his or her ability and in accordance with the couple's expectations. The gains attributable to the party who is responsible for economic growth are usually tangible. The gains attributable to the party who is responsible for maintaining the home are usually intangible. Just because the gains are intangible they should not be undervalued.*

*Both parties benefit from the efforts of the spouse who maintains a home. The value of that labor must be recognized and translated into monetary value at the time the marriage is dissolved.*

Now, the reason I've taken the time to discuss the *Johnson* case and Judge Beck's concurring opinion is that I believe it represents the wave of the future in equitable distribution cases insofar as the homemaking contribution is concerned. Too many equitable distribution judges look at a man's business as something *he alone* created and therefore award his wife a smaller percentage of the marital assets than she is entitled to.

The Beck opinion has pointed the way to determining the true value of a woman's contribution to the marriage partnership. Let's hope that other judges follow her reasoning.


## How the Judge Arrives at Your ED Percentage

If no mathematical weight inures to the various EDFs, how does the judge decide how much of the pot you get? Very simply, in an equitable distribution state you simply get whatever the judge *feels* you're entitled to.

Well, you may say, this is vague. Sure it is! But you're entitled to *equitable* distribution and family court judges are bound by the decisions of the appellate courts in your state, and they're *not* vague.

This body of law contains guidelines to the Family Court judges as to what is fair and what isn't. These guidelines are expressed in percentages of the marital assets, and trial judges generally follow them. Therefore, you've got to read as many of the equitable distribution cases as you can. Learn the percentages in your state.

However, each state has different perceptions of what is equitable. Using three eastern states as examples, we'll examine a 20-year marriage where the wife has raised three children, has always been a homemaker, and has little or no assets in her own name. Her health is poor.

Her husband owns a business and is in good health. His business becomes more successful each year.

| State | Wife's Probable Award |
|-------|----------------------|
| Pennsylvania | 50–55% |
| New York | 35–40% |
| New Jersey | 45–50% |

Why should these percentages be different? After all, the demographics of all three states are similar, as are the divorce codes, all of which were adopted within a dozen years of each other (New Jersey, 1969; New York and Pennsylvania, 1980).

I don't know, but I can tell you this—you and your lawyer have got to prepare your ED testimony as if you were preparing to stand trial before a judge for first-degree murder.

The point is, know your state's percentages and never mind what the "perception" is. If your lawyer believes you're entitled to 55 percent of the marital assets, go for it. The law is on your side, so prepare thoroughly and carefully to maximize your award.

(Actually, the extent of judicial discretion in awarding a percentage of marital assets to either party is almost absolute. Consider *D'Arc v. D'Arc*, New Jersey (1978), where a court awarded a woman almost 100 percent of the marital assets and her husband 0 percent. Why? Because he hired someone to murder her! (Who says he didn't get *equitable* distribution?)

In states where the "new" divorce code has not yet sunk into the judicial consciousness and where family court judges still operate under the "old law," your lawyer has got to fight like hell. He or she must wave the divorce code in the judicial face and say:

Judge, here is the new law—it's *equitable distribution* now. My client is *entitled* to, 50 percent, 55 percent, 60 percent of the marital assets based on these factors you *must* consider. The old law is gone. *You must follow the new law and apply it fairly.*

I recently argued to a judge that my client should get 100 percent of the marital assets because her husband was a compulsive gambler and would take whatever percentage he was awarded down to Atlantic City and deposit it at his favorite casino. Here is what part of my brief said:

> If this Honorable Court should decide that Mr. Jones is entitled to, say, 15 percent of the marital estate, or $20,000, it is respectfully suggested that the Court save the Defendant (husband) some wear and tear on his nerves, not to mention his tires, by just sending a check in the amount of $20,000 directly to the Sea Side Casino.

It didn't work. My client got 65 percent and the gambler got 35 percent.

Let's go back to the homemaker factor—401(d)(7) in the Pennsylvania Divorce Code—what I believe to be your make-or-break factor. I've always wondered whether a judge would mind if I had a drum and bugle corps march into the courtroom as I was about to ask my client about her contribution as a homemaker.

Let's look at how the factor is actually developed and explained by a woman in court. The story will also help you realize how much work you and your attorney will have to do to prepare for this one small part of your case.

## STORY

I represented Myra whose husband, Frank, was a highly successful orthopedic physician. Upon separation, they'd been married for eighteen years and had three children, ages 16, 15, and 13.

Myra met Frank at the hospital where she was a physical therapist and he a resident. What had Myra done to increase Frank's earning power? "Not a damn thing," said Frank.

When they met, Myra was earning $12,000 a year while Frank's salary as a resident was only $8,000. Five years later they had three children and had purchased a small suburban home. Myra's salary had increased to $15,000 and Frank had just begun his private practice but was earning very little. Knowing that they needed her income and that without it her husband might not be able to pursue his specialty, it was Myra who supported and looked after the family.

She got up at 6 A.M., made breakfast, got the children dressed, and to the babysitter, went to work, came back at 4 P.M., spent time with the children, shopped, cooked and did the dishes, helped the children with their homework, and, when necessary, mowed the lawn. When Frank came home the house was clean, the children were quiet, and he had only to go into his den, do paperwork, and study. At 9 P.M. the children—cleaned, bathed, fed, and happy— came in so Daddy could kiss them goodnight. Then Myra collapsed into bed. Frank was very content.

Even after Frank's practice began to grow, Myra kept working. Most medical specialists depend on referrals from other physicians, so it took a long time for Frank to build up his practice. Therefore, Myra couldn't quit her job because they still needed the money. She got more tired each year, while each year Frank's practice began to prosper.

Not only did Myra keep working so Frank could succeed, but she kept working for the same physical therapist, earning a salary and, from time to time, raises. Eventually she gave up the idea of developing her own private practice because she and Frank feared she might not succeed, that it would take too long to build up her practice, or that they would suffer from the loss of her steady salary. By the time Frank's practice began to prosper, it was too late for her to go into private practice; she was a little older and did not have the same energy of her early years.

Myra's hard work paid off. Frank became a successful orthopedic physician with a lucrative group practice. When he got very rich, he walked out. (Actually he drove away in his new Jaguar.)

Therefore, Myra's final ED testimony was very convincing:

"Your Honor, when I started working as a physical therapist I made $5,500 a year. I now make $18,500 a year. My husband, on the other hand, is making over $200,000 a year in his practice.

"If I had gone into private practice, I might now be making $30,000 or $40,000 per year. What I did was give up my chance of owning my own physical therapy practice so that my husband and I would be able to feed and clothe ourselves and the children during the early years of his practice. This enabled Frank to develop *his* practice.

"Now it's too late for me to go into private practice and therefore

I feel that I have contributed a great deal to the development of my husband's practice. In a real sense, I sacrificed my economic future for his.

The courts call this contribution homemaking. (If Myra had quit her job, Frank would have become a general practitioner—no specialty.)

One of the most significant assets that had to be valued by the court was Frank's medical practice (after all, if Myra had quit her job there'd be no specialty). Myra told the ED judge the complete story of the early years of their marriage, and she received 50 percent of the marital assets, which included the value of Frank's interest in his group practice.

---

## TIP

If your husband is a professional, i.e., a doctor, dentist, lawyer, accountant, etc., ask your lawyer whether his practice can be listed as a marital asset in your state. *In some states a professional practice, unlike a manufacturing or service business, can't be bought and sold and therefore may not be valued for purposes of equitable distribution!* The rationale is that a surgeon's practice, for example, is based entirely on his skill and reputation, which can't be transferred. Even the Myra-Frank story might be different today, since Pennsylvania is currently reconsidering its views.

If you live in one of these states and your husband has a professional practice, you can't include his practice as a marital asset. You can, however, include his tangible assets—cash in bank, equipment, receivables, etc., and should go for big alimony, a topic we'll cover in Chapter 16.

---

## You Must Understand and Articulate Your Economic Horizon

Here's what Margo Henderson will say at the final hearing when she gets to the ED testimony:

Me: Mrs. Henderson, please tell the court the nature of the assets you have in your own name.

Margo: A checking account with about $200, some jewelry worth about $2,000, I suppose. I'll be getting some furniture and my car, but that's about it.

Me: Now your liabilities.

Margo: Well, I owe you over $20,000. I owe expert witnesses about $5,000. I owe my parents $5,000 I've borrowed for court costs and expert witnesses, and some bills had run up before the separation—say another $6,000. I've also borrowed $6,000 from a retired uncle for my first year's college tuition.

Me: Is there anything you can do to improve your financial situation, either increase your assets or pay off your liabilities?

Margo: Not without the court's help, no.

Me: Do you have a business you can use for pay for your personal needs?

Margo: Of course not.

Me: Do you have a profit-sharing plan or pension plan for your old age?

Margo: No.

Me: Do you have any opportunity at all to acquire capital or additional assets?

Margo: None whatever.

Me: How long will it take for you to be self-supporting?

Margo: Well, now I've enrolled in the university for a degree in public relations. But it'll be six or seven years before I can get a job paying, say, $30,000 to $35,000 a year.

Me: What is the present state of your health?

Margo: Not so good. I'm still seeing Dr. Baker, my psychiatrist, but the stress of this litigation and my financial insecurity is making it difficult. I can't pay you or any old bills, and I can't see how I'll ever get out of this hole I'm in. And of course, while I litigate, I've got to take care of two small children.

## You Must Be Able to Describe Your Economic Health

It's up to you to present your case. Remember, your lawyer doesn't testify for you. He helps you by the questions he asks you, but *you* take the stand, and you have to convince the judge that you're entitled to 40 percent, 50 percent, or 60 percent.

In fact, the judge will not be able to make any decisions in your favor on the I, V, and D factors unless you present testimony on each and every factor, and then corroborate your testimony by other witnesses or by producing relevant documents.

Examples:

- You want to prove you have no real vocational skills. (401(d)(3) in the Pennsylvania EDF). Not only must you testify about your entire vocational history, or lack of it, but you should also have a vocational counselor testify on your behalf.
- You want to convince the judge you've been a good homemaker [Pennsylvania 401(d)(7)]. Not only should you tell the judge what you did during an average week from 6:00 A.M. to 10 P.M. each and every day, but you should also find witnesses (friends, neighbors, relatives) who can testify how hard you worked as chief cook, bottle washer, nurse, etc.
- You want to prove your health is poor and that you suffer from phlebitis. If you're being treated for phlebitis, bring your physician to court. It's one thing to say, "Your honor, I've got phlebitis," and another for a doctor to say you've got it. (Nor do you want your husband's attorney to say that you've got phlebitis; you want your doctor to say it. Not only is it more effective to have the doctor in court, but you're not really capable of answering questions about medical matters.)

*In order to prove anything, you must testify and find corroboration for your testimony.*

You and your attorney will probably spend anywhere from twenty to forty hours just on the EDF. If your attorney doesn't insist on this depth of preparation, he's ripping you off.

## Document Your Economic Health

You and your lawyer must take the time to paint a picture of your economic health—your future in dollars and cents. You must prepare so you can accurately describe your economic health and then compare it to your husband's economic health.

At the final hearing, your attorney, if he's good, will question you for hours. It will be like a Broadway opening for a show called *Margo Henderson and the EDF.* When your attorney asks your husband the same questions on cross-examination, the numbers 60-40 or 55-45 will begin to flash in the judge's brain like a neon sign.

In equitable distribution states, judges can award a spouse almost any percentage they think is fair. I've seen judges award women anywhere from 30 percent to 70 percent of the marital assets. It depends on the facts of the case, the extent of your preparation for trial, and your lawyer. Mostly, though, it depends on *you.*

## Your "Misconduct" During the Marriage May Affect How Much You Get for Equitable Distribution

Earlier on, I said that almost all of our states distribute marital property by equitable distribution or by community property. I'd also said that the granting of a divorce can now be accomplished without reference to fault or misconduct. But there are some states where this may not be the case. Let's take Missouri as an example: If you had a long affair while you were married, the court can consider your misconduct in distributing marital property.

Please check with your attorney to find out if you live in one of these states with the "middle ages" mentality toward distributing marital property. If you do live in one of them, you'll have to sit down with your attorney and tell him chapter and verse about your misconduct.

Let's not waste any time on *why* your legislature included this stupid clause in its equitable distribution statute—especially since equitable distribution is supposed to recognize the economic partnership of marriage, not encourage a mud-slinging contest. But if you live in a state where the statute includes misconduct, let's talk about it.

If you had a fairly long marriage (say fifteen to twenty years), raised children, helped your husband by working now and then, and were a good homemaker, most judges will not pay too much attention to a single lapse of marital morality. Likewise, if your husband takes the stand and accuses you of turning the air-conditioning up too high or burning his toast, the judge will yawn.

On the other hand, if your husband worked diligently in the coal mines for forty years while you "ran around" and left the children hungry and crying, the judge will listen to every sordid detail, and *your misconduct will affect how much you get.* If he has dated his secretary for the past eight or ten years and you had a brief affair fifteen years ago—very brief, and very private—or if your husband physically abused you during the marriage, the misconduct element will cancel out or may result in your getting *more* of the marital pot.

Even if you live in one of the misconduct states, on balance it usually won't affect your award. All the same, *you must tell your attorney everything you can think of that your husband might bring up under "misconduct."* Full disclosure to your attorney may be more important than the misconduct itself. (See Chapter 25, "Preparing for Trial.")

A brief word about New York State. Unlike the other "misconduct" states, the New York statute doesn't list misconduct as a specific factor in deciding equitable distribution. In 1985, though, the New York Court of Appeals (the highest appellate court in that state) decided that if any party was guilty of "egregious conduct," such conduct could be considered by the equitable distribution judge. If your misconduct may be a factor and you live in New York State, check with your attorney.

## Will Your Home Be Sold as Part of ED?
It depends. Let's look at some different cases.

### Case #1
Let's take the case of a long marriage, where you and your husband are in your fifties, the children are emancipated, and there are only

two major assets—a home, clear of mortgage, worth $100,000 and your husband's pension, which your pension expert says is worth $95,000 on the day of the trial. You will be awarded the home and your husband will be awarded his pension. You can live in your home as long as you want to or sell it. It's all yours.

## Case #2

Same couple, only the assets consist of the home at $100,000, his pension at $95,000, bank accounts at $10,000, a vacation home with equity of $50,000, two cars at $5,000 each, and furniture of $7,500. Your health is poor to fair; his is good. You have never worked outside the home but have raised three children and helped him in his job. There are no marital liabilities. The marital pot, therefore, totals $272,500. You will get your home and more. If you are awarded 50 percent of the assets, or $136,250, you will get your home, your furniture, the bank accounts, your car, and $13,750 in cash.

## Case #3

You have been married for ten years. The children are ages 8, 6, and 3. The only assets are your home, worth $100,000 with a $40,000 mortgage remaining (equity = $60,000), and your husband's pension, worth only $20,000. Total marital assets are $80,000. You are unemployed.

The court can't divide the assets at the final hearing. If you were awarded 50 percent of the marital assets, you would be awarded $40,000, but the house would have to be sold to raise the cash. And the court realizes that you need a home in order to raise the children.

For such cases, *most divorce codes contain a clause permitting an equitable distribution judge to award either spouse exclusive possession of the marital residence for a reasonable number of years.* Therefore, the judge will probably award you and the children exclusive possession of the marital residence until the *youngest* child is emancipated. At that time the home will be sold and the proceeds divided on a 55–45 or 60–40 basis—whatever the judge believes to be fair, taking into account the fact that your husband will keep his pension.

Incidentally, you will almost certainly receive enough alimony and child support for the next fifteen years, so that you can pay the mortgage and maintain yourself and the children.

### Case #4

You have been married for six years, no children. You work, your husband works, and both of you are in good health. The only asset is the equity in your home, say $40,000.

The judge will almost certainly order the house sold and the proceeds divided on what is deemed an equitable basis, depending on who put up the lion's share of the down payment. (If the judge awards you $20,000 and your husband $20,000, you can negotiate to buy your husband out, or vice-versa, and the house will not have to be put on the market. You and he could engage in a private sale.)

## You Don't Pay Taxes on Your Equitable Distribution Award

Later in this book we'll talk about temporary and permanent alimony (in some states it's called maintenance). Whereas community property and equitable distribution deal with the division of marital *property*, alimony deals with the division of marital *income*. The good news is that you can ask the court for alimony while you're still litigating your divorce, as well as for a period of time after the case is over. The bad news, however, is that you pay income taxes on alimony payments.

The I.R.S. says that alimony payments to a wife are deductible by a husband and must be included by the wife as income in her personal income tax return. *However, you don't pay income taxes on your award of equitable distribution or community property.*

Say you and your husband agree on a settlement or the court orders one where you get the following:

| | |
|---|---|
| The marital residence with a net value of | $150,000 |
| Cash | 10,000 |
| Furniture | 5,000 |
| Your car | 7,500 |
| Your IRA | 6,000 |
| ½ of a stock account | 21,500 |
| Total settlement (or Award) | $200,000 |

You don't pay any taxes on the $200,000!

Therefore, as a negotiating tip, you should go for more property division and less alimony when you get to court or during your negotiations.

## Who Pays the Capital Gains Tax Upon the Resale of the Marital Residence?

Simple rule: If you get the home, you do. If he gets the home, he does.

Suppose you get the marital home as part of a settlement agreement or after the trial. Your husband signs a deed conveying his interest in the property over to you, you record it, and the house is yours and yours alone. You can sell it at any time and the proceeds are all yours.

Let's say you and your husband paid $50,000 for the property in 1965, and that the house is worth $150,000 on the date of the settlement or judicial award. Ten years go by and your home is worth $200,000. *If you're under 55*, you owe the government *capital gains taxes* of 28% (1989 rates) on the gain as follows:

| | |
|---|---:|
| Sales price | $200,000 |
| Purchase price | 50,000 |
| Capital gain | 150,000 |
| Capital gains tax (1989) | 42,000 |
| Net Proceeds | $108,000 |

Under present tax law, *if you're over 55* when you resell your home, you can claim an exclusion of $125,000. Therefore, you'll only pay the capital gains tax on $25,000.

## You Can Reduce Your Capital Gains Tax by Deducting Improvements to Your Property from the Day of Purchase

Let's take the capital gains tax illustration I used above. The capital gain of $150,000 can be reduced by deducting all improvements to the property since the day you bought it. And it doesn't make any difference whether you or your husband, or both of you, paid for the improvements. All that the I.R.S. cares about is whether they are actual improvements to the property rather than ordinary repairs.

I don't want to spend more time on this now because your C.P.A. will help you when the time comes, but there are two very important tips I want to pass along:

---

## TIP ONE

When you are settling your case or during the trial, insist that your husband provide you with all of the data regarding home improvements from the date of purchase. He may have all of the records of contracts, cancelled checks, invoices, etc. and you've got to get these documents *before* he gets his divorce.

On the other hand, if you wait until you actually resell your home and *then* ask your ex-husband for this data, he'll probably tell you to get lost. I've never seen a husband refuse to turn these records over to his wife, or a judge refuse to order their turnover if you bring it up *before* the case is over.

Don't let your attorney forget this. It could cost you thousands of dollars.

---

## TIP TWO

As part of your new single life after the divorce, you'll start to keep your own tax records, including, of course, records on home improvements. Remember you're on your own after the divorce, so ask your C.P.A. to help you set up a system of keeping your tax records.

---

### Can You Ask Your Husband to Pay the Capital Gains Tax When You Resell Your Home?

You can ask but he'll say no. So will the judge if you ask him. After all, they'll say, *you* get the gain in increased value, so why shouldn't you pay the tax?

## How Much Will You Get For ED?

*It depends* on how well you are prepared on your EDFs; how good your experts are; and how good your attorney is.

You can see how important equitable distribution is to you, particularly where your husband has a business or profession. But don't be frightened by its importance. It's your stubborn husband who should be frightened by it. Why?

Your husband is afraid of equitable distribution because he can't change the facts; he can't change the law; he can't hide his records forever; and he will have to divide the assets of the marriage with you, whether he likes it or not. And he won't like it. Not only will he not like it, he'll refuse to believe that everything you and he acquired during the marriage is a marital asset; that his business or profession is a marital asset and must be valued at *fair market value*, not book value; that assets he "created" and put in his name, without any monetary contribution from you, the "li'l ole home-maker," are going to be divided up; that you're going to turn down an offer to "split" the house and "get it over with"; and finally, that the law means what it says—*equitable distribution*. So what the hell are *you* scared about?

---

## CHECKLIST: EQUITABLE DISTRIBUTION

1. Give your lawyer a notebook filled cover-to-cover on the equitable distribution factors and how they apply to you.
2. Rehearse, rehearse, and rehearse some more before the final hearing. It will be up to you to convince the judge to award you a greater percentage of the marital pot than your husband is awarded.
3. Understand your "economic horizon"—what the next ten, fifteen, or twenty years of your economic future look like and be able to articulate it in a courtroom. Your lawyer will help you in this.
4. If "misconduct" is an equitable distribution factor in your state, be sure to tell your lawyer *everything* that might fit in that category.

5. Make sure your lawyer explains *every* major equitable distribution case decided by your state's appellate courts since the adoption of equitable distribution. Know the percentages!
6. Make sure your attorney has a large chart prepared for court to show the judge what the marital pot looks like.
7. Don't skimp on expert witnesses to prove your economic horizon.

The secret to getting a fair award is *preparation*, hours of rehearsal with your attorney, and conference after conference with your witnesses.

Now let's talk about getting your husband to pay for the expense of all this preparation. We're not through with him yet!

NOTE: Please note that community property law is not as simplistic as it would appear. While the end result is 50-50, getting there can be very complex. You just don't walk into the courthouse and say "I want my half." However, I emphasize equitable distribution in this book because most of my readers reside in equitable distribution states.

# Thirteen

# Does Your Husband Have to Pay for Your Lawyer and for Litigation Expenses?

## *Chronology: Henderson v. Henderson, April 1987*

Margo:   Sidney, I got your March bill and I'm shocked. I didn't realize you had to spend so much time on my case.

(Figure 13.1 on page 148 is Margo's bill dated March 31, 1987.)

Me:   Did you check the time slips, Margo?

Margo:   Oh sure, they're OK. What I'm saying is that the case is going to cost much more than I thought. And we haven't really started, have we?

Me:   Not really. We'll probably go to court in a few months for your temporary alimony and child support order, then we'll spend a year or so fighting the "Petition Wars" for discovery and, say, in '89 or early '90 we'll start getting ready for the final hearings.

Anyhow, today we've got to talk about hiring a CPA, your first expert.

Margo:   Why do we need one?

## FIGURE 13.1

## SAMPLE BILL FOR LAWYER'S FEES

---

**SIDNEY M. DeANGELIS**
Attorney At Law
Main Street Professional Building
Smithdale


                                           March 31, 1987

Professional Services Rendered:


Mrs. Margo Henderson
576 Oak Drive
Smithdale, _____


Re: Henderson v. Henderson


January 15, 1987 - March 31, 1987
(54.5 hours at $150/hr. based upon time slips
on file)                                    $ 8,175.00

Out-of-Pocket costs:

  Filing Complaint        $150.00
  Service of Complaint      20.00
  Miscellaneous expenses    12.50
                          _____
                                                182.50

Total . . . . . . . . . . . . . . . .       $ 8,357.50

---

**Me:** Well, Fenster tells me that Roger reports a gross annual salary of $25,000. If we don't have a CPA to attack that, you'll be stuck with asking for alimony and support from *net* income of about $18,000 a year.

**Margo:** That's ridiculous—he makes about $75,000 a year.

**Me:** I know that and you know that, but the judge doesn't. We have to prove Roger's *real earning capacity*, not what he reports.

**Margo:** How much will a CPA cost?

**Me:** Margo, it's not *a* CPA but *an investigative CPA* you need, someone who can go through his records and testify in court. They're expensive. Say a retainer of $1,000.

**Margo:** But I don't have it. And he doesn't have to hire a CPA, does he?

**Me:** No, he can use the company accountant who will swear he makes $25,000 a year gross, and $18,000 or so net. But if you don't have a CPA to testify, you'll get a very low alimony and support order.

Margo:  But can't we just subpoena his records for the hearing? And won't that be cheaper?

Me:  Sure we can and sure it would be cheaper. But let's carefully analyze what you've just suggested.

Look, your alimony and support case isn't scheduled yet, but let's assume we get a date for June 1. It will start at 9:30 in the morning. If I serve a subpoena on Roger for his books and records—you remember the list we sent Fenster last month—he'd have to comply with the subpoena—but not until 9:30 A.M. on June 1!

He'd bring in five cartons of records and turn them over to me at 9:30 A.M. You'll be up on the stand then and I'd be questioning you about your needs. Then I would have to call Roger and begin to question him *while I looked through the records for the first time.* Get it?

Margo:  Yep. It wouldn't work. So you need them ahead of time so you and the CPA can examine them and be prepared to cross-examine Roger.

Me:  Margo, go to the head of the class.

So that day I filed a petition for Roger to come up with $3,000 for a CPA, $3,000 for a business valuation expert, and $5,000 for interim counsel fees. Margo's petition alleged that Roger *reported* $25,000 gross but his actual earning capacity exceeded $75,000 (see Figure 13.2, page 150).

Within a few days, Fenster filed an answer to our petition, stating:

1. Margo doesn't need an accountant because she signed the joint income tax returns and is bound by them.
2. Roger doesn't have money to pay for a CPA or attorney's fees for Margo.
3. Margo is just driving up costs and fees to "harass" poor Roger. She should settle the case, not litigate.

Shortly thereafter, the court administrator scheduled our petition for hearing on May 25, 1987 (and our discovery petition for June 8).

## FIGURE 13.2

## PETITION FOR INTERIM EXPENSES

In the Family Court of Smith County

Margo Henderson                                    No. 87-1234
            Plaintiff
    vs.

Roger Henderson                                    In Divorce
            Defendant

                Petition for Interim Counsel
                Fees and Litigation Expenses

         Comes now Margo Henderson, by her attorney Sidney M.
De Angelis, Esquire, and petitions this Honorable Court for
Interim Counsel Fees in the amount of $5,000 and Interim
Expert Witness Fees in the amount of $6,000 and in support
thereof alleges the following:

1.  That she is the Plaintiff in the foregoing action in
    divorce filed January 16, 1987.

2.  That, to date, her counsel has incurred 54.5 hours of
    professional services on her behalf at $150 an hour
    plus out-of-pocket costs of $182.50, a total of
    $8,357.50, but she is unable to pay for same;

3.  That the Defendant, Roger Henderson, a self-employed
    businessman with an earning capacity in excess of
    $75,000 annually, possesses various assets with a value
    in excess of $100,000;

4.  That she requires the services of an investigative
    Certified Public Accountant to inquire into the earning
    capacity and net worth of the Defendant;

5.  That she further requires the services of a business
    valuation expert to value the Henderson Electronics,
    Inc., all stock of which is owned by the Defendant;

6.  That without interim counsel fees for her attorney and
    without the funds to employ a Certified Public Accountant
    and business valuation expert, she will be unable to
    secure the economic justice provided for in the Divorce
    Code of this State;

7.  That the Defendant, Roger Henderson, can afford to pay
    the sums requested in this Petition;

8.  That the denial of this petition would amount to a
    denial of economic justice to the Plaintiff.

# DON'T COUNT ON COUNSEL FEES
# FROM YOUR HUSBAND

Many women who come into my office ask, "Is it true, Mr. De
Angelis, that my husband has to pay for your fees?" My answer is
always, "Maybe, but let's not depend on it."

Although you are entitled to an award of counsel fees, both during the proceedings and at the final hearing, you should look to your own resources and your own equitable distribution award to satisfy your fee obligations to your attorney, who will get paid out of the assets awarded you by the court, unless you have the wherewithal to pay him as you go along.

In some states, particularly New York, Texas, and California, family court judges appear to be more generous in awarding counsel fees in divorce cases. In most states, however, it's very, very difficult.

There are a number of reasons for this judicial reluctance. In the first place, awarding counsel fees in a divorce case is a relatively new concept for many judges, especially those who can remember when only rare cases permitted counsel fees to be extracted from the other party. (The first equitable distribution law was enacted in 1969.) Also, the judicial system is, by and large, still male-dominated. Many male judges (and some female judges) hesitate to force a husband to pay to have his financial throat cut.

Your tenacious lawyer, however, will do the following:

1. File for interim fees and expenses soon after the complaint in divorce is filed;
2. Remind your husband's lawyer from time to time what your fees amount to and how much you've spent for expenses;
3. Keep going back to court, ideally before the same judge, to argue that you are being deprived of the right to counsel if your husband doesn't pay for your lawyer.

---

## TIP

If you're turned down time after time or awarded piddling amounts for counsel fees or expenses, have your attorney file a petition to *stay all proceedings*—to stop the litigation until you can pay your lawyer. At the very least this will get your husband's attention. He wants to get the case over with as soon as possible.

---

Is it easier to get fees later on? I'm afraid not. Let's consider a childless couple who own a house worth $100,000 (free and clear of any mortgage), bank accounts of $15,000, two cars worth $15,000, and a business operated by the husband and valued by the court at $150,000. The total marital assets, then, are $280,000.

Assume that the court awards one-half of the marital assets to the wife, or $140,000. Therefore, she'll get the home at $100,000, the bank accounts at $15,000, her car at $7,500, and her husband will owe her an additional $17,500 to make up her $140,000. The wife's counsel fees total $30,000. Will a judge make the husband pay an additional $10,000 to $12,000 for his wife's counsel fees? No.

Considering the equitable distribution ordered and the fact that the wife now has $15,000 in cash and a home worth $100,000 that she could sell, it would be inequitable for the judge to make the husband pay for attorney's fees. Her attorney has performed so well as to effectively prevent any award of counsel fees! Translation: the more he gets for you in cash and liquid assets, the less likely it is that the court will award him counsel fees. On the other hand, if he does a lousy job and you're left with very little in equitable distribution, it is likely that the court will make your husband contribute something to your counsel fee bill.

In a tougher example, suppose a couple separates on January 1. The only assets are the marital home and the husband's business. The wife lives in the marital home with three young children and has borrowed $3,500 for her attorney's retainer, which is used up by March 1, but the judge tells her she must wait until equitable distribution is completed before counsel fees are decided. She waits three years, during which time her counsel fees increase to $22,000. At the final hearing, she is awarded the house, worth $125,000 after the mortgage, and her husband is awarded the business, valued at $100,000. The judge denies her any counsel fees because she received a "substantial portion" of the marital assets.

*Now what happens?* She owes her attorney in excess of $20,000 and has been told by the court that she can pay her fees out of the substantial portion of marital assets she received. How? Does she sign over the spare bedroom to her attorney? Does she sell the house and pay her attorney out of the proceeds? To say it's not fair doesn't help much. Your lawyer must convince the various judges who hear these counsel fee petitions throughout the litigation that it's not "economic justice" to sweep these petitions under the rug and that the money he is seeking is not for him *but for you.* He must articulate that, if your husband is in better "economic health" than you are, or controls more liquid assets, you're entitled to have him contribute to your counsel fees.

Finally, he must convince the judge that you can't get the economic justice guaranteed you by the state divorce code if you can't hire CPAs, business valuation experts, real estate appraisers, and so forth.

Some time ago, I was asked by the Pennsylvania Chapter of N.O.W. (National Organization for Women) to recommend changes to our state's divorce code. My first suggestion was for stronger language instructing judges to award counsel fees to "dependent" wives so that *both* husband and wife would have access to effective counsel.

Maybe there's a need for strong lobbying on this issue.

## When Will the Court Make Your Husband Pay Large Counsel Fees?

Will the court ever lift some of the counsel fee burden from your shoulders? The answer is yes, if your attorney:

- Documents hourly charges carefully and fairly;
- Can get across to the judge that your husband and his lawyer were playing dirty tricks throughout the case and delaying the final result;
- Subpoenas your husband's canceled checks for the final hearing, showing the judge that your husband paid $15,000 or $20,000 for his attorney;
- Can, with the help of your CPA, show the judge that your husband is guilty of *economic sin*—that is, hiding assets and income or (worst of all) paying his counsel fees through his business.

In these and other cases where your husband's slippery methods become apparent to the judge, where his own greed and venality come back to haunt him, the judge will make him pay much, if not all, of your counsel fees and expenses.

## If Your Husband Wants to Settle, He Might Pay Most or All of Your Lawyer's Fees

While your chances of getting your lawyer paid through the courts are generally dismal, the story changes when your husband wants out before the case is over and decides to settle.

Let's remember that, in most states, your husband can't get a divorce decree until the entire economic case is over. If he doesn't like the judge's economic decree and decides to appeal, he'll have to wait another few *years* before he's free to remarry.

For these and other reasons, many husbands decide to cut their losses and negotiate an end to the divorce litigation. They accomplish three things by a negotiated settlement:

1. They put an end to their own lawyer's fees.
2. They get an immediate divorce.
3. They limit what they pay you by negotiating instead of submitting themselves to the mercy of some hard-hearted judge. They decide to cut their losses.

Under these circumstances, your lawyer will enter into negotiations for an "amicable" settlement of the economic litigation. He will ask your husband's lawyer for a settlement based on what you're entitled to: equitable distribution of the marital assets; child support; post-divorce alimony; and his counsel fees, your expert witness fees, and your court costs (filing fees, service of subpoenas, cost of depositions, and the like).

If your husband has seen the economic writing on the wall, if he wants out sooner rather than later (if Tracey is getting impatient), if, if, if, then he may agree to pay all your lawyer's fees, or most of them, when he agrees to settle.

## CHECKLIST: ASKING THE COURT TO MAKE YOUR HUSBAND PAY FOR YOUR LAWYER'S FEES AND EXPERT WITNESS COSTS

1. Make sure your lawyer files the first petition for interim counsel fees soon after your complaint is filed.
2. Don't be upset if you don't get what you expect the first time. Your lawyer can always go back and file another petition as the case goes on.
3. Keep accurate records of your expenses for expert witnesses and court costs.
4. Be patient. Don't give up. There's always the final hearing.
5. Try to prove that your husband is guilty of "economic" misconduct (paying his counsel fees through his business, hiding assets, delaying discovery, etc.).

Now let's see how a family court judge actually reacted to Margo Henderson's first petition for interim counsel fees and expenses.

# Fourteen

## *Henderson v. Henderson*: Margo "Loses" Round One

In most states, and in most counties, petitions for interim counsel fees and litigation expenses are heard by judges in a courtroom where you, your husband, and other witnesses actually testify. In large metropolitan areas, New York City and its suburbs, for example, these petitions are not heard in open court but are submitted to the assigned judge who, based on supporting affidavits, decides on the wife's petition and the husband's answer. (In *Henderson v. Henderson*, Smith County, the family court motion judges held hearings in open court.)

Each county, depending on its size, has a certain number of judges assigned to its family court to hear divorce, support, custody, and juvenile cases. In Margo's county, there were four judges sit in family court. The *Henderson* case was assigned to Judge Greene who was known to have a pro-husband bias.

### *Chronology: Henderson v. Henderson, 9:30 A.M., May 25, 1987*

Remember, this is the first time Fenster and I have met in a courtroom (in your case) and the first time any judge has listened

156

to any part of your case. You and Roger sit in the courtroom trying
not to look at each other and wait for the informal conference to
end. Judge Greene has called Fenster and me into his anteroom for
an off-the-record discussion.

Judge:      Gentlemen, before we go on the record what's this all about?
  Me:       Well, Judge, my client has a few dollars in her checking
            account and her assets consist of a wedding band and a
            collection of used books. She owes her parents $2500 for
            various litigation expenses they have advanced to her, and she
            just gets by on the $200 a week Mr. Henderson is sending her
            as voluntary support. My time records show 54.5 hours, or
            $8,175, and we need an investigative CPA. Mr. Henderson has
            a wholly owned corporation. And Joe here won't agree to
            discovery. That's before you on June 8—
Fenster:    Judge, let me interrupt. Sidney thinks that my client is a
            millionaire. No way.
Judge:      What does he do, Joe?
Fenster:    They sell electronic components to manufacturers, but the
            business has gone bad because of competition. Everybody and
            his uncle are in the business now. Anyhow, the net profit of the
            corporation for '86 was $8,221. In addition, Mr. Henderson
            had to borrow money for my retainer and get an apartment—
            she threw him out—and he's paying $200 a week and all the
            bills—mortgage, utilities, insurance, everything. She has no
            expenses. She's in Fat City.
Judge:      Sidney, what's his business worth?
  Me:       We don't know, Judge Greene. We don't have enough money
            to hire a business valuation expert and, as I said, Joe won't
            agree to voluntary discovery, so we haven't looked at any
            relevant books and records, and—
Judge:      (interrupting) Well how can I determine whether to grant your
            petition if I don't know what the relative assets are?
  Me:       That's a good question, Judge. But I have a better one for you.
            How does a dependent spouse hire a good CPA to get you the
            information you need so you can make an informed decision
            unless you give her the money for a retainer in the first place?
            Make Henderson put up the $1,500 retainer for the CPA and

I'll wait for my fees. Then we can get moving on this case.

Fenster:   Look Judge, Sidney doesn't need an accountant. We'll give him the corporate tax returns and the financial statements prepared by our accountant. Why waste $1,500?

*Translation of what Fenster said*: We don't want Sidney and his CPA looking at our original books and records. We want to keep him out of the corporate checkbook. But we'll give him the corporate tax returns and financial statements because they're fudged anyhow.

Judge:   Well, I think we'll have to hold a hearing on this—I can't make a decision based on what counsel says in chambers. Let's go.

After chambers, I cross-examined Roger Henderson for forty-five minutes. He testified that his *draw* was $25,000 a year; that the company paid for all of the expenses for the "company car," a 1986 Mercedes; that the company's financial condition had steadily improved over the past five years; and that he had given Fenster a retainer of $5,000.

The judge ordered Roger to pay $750 for Margo's accountant and $500 to me for interim, or temporary, counsel fees. He didn't even mention the business valuation expert.

But Judge Greene gave us another shot to the head:

Judge Greene:   OK gentlemen, that's my order on Mrs. Henderson's petition for interim counsel fees and expenses. While you're both here, I'll also rule on her petition to take Mr. Henderson's depositions, so you won't have to come back on June 8. Petition denied. Plaintiff's counsel can submit written interrogatories to defendant, which must be answered within twenty days. If plaintiff's counsel feels the answer's are unsatisfactory, he may resubmit the petition for depositions.

Margo and I walked back to my office without saying a word, in fact, not even looking at each other. I expected her to start crying, but she kept biting her lip and bottled up the tears, temporarily.

When we walked into my office, I immediately called Barbara Ann Gordon, the CPA I like to use in these "trench warfare" cases. Barbara, whose hourly rate was $60, agreed to take the $750 and wait until the case was over for her final fee. Barbara talked to Margo on the phone for a few minutes, and they agreed to meet at Barbara's office the next day.

Then Margo began to cry.

Me: What's wrong, Margo?

Margo: *I hate it! I hate it!* He sits there and smirks—he doesn't give a damn about me or the kids. He has all the money he needs for Fenster and his CPA, and I have to grovel in the dirt to get a lousy $750 for my CPA and the whole damn thing stinks. You'll charge me $600 or $700 for the day and we got $1250. What a system! It stinks! We lost, didn't we?

Me: Not really, Margo. Judges are reluctant to award large sums for experts and counsel fees in the beginning of the case. Anyhow, what counts is how Roger perceives the outcome, not so much how you do.

Margo: What do you mean—he knows we lost, doesn't he?

Me: No Margo, he doesn't think that at all. Sure, Judge Greene had him pay only $1,250, and yes it cost you $600 or $700, but you've got to remember the dynamics of divorce litigation.

In the beginning of the case, on Day One, Roger believed he was in a superior bargaining position, that he was invincible. He had money, something he believed to be "litigation" or "staying power." He had you in a subservient position—broke, scared, believing you would lose. And he was firmly convinced that you would settle for a quick divorce on his terms.

It hasn't happened. It's not going to happen. It's going the other way. Sure, it's slow. And sometimes we only move ahead a few inches. But we're moving. Do you think Roger was overjoyed to pay you $1,250 today? I don't think so.

Look, Margo, let me draw you a diagram. I'll call it Climbing the Settlement Mountain. (I walked over to my blackboard and drew the diagram shown in Figure 14.1 on page 160.)

As you climb upward on the Settlement Mountain, he automatically descends. It may be imperceptible, but I can see

## TABLE 14.1

## CLIMBING THE SETTLEMENT MOUNTAIN

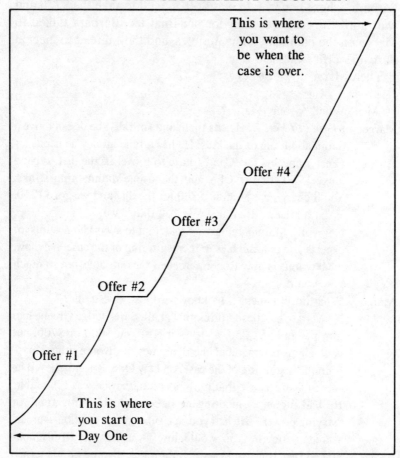

This is where ⟶
you want to
be when the
case is over.

Offer #4

Offer #3

Offer #2

Offer #1

This is where
⟵ ——— you start on
Day One

the movement very clearly. Be patient—you're in control,
whether you know it or not. What's more important, I believe
Roger knows it.

Margo:   It's going to take a long time, isn't it?

Me:   Yes it will. But what else do you have to do these days that's
more important?

Margo:   Well, it may not be important to you, but you don't know what
it's like to handle this damn litigation, worry about the kids,

run the household, wait for the lousy support checks so I can go to the supermarket. And then see that smiling bastard drive up in his Mercedes with that young strumpet wearing her $800 suit, all smiles, to pick up the kids to go to another expensive dinner and then a movie.

I hate it! I don't like taking care of the house and the kids all day long and doing "homework" for you at night. I don't like getting bills from you I can't pay. I don't like not being able to hire experts without begging them to please take my case— "I'll pay you later." I want to go back to school. I want to get on with my life! (in a lowered voice) You know, Roger and I met for a drink right after I filed. He said he'd give me the house and pay your fees—it was late January. I told him I couldn't talk about settlement because you told me not to. Roger reacted like he always does when he doesn't get his way. He gulped his drink down, cursed, and then pointed his finger at me and said: "Listen here, Margo—if you don't take this offer you'll regret it. You don't have two dimes to rub together. You're broke, kid, and your lawyer'll drop you if you can't pay him, understand?"

Me:      What did you say?

Margo:   Nothing. I got nervous and began to cry.

Me:      Why didn't you tell me about it before?

Margo:   Sidney, I was afraid to bring it up. Will you drop me if I can't pay?

Me:      Of course not, Margo. There are two big reasons why I won't drop you. First of all, we have a written contract that says I'll wait until the case is over for all fees over and above the initial retainer.

More importantly, I feel there's a professional obligation to you that I have to fulfill.

And I guess there's another reason too. Your husband is a wise-guy, and I can't wait to get at his books.

Anyhow, let's make a deal. You take care of the kids and the house—and that *is* important to me—and do your homework. I'll work like hell to get you what you're entitled to. And please, from now on, tell me about any conversations you have

## FIGURE 14.2
## STRATEGY LETTER

**SIDNEY M. DeANGELIS**
Attorney At Law
Main Street Professional Building
Smithdale

April 8, 1987

Joseph Fenster, Esquire
Suite 500
Fidelity Building
Smithdale, _____

Re: <u>Henderson v. Henderson</u>

Dear Joe:

　　With all due respect, I think you should advise your
client that his "stonewalling" may cost him a great deal of
money before this case is over.  As I have told you before,
Mrs. Henderson and I have entered into a fee agreement whereby
she has agreed to pay me $150 per hour.

　　Since January 15 of this year I have incurred approximately
fifty hours on her behalf, most of which I must say has been
occasioned by your client's refusal to agree to a voluntary
exchange of financial data.

　　At the same time, his refusal makes it necessary to
retain a Certified Public Accountant to examine those books
and records which the Court will direct him to produce.

　　The point I am making is that your client is running up
large legal fees and he may have to pay Mrs. Henderson's as
well as his own.  Why don't you talk to him, Joe, and let us
get this case out of litigation and into the settlement stage.

Sincerely yours,

SIDNEY M. De ANGELIS

SMD:e
cc:  Mrs. Margo Henderson

with Roger, OK? Actually, you shouldn't talk to him about the case at all.

Margo:  OK, Sidney, I'm sorry. But when can you go back and ask for more fees and expenses?

Me:  Anytime I want to. I'll wait a few months, keep careful records, write a few letters to Fenster telling him his refusal to go along with discovery is only driving up my fees, and when I think it's the right moment, I'll go back again. As they taught me in law school: tenacity, tenacity, tenacity!

Margo:  Did they really teach you that at law school?

Me:  No, I learned it the hard way. Anyway, Margo, this was only the first battle, a skirmish really. After I get some discovery, after I learn what he's hiding, we'll go back for counsel fees with real ammunition.

Margo:  But why would the judge give me more than I got today?

Me:  Because we'll be able to prove Roger's a sinner.

Margo:  A sinner—uh—what do you mean?

Me:  Once we prove he's guilty of *economic sin*, that he's lying about income or expenses or hiding assets, the judge will hang him by his ears, and he'll have to come up with big bucks for me and for your expert witnesses.

    (Margo smiled for the first time that day.)

Margo:  OK, Sidney, let's go!

Figure 14.2 is a letter to Fenster, accusing him of driving up counsel fees and stating the results of his client's refusal to pay for expert witness expenses.

Now, let's get you some temporary alimony and child support.

# Fifteen

# Temporary Alimony

Under the old divorce laws, when a husband and wife were divorced virtually all support for the woman ended, since very few states had alimony laws. If her husband convinced the court that he was entitled to a divorce, that was the end of her support, regardless of how long the couple had been married, what the wife's health was, or what she had done to help him. If she had a career or was wealthy in her own right, fine. But, if she was dependent on him, she would receive nothing. Except for having to support the children, he got out scot-free.

The social revolution that led to equitable distribution made it clear that no longer is a husband allowed to take his earning power with him, inviolate and untouched by his wife. Nor can he take his business or pension plan. The new divorce laws provide that marital assets will be equitably distributed and that marital income may be divided as well.

Except for Texas, every state has adopted an alimony clause in its divorce code. Texas permits temporary support until the final decree of divorce is entered but does not order post-divorce alimony unless the parties agree to it. If you're a Texan, check with your attorney.

## THE DIFFERENCE BETWEEN YOUR TEMPORARY SUPPORT ORDER AND A TEMPORARY ALIMONY AWARD

Let's go back to when your husband agreed to a temporary order to pay you $200 a week, to pay your mortgage and utilities, to allow you to use the automobile, and to pay for your homeowner's and medical insurance. Although this temporary order was for you and the children, it was not allocated, i.e., so much for you and so much for them. It had nothing to do with the temporary alimony and child support counts in your divorce complaint.

Your husband didn't agree to this out of compassion; he agreed to the voluntary order because:

1. He was told by his lawyer that the judge might "kill" him when the alimony and support case was heard if he hadn't fairly supported you and the children in the meantime;
2. He also knew you could get an "emergency" order for, say, $150 a week if he didn't agree to pay you anything; and
3. He couldn't figure out how to starve you without starving the children at the same time.

Anyhow, this voluntary order was "without prejudice"—it could go up or down at the alimony and child support hearing, depending on the testimony. It was a court order, meaning your husband had to comply with it or be held in contempt by the judge, but it wasn't a *final* order based on testimony in open court.

Now the date for your temporary *alimony* hearing is approaching. The hearing will include your request for temporary alimony *and* child support (unless, of course, you have no children). This is because you're dealing with the same formula—your needs, their needs, your husband's earning capacity, and yours. Separate hearings based on the needs of one family would be a waste of time.

The first few months of litigation will be spent getting ready for this court hearing, your first formal battle with your husband before a judge. Again, in some counties your petition for temporary alimony and child support may not be heard by a judge in a court hearing but may be decided just on the papers and briefs

filed. Of course, your attorney will tell you which procedure is
followed in your county.

There are some tactical considerations for you to keep in mind
at this point, so you can understand the game of hide-and-seek you
and your lawyer are about to play with your husband and his
lawyer.

## WHY IT'S IMPORTANT FOR YOU TO GET
## DISCOVERY AT AN EARLY STAGE

If you're in a state that doesn't have mandatory discovery, your
attorney will try like crazy to get discovery *before* you go to court.
*Otherwise he's flying blindfolded.* At the same time, your husband's attorney will try just as hard to keep your team from
looking at anything except an income tax return (which most
counties require your husband to show at this time).

### Your Lawyer *Can* Subpoena Your Husband's Records
### for the Alimony and Child Support Hearing

Realizing the game your husband and his lawyer are playing, your
attorney will issue subpoenas for the financial data needed to try
your case, and your husband will have to comply. Now, your
attorney won't get those records until the day of trial, but he won't
want to postpone the hearing until the court makes up its mind on
discovery.

Keep in mind that this game of hide-and-seek isn't played if
your husband works for someone else; in that case, his W-2
statement shows what his employer paid him and what federal,
state, and local taxes were withheld. If your husband works for
himself, however, his personal income tax return is meaningless; it
merely shows what he wants it to show (that's another reason you
need a CPA).

### Why You Should Go Ahead With the Alimony and
### Child Support Hearing Even If You Don't Have
### Discovery

If heard before a judge, the first temporary alimony and child
support hearing will be the first chance your attorney has to cross-

examine your husband on the record. Of course, your attorney would have preferred to take your husband's depositions before trial. (Depositions, part of the discovery your attorney tries to get immediately after he files your divorce complaint, require your husband to swear to tell the truth and answer all questions about his finances as they are transcribed into a permanent record.)

In some states, court approval is required for depositions, and not all judges automatically allow the husband to be deposed on his financial records.

Absent depositions, your lawyer can subpoena your husband's records, which have to be produced on the day of the hearing. Which means your lawyer has only *a few seconds* to study the records before asking questions.

Of course, your lawyer hopes that the judge will begin to realize that hide-and-seek is prejudicial to you and takes up too much judicial time. Here's what happens—*sometimes.*

### *Chronology: Courtroom, First Day of Temporary Alimony and Child Support Hearing, 11:15 A.M.*

I have been handed several boxes of Roger's financial records, in accordance with a subpoena and have called Roger to the stand for cross-examination. His accountant has seen to it that the papers are disorganized, but I know what the game is. I painstakingly pick up one paper at a time and question him about each document.

|  |  |
|---|---|
| Me: | Now, Mr. Henderson, can you identify this document? |
| Roger: | Well, I really don't know what it is. |
| Me: | Sir, isn't this the corporate tax return for your company for the fiscal period June 30, 1985 to June 29, 1986? |
| Roger: | (stalling) I'm not sure. I'll have to look at it. |
| Judge: | (realizing this could go on forever) Gentlemen, can I see you both in chambers? |
| Judge: | (in the anteroom, looking at Fenster) Do you really believe I'm going to sit here while De Angelis looks through 10,000 documents and your client says he doesn't know what they are? |
| Fenster: | Judge, we gave De Angelis copies of the tax returns and |

financial statements. He's just fishing. We just can't turn over
our entire business records to him.

Me:  Your Honor, we filed for discovery in January, but Fenster
won't cooperate. He's playing hardball.

Judge:  Well he's not going to play hardball in my courtroom. I've got
six other cases on my list. OK gentlemen, this case is temporarily adjourned while De Angelis goes through those boxes
and looks at everything. Sidney, when you're finished let me
know and we'll resume. (turning to Fenster) And if De
Angelis doesn't have enough time to look through them today,
he can keep the records until he *is* ready, and we'll schedule
another day for the hearing. You guys may have time to play
games, but I don't!

## The Generally Accepted Formula for Awards of Temporary Alimony and Child Support

The judge who hears your request for temporary alimony and
child support will base the award on a consideration of these
factors:

- Your needs;
- The needs of your children;
- Your husband's earning capacity;
- Your earning capacity;
- The assets each of you controls.

The formula more-or-less in general use throughout the country is
as follows:

- One-third of your husband's net earnings for your temporary
  alimony (reduced by your net earnings) where there are no
  children;
- Fifty percent of his net earnings where there are one or two
  children (again, reduced by your net earnings);
- 55 percent and up where there are more than two children and
  where you or they have special medical problems.

Therefore the first thing you have to work on are your needs and
the children's. How much do you and they need to live on?

## Preparing Your Income and Expense Statement

Soon after you file for divorce, or your husband files and you file a counter-claim, your attorney will help you fill out a budget, or income and expense statement. The purpose of this expense statement is to provide the court (and your husband) with a weekly or monthly breakdown of what you need to live on in order to enjoy the same standard of living you enjoyed before the separation. To the best of your ability, you'll have to allocate all of your expenses between you and the children. For example, if your mortgage payment is $450 per month and you have two children, you might allocate $150 for you and $300 for them.

In a way, the first hearing for temporary alimony and child support is a mini-equitable distribution hearing. It will set the tone for future negotiations, and it will show your lawyer how your husband handles himself on cross-examination. Its importance transcends the dollar-and-cents award you'll receive, for it is the first time you really take control. Accordingly, you've got to prepare your income statement very, very carefully.

Your lawyer will help you do this and get you ready for the first court battle.

### Chronology: Henderson v. Henderson, May 1987

Me: Margo, let's prepare your income and expense form. You'll have to testify about your needs soon, and you've got to be prepared.

Margo: It looks complicated.

Me: No, it's fairly simple. You just fill in the amount of money you need each week for each category—mortgage, utilities, telephone, and so on. It'll probably be easier if you come up with a monthly figure and divide it by 4.3, the actual number of weeks in a month.

Margo: How do I get the figures?

Me: Well, it isn't difficult. You go through your checkbook for the past year before separation. Get twelve telephone bills, for example, add them up, and divide by twelve. That's the monthly average.

Margo: How about things like food and clothing?

Me:    You'll have to estimate a weekly food bill. Count the super-
       market, things you buy at convenience stores, bakery, and so
       on.

            Clothing'll be a little more difficult. Figure out what it costs
       to clothe the kids through four seasons, and then yourself. But
       remember to base these figures on what things cost while you
       and Roger lived together, *not what you're spending now*. It's
       your *prior* standard of living that counts, except that now your
       expenses are for three people, not four (see Illustration 1).

## ILLUSTRATION 1

ROGER        MARGO      JEFFREY  JENNIFER

            What was the total cost of living for the four of you *before*
       the breakup—food, clothing, mortgage, utilities, vacations,
       repairs, auto expense, insurance, piano lessons, everything?
Margo:  Well, I guess—
Me:    No, you can't guess. Think.
Margo:  OK. Roger brought home about $25,000, but the company
       paid for a lot of things—
Me:    Now you're thinking.
Margo:  I'd say another $10,000 or $15,000 came from HEI—$35,000
       to $40,000.
Me:    Now, what does it cost to maintain you, Jennifer and Jeffrey
       for a whole year? $20,000? $30,000? The only change is that
       Roger is gone. Get it? (See Illustration 2.)
Margo:  OK, Sidney, I can do it. But what about this item—vacations?
Me:    Well, you do another notebook called *How We Lived: Our
       Standard of Living* and tell me about every trip, vacation, who

## ILLUSTRATION 2

MARGO        JEFFREY        JENNIFER

went, what it cost, and how much was paid for by HEI. Then estimate what it would cost for you to take a similar vacation by yourself for, say, ten days in the winter and a two-week vacation with the kids in the summer. Then divide by fifty-two.

Margo:  It's a lot of work.

Me:  You can do it, Margo—we've got time. But remember, this will be your first time on the witness stand, and you've got to know your expense statement backwards and forwards. And don't forget that Roger's attorney must get a copy of it by the end of the month. So do your homework and call me Monday. I'll go over it with you.

At the end of May Margo brought me her income and expense statement (see Table 15.1, pages 172–74) and we spent a few hours working on it.

## The Difference Between Temporary Alimony and Permanent Alimony

You and your husband separated on January 1, and you filed for divorce on January 16. In your complaint you asked for temporary and permanent alimony.

Temporary alimony (or *alimony pendente lite*—Latin, for pending the completion of the case) is the support you are awarded at a hearing (or by court order without an actual hearing), which carries you through to the final divorce decree.

# FIGURE 15.1

## MARGO'S INCOME AND EXPENSE STATEMENT

**SMITH COUNTY DOMESTIC RELATIONS SECTION**
**THIS FORM MUST BE FILLED OUT**

(If you are self-employed or if you are salaried by a business of which you are owner in whole or in part, you must also fill out the Supplemental Income Statement which appears on the last page of this Income and Expense Statement.)

Docket # 87-1059

**INCOME AND EXPENSE STATEMENT OF**

Name   MARGO HENDERSON, JENNIFER & JEFFREY HENDERSON          Case #_____

**INCOME**

Employer:____NONE
Address:_____
Type of Work:_____
Payroll Number:_____
Pay Period (weekly, biweekly, etc.):_____
Gross Pay per Pay Period:          $ _____

Itemized Payroll Deductions:

| | |
|---|---|
| Federal Withholding | $ _____ |
| Social Security | _____ |
| Local Wage Tax | _____ |
| State Income Tax | _____ |
| Retirement | _____ |
| Savings Bonds | _____ |
| Credit Union | _____ |
| Life Insurance | _____ |
| Health Insurance | _____ |
| Other (specify) | _____ |
| _____ | _____ |

Net Pay per Pay Period:          $ −0−

Other Income:

| | Week | Week Month (Fill in appropriate column) | Year |
|---|---|---|---|
| Interest | $ _____ | $ _____ | $ _____ |
| Dividends | _____ | _____ | _____ |
| Pension | _____ | _____ | _____ |
| Annuity | _____ | _____ | _____ |
| Social Security | _____ | _____ | _____ |
| Rents | _____ | _____ | _____ |
| Royalties | _____ | NONE | _____ |
| Expense Account | _____ | _____ | _____ |
| Gifts | _____ | _____ | _____ |
| Unemployment Comp. | _____ | _____ | _____ |
| Workmen's Comp. | _____ | _____ | _____ |
| | _____ | _____ | _____ |
| Total | $ _____ | $ _____ | $ _____ |
| TOTAL INCOME | | $ −0− | |

**EXPENSES**

| | Weekly | Monthly (Fill in appropriate column) | Yearly |
|---|---|---|---|
| Home | | | |
| Mortgage/rent | $ _____ | $ 687 | $ _____ |
| Maintenance | _____ | 75 | _____ |
| Utilities | | | |
| Electric | _____ | 100 | _____ |
| Gas | _____ | 60 | _____ |
| Oil | _____ | 125 | _____ |
| Telephone | _____ | 75 | _____ |
| Water | _____ | 20 | _____ |
| Sewer | _____ | _____ | _____ |
| Employment | | | |
| Public Transportation | $ _____ | $ −− | $ _____ |
| Lunch | _____ | −− | _____ |
| Taxes | | | |
| Real Estate | $ _____ | $ 85 | $ _____ |
| Personal Property | _____ | _____ | _____ |
| Income | _____ | _____ | _____ |

| | Weekly | Monthly (Fill in appropriate column) | Yearly |
|---|---|---|---|
| **Insurance** | | | |
| Homeowners | $ _____ | $ 40 | $ _____ |
| Automobile | | 100 | |
| Life | | | |
| Accident   * | | | |
| Health )   * | | | |
| Other  ) | | | |
| **Automobile** | | | |
| Payments | $ _____ | $ _____ | $ _____ |
| Fuel | | 80 | |
| Repairs | | 50 | r |
| **Medical** | | | |
| Doctor ** | $ _____ | $ 50 | $ _____ |
| Dentist | | 30 | |
| Orthodontist | | | |
| Hospital | | 20 | |
| Medicine | | | |
| Special needs (glasses, braces, orthopedic devices) | | 15 | |
| **Education** | | | |
| Private school | $ _____ | $ _____ | $ _____ |
| Parochial school | | | |
| College | | | |
| Religious | | | |
| **Personal** | | | |
| Clothing | $ _____ | $ 150 | $ _____ |
| Food | | 450 | |
| Barber/hairdresser | | 20 | |
| Credit payments | | | |
| Credit card | | | |
| Charge account | | | |
| Memberships   (Health Club) *** | | | |
| **Loans** | | | |
| Credit Union | $ _____ | $ _____ | $ _____ |
| Remodeling Loan **** | | | |
| Parents   ***** | | 100 | |
| | | | |
| **Miscellaneous** | | | |
| Household help | $ _____ | $ 75 | $ _____ |
| Child care | | 30 | |
| Papers/books/magazines | | 10 | |
| Entertainment | | 100 | |
| Pay TV | | 20 | |
| Vacation | | 150 | |
| Gifts | | 20 | |
| Legal fees ****** | | | |
| Charitable contributions | | 30 | |
| Other child support | | | |
| Alimony payments | | | |
| **Other** | | | |
| Restaurants | $ _____ | $ 100 | $ _____ |
| Gardener | | 50 | |
| Pet Supplies & Veterinarian | $ _____ | $ 20 | $ _____ |
| Total Expenses | | $   2,937.00 | |

      *    It is assumed that the Court will direct Mr. Henderson to continue the maintenance of Blue Cross and Blue Shield coverage.

    **   The Plaintiff is presently being seen by Dr. James Baker, a psychiatrist, who charges $80 per visit. It is requested that the Defendant be directed to make these payments until the entry of the final Decree of Divorce.

  ***  For several years the Plaintiff and Defendant enjoyed the benefits of the Central Valley Health Club. The Defendant then cancelled the family membership. The Plaintiff requests that the membership be reinstated so that she and the children can participate in their facilities. The cost is approximately $600 per year.

 **** Some years ago the parties borrowed approximately $9,500 to remodel their kitchen. The Defendant has been making the bank payments for this loan, and should be directed to continue to make them.

***** The Plaintiff had to borrow $2,500 from her parents for a retainer for her attorney. She would like to pay this back at the rate of $100 per month.

****** The Plaintiff is in the midst of divorce litigation with the Defendant, and will be applying to the Court for counsel fees.

Let's say that on May 15 the judge awards you $150 a week for temporary alimony and $200 for child support (this order is ordinarily retroactive to the date you filed your complaint). Now if, say, two years go by while you prepare for the final equitable distribution hearing and—unless something catastrophic occurs—you get by on the $350 until the final hearing. Then your temporary alimony ends. At that time the judge decides whether or not you get alimony *after* the divorce and if so, how much and for how long. (It's called permanent alimony, but it's really not "permanent," as we'll see in Chapter 16.)

### Temporary Alimony Is Practically Automatic

Let's make some basic economic assumptions so you can clearly understand the nature of temporary alimony. Let's assume your husband's salary is $35,000, that he controls some bank accounts, has a pension plan, and has no major debts. Let's also assume that you're a "dependent" spouse—a homemaker 100 percent of the time or you take care of the home and have a low-paying, part-time job ($3,500 to $7,500 annually). In addition, you're raising two minor children so you can't work full time. Finally, let's assume that you have only a small checking or savings account and no other assets.

With these assumptions in mind and further assuming your husband is in good health, *you will get temporary alimony merely because you are involved in a divorce case.* It will be almost automatic.

How much will you get? Let's go to the blackboard again.


### Husband's Ability to Pay Temporary Alimony

| | |
|---|---|
| Gross Salary | $35,000 |
| Estimated Federal, State, and Local Taxes | 8,000 |
| Annual Net Salary after Taxes | $27,000 |


### Your Weekly Needs Based on the Living Standard You Enjoyed Prior to the Separation (Not including the children)

| | |
|---|---|
| Shelter (½ of the mortgage payment, $400, divided by 4.3) | $ 47 |
| Food | 75 |
| Utilities (½) | 20 |
| Clothing | 40 |
| Telephone (½) | 5 |
| Doctors, Dentists (not reimbursed by medical insurance) | 15 |
| Pharmacy Items (prescriptions, shampoo, etc.) | 5 |
| Car Payments (½) | 15 |
| Fuel, Oil, Repairs (½) | 10 |
| Entertainment (movies, swim club, etc.) | 10 |
| Vacations | 10 |
| Beauty Parlor | 5 |
| Books and Magazines | 2 |
| Total Needs per Week (exclusive of children) | $259 |

*Your Present Earning Capacity or Potential:* $5,000

You should get approximately $165 a week as temporary alimony based on the following calculation. (*We're not considering child support in this example.*)

| Husband's Annual Net (after taxes) | $27,000 |
| Wife's Annual Needs (52 × $260) | 13,520 |
| Wife's Earnings | 5,000 |
| Wife's Net Needs | 8,520 |
| $8,520 ÷ 52 | 164 (±) |

Temporary alimony is almost automatic, or as automatic as any legal concept is. You should file for temporary alimony promptly after you file for divorce, and prepare constantly for the first encounter with your husband. You're entitled to it.

---

## CHECKLIST: TEMPORARY ALIMONY

---

1. Try to get discovery before you go to court for temporary alimony. If your state provides for mandatory discovery, build a fire under your attorney's backside until he gets to work on your husband and his records.
2. Work on your expense statement or budget until you know it by heart.
3. Make sure you base your needs on your prior standard of living, not on what your husband is giving you now (but don't exaggerate your needs).
4. Allocate your expenses between yourself and your children fairly. (Suggestion: One-half for one child; two-thirds for more than one child.)

So much for temporary alimony. Let's talk next about permanent or post-divorce alimony and how you get that.

# Sixteen

# Permanent Alimony and How to Get It: The Alimony Factors

After you filed for a divorce and asked for both temporary and permanent alimony, your husband said, "Hell no, I won't pay," and your lawyer had your request for temporary alimony scheduled before a family court judge, along with your petition for child support. You went to the hearing on June 15, and the judge ordered your husband to pay you $150 a week as temporary alimony and $200 a week for child support, both orders retroactive to January 16. Two years go by while your team fights for discovery and fails to settle the case. All this time your husband has been paying you temporary alimony at $150 a week and child support at $200 a week.

There have been no major economic complications—no serious health problems affecting you or the children—so you haven't gone back to court to modify the $350. Now you're getting ready for "D" Day, the equitable distribution hearing. Where does permanent alimony fit in? The first thing you should know is that at the final hearing the judge will hear equitable distribution (or community property) first, going through the *IVD* formula and hearing all that testimony before your lawyer gets to your alimony claim. (The judge won't *decide* equitable distribution at that point, merely hear the testimony.)

Suppose your equitable distribution hearing begins on July 1, 1989, and there is so much testimony from you, your expert witnesses, your fact witnesses, and from your husband and his witnesses that the case runs over into three more full-day hearings until, say, September 15. The judge will wait until the entire testimony is transcribed, then ask the two lawyers to submit briefs.

After reading the briefs and the transcribed record (or parts of it), the judge will write an opinion called an *adjudication*, a copy of which will be mailed to your attorney, who will call you. That's how you'll find out what you got.

In that adjudication, the judge will first deal with how much property you get, *then* how much permanent alimony you get, if any, and for how long. Next, counsel fees, expenses, and everything else in dispute will be decided. Finally he will issue a decree of divorce. You'll be single again and maybe collecting alimony.

Remember, you will have to testify in support of your claim for alimony just as you did on your claim for equitable distribution, which is where the alimony factors come in. Every divorce code has set forth certain factors that *must* be considered by the trial judge when hearing your alimony case. These alimony factors, carved in granite, are legislative guidelines the judge must follow in deciding whether you're entitled to alimony after the divorce. (They play the same role as the EDF play in your equitable distribution award.)

Let's look at the seventeen alimony factors in Pennsylvania to make this more concrete. Please remember that these alimony factors apply only in Pennsylvania, and that I'm discussing them with you only to give you an idea of the factors and their scope. Be sure to get a copy of *your* state's alimony factors from your own attorney.

## ALIMONY AND SUPPORT:
## SECTION 501. ALIMONY.

In determining whether alimony is necessary, and in determining the nature, amount, duration, and manner of payment of alimony, the court shall consider all relevant factors including:

1. The relative earnings and earning capacities of the parties;

2. The ages and the physical, mental, and emotional conditions of the parties;

3. The sources of income of both parties including, but not limited to, medical, retirement, insurance, or other benefits;

4. The expectancies and inheritances of the parties;

5. The duration of the marriage;

6. The contribution by one party to the education, training, or increased earning power of the other party;

7. The extent to which the earning power, expenses, or financial obligations of a party will be affected by reason of serving as the custodian of a minor child. It would be inappropriate for a party, because said party will be custodian of a minor child, to seek employment outside the home.

8. The standard of living of the parties established during the marriage;

9. The relative education of the parties and the time necessary to acquire sufficient education or training to enable the party seeking alimony to find appropriate employment;

10. The relative assets and liabilities of the parties;

11. The property brought to the marriage by either party;

12. The contribution of a spouse as homemaker;

13. The relative needs of the parties;

14. The marital misconduct of either of the parties during the marriage; however, the marital misconduct of either of the parties from the date of trial separation shall not be considered by the court in its determinations relative to alimony.

15. The federal, state, and local tax ramifications of the alimony award;

16. Whether the party seeking alimony lacks sufficient property including, but not limited to, property distributed under Chapter 4 (equitable distribution) to provide for the party's reasonable needs;

17. Whether the party seeking alimony is incapable of self-support through appropriate employment.

The court ordering alimony shall determine the duration of the order, which may be for a definite or an indefinite period of time which is reasonable under the circumstances.

I'm sure you'll notice immediately how similar the alimony factors are to the equitable distribution factors. They're practically identical but with one major exception. Most alimony factors include "relative assets and liabilities" (Item 10 in the Pennsylvania list). This means that the judge must consider how much you were awarded in equitable distribution before deciding how much alimony you'll get, if any. As we'll see, the greater your equitable distribution award, the less likely you are to get alimony.

## KNOW YOUR ALIMONY FACTORS BY HEART

What the alimony section of the divorce laws tells judges is that they must carefully analyze the *entire history* of the marriage and determine whether the dependent spouse (it is usually the wife, although it can be the husband) is in need of support and maintenance for a period of time following the termination of the marriage. (Yes, your husband can get alimony from you if the factors weigh in his favor and if he has asked for it in his pleadings.)

Therefore you will need another notebook called *Alimony Factors*. Again, you must be acquainted with every factor and begin to work on the narrative involving each one so that your lawyer will know how to present your case. You and your lawyer are likely to spend a minimum of twenty hours on the alimony factors alone.

### Do the Alimony Laws Mean You Can Get Alimony Only if You Go Back to School?

In those states where the divorce code appears to limit post-divorce alimony to "rehabilitative alimony," or just enough support to put you through a retraining program, the courts—at least in the earlier cases—got carried away. They decided that a woman was never entitled to lifetime alimony, or even to alimony for five or ten years, following the divorce. Their pitch was that *every woman* could be "retrained"; so a woman in her late fifties who'd been married for twenty-five years would get alimony only while she "rehabilitated." But this was unfair to women who could not increase their income no matter how much "retraining" they got. It was also unfair to women who were emotionally insecure after a long and often traumatic marriage. They just couldn't become CPAs at the age of 57.

Well, I finally have some good news to pass along. The trend of these earlier cases is being reversed, and reason and common sense have begun to prevail.

Let's look at another divorce case decided in Pennsylvania in 1986 (*Teribery v. Teribery*). While it's a law only in Pennsylvania, I pass it along to you to show which way the wind is blowing.

### TERIBERY v. TERIBERY

Jennie and George Teribery had been married for 31 years. Jennie was 51 and George 52 when they litigated their divorce before a county judge in the western part of the state.

George earned $33,000 at his job, which he'd held for 32 years. His pension plan had been valued at $43,000 as of the time of the divorce hearings. George's health was fine.

Jennie, however, wasn't fine. She'd raised six children, taken care of George, and had no real employment skills. For the five years prior to separation, she had worked as an assembly line packer of dairy products, but had been out of work an average of six months each year.

Moreover, Jennie had been admitted to a mental health facility on four occasions during the year following their separation.

After hearing these facts and valuing the marital assets at $81,500, the county judge awarded Jennie $59,000 of marital assets (including half of George's pension), or 72 percent. George got $21,500, or 28 percent.

George didn't like this award and appealed to the Superior Court of Pennsylvania, which dismissed George's appeal, stating that an analysis of the EDF warranted a 72–28 split in Jennie's favor.

But the county judge hadn't stopped at equitable distribution. He also ordered him to pay Jennie alimony of $180 a week (50 percent of George's net income) *on a permanent basis*, to be reduced only as Jennie earned income from her own employment. Lifetime alimony, he said.

George also screamed in his appeal that it was unfair to award permanent alimony, especially to the tune of *50 percent* of his net income, and that Jennie should go to work or get retraining.

*The Superior Court threw him out on his alimony appeal as well.* In its opinion the Superior Court noted:

> *Appellee's [Jennie's] age and personality diminish her opportunities for better employment. At age fifty-one, she is unlikely to upgrade her salary even with retraining. Furthermore, her treating psychiatrist testified that she was insecure and dependent. He also noted that her separation from appellant caused her to suffer from severe depression. She had been admitted to a mental health facility as an inpatient on four occasions during the year following separation. Her psychiatrist prescribed heavy dosages of antidepressant medication to combat her occasional suicidal inclinations. The psychiatrist expected appellee to recover from her mental disorder, but her timidity and dependent nature were irreversible.*

> *In light of the parties' respective incomes, earning capacities, ages, health, education, standard of living, assets, and needs, we find no error in the award of alimony . . . . Moreover, appellant's departure from the marital home is not the only evidence of misconduct. Depending on the circumstances, leaving the marital home may not constitute misconduct.*

> *However, appellant overlooks evidence of his infidelity. Although appellant denied his extramarital affairs, appellee testified to the contrary. The trial court obviously considered appellee's testimony more credible.*

Are you entitled, or what?

## The Relationship Between Both Kinds of Alimony and Child Support

Keep in mind that the alimony laws are completely independent of child support. Alimony, both temporary and permanent, is a "maybe." You may or may not get an alimony award, but child support is an absolute so long as the children live with you and you maintain and care for them. (We'll talk about child support in some detail in the next chapter.)

However, it is also true that a judge will consider how much child support you are receiving. For example, Richard and Jean separated after thirteen years of marriage. Richard works for an advertising agency and earns a gross salary of $70,000, or $52,000 after taxes. Jean is a part-time computer programmer and nets $10,000 for thirty hours' work per week.

There are three children, ages 10, 8, and 5. Everyone is in fairly good health. Other than the marital home and Richard's pension plan, there are no major assets.

After the separation, Richard and Jean agree that Richard will pay the mortgage, utilities, car insurance, and Blue Cross and will give Jean $200 a week for child support. Jean agrees to take the $200 as a "preliminary" or stop-gap payment, but tells her attorney it isn't enough. Three months later Richard and Jean appear before a family court judge for temporary alimony and child support.

The usual arguments take place. Jean testifies that she needs $500 a week for herself and the children to live on the same scale they enjoyed prior to the separation. Richard says it can't be done. He has to pay for an apartment, his own food, and so forth, on the same salary he had before. Anyhow, his lawyer argues, Jean can work full time and earn enough to support herself.

Jean's lawyer responds by saying that the kids need Jean when they come home from school so she can't work full time. She needs temporary alimony as well as child support, he says.

The judge orders Richard to pay Jean $300 per week for child support, plus all of their medical and dental expenses, and $50 per week as temporary alimony for Jean.

The judge's notes on his yellow legal pad form the basis for his order:

Richard earns $52,000 net. Richard will pay $300 per week, or $15,600 ($\pm$) for the kids as child support.

This leaves Richard with $36,400 a year for his own needs.

Jean earns $10,000 net for her part-time work. She will get

$15,600 as tax-free child support from Richard and will therefore have a base of $25,600 until the equitable distribution hearings.

But Jean will be supporting herself and three children while Richard has only himself to support.

So we'll give Jean another $50 a week as temporary alimony. That will give her $28,200 and Richard $33,800 a year.


Neither Richard nor Jean is happy with the judge's decision, but it's only a temporary order and Jean will get by until the equitable distribution hearing. At that time she may get the house by way of equitable distribution and she may get permanent alimony depending on the alimony factors.

Two years later when they appear before the equitable distribution judge, Jean's lawyer argues that there are two major assets:

1. The martial home worth $95,000 with a current mortgage balance of $35,000, which costs $450 a month not including taxes; and
2. Richard's pension plan, which has a current value of $50,000, as stated by a pension plan expert.

So Jean's lawyer argues that *equitable* distribution would require the court to award the house and contents to Jean (net value $60,000), the pension to Richard ($50,000), and divide the small bank accounts, IRAs, etc. on a 50–50 basis. Richard's lawyer says that this wouldn't be fair. He suggests the home be sold, the proceeds divided 50–50, and that Richard keep his pension.

After the judge hears all of these arguments about equitable distribution, then Jean's lawyer begins the alimony phase of her case. Jean takes the stand and begins to testify about her alimony needs. She shows an expense statement (*for her needs only*), which demonstrates that she requires a total of $20,000 a year for support and maintenance so that she can continue the same standard of living she enjoyed when she and Richard lived together. Richard testifies that Jean can work full time and earn enough to support herself. The judge, convinced that Jean cannot work full time because it would be harmful to the children, is also convinced that Jean's needs of $20,000 a year are reasonable.

Furthermore, the judge knows that Jean won't have any *liquid assets* even after she's awarded the home. Sure, she'll own the house in her own name, but she can't sell it—she has to maintain a home for the three kids for at least ten to fifteen years.

Finally, the judge realizes that the home is a liability now—the mortgage payment is $450 a month. Then there are the taxes and ever-present repairs. How will Jean be able to manage that without substantial alimony?

If there were no children, the judge could easily award Jean $15,000 a year as permanent alimony but, under the facts of the case, he can't. (If he did, Richard would be paying $15,600 for child support and $15,000 for alimony, or $30,600, and be left with $19,000 of his net income while Jean would have $40,600.)

Maybe as the kids get older, the judge thinks, Jean will be able to work full time and support herself but when? Maybe when the youngest, now seven, is ten, or eleven, and the other children thirteen and fifteen.

So it looks like Jean will need alimony help for about four or five years so she can maintain the home for the children.

The judge finally decides to award Jean the house, subject to the mortgage, and $125 a week as post-divorce alimony for a period of six years. By then, she'll be able to make it on her own.

I've gone into some detail on the subject of post-divorce alimony because of its importance where your husband works for someone as opposed to owning his own business or profession in a state that doesn't consider a profession as a marital asset. *Where this is the case and where the major marital assets consist of the marital home and your husband's pension plan, permanent alimony is your biggest weapon.*

## You're Entitled to Your Own Career

The cost of tuition, books, etc. is a necessary and integral part of post-divorce alimony. Let's suppose you have been the "classic housewife" and have not worked since early in the marriage. Your husband has reached his career potential, whether he's working for IBM or running his own business or profession. You too are entitled to your dream of a career in real estate, the stock market, nursing, public relations, commercial piloting, engineering—you name it. *You're Entitled!*

Here's what you do.

1. You decide whether you want to study at a university, full time or part time, day or evening, or to attend a vocational school to enable you to get a good job.
2. You talk to a vocational guidance counselor.
3. You calculate the total cost for college or vocational school, including tuition, fees, books, and any other incidentals.
4. You and your vocational counselor (cost, $350–500) will testify at your alimony hearings that you need $X$ thousand dollars a year for so many years for this career training so that you can achieve your potential;
5. Your attorney will prepare a schedule of your "retraining" needs, which he will admit into evidence along with your "regular" needs.

If your alimony needs, *without retraining*, are $200 a week for five years, let's assume you need another $3,000 per year for the four-year vocational school or college you want to attend. $3,000 a year is $60 ($\pm$) a week. Your alimony needs are now $260 a week for four years and $200 a week for a fifth year. Will you get it? You know the answer by now. It depends. If you prepare properly and retain a convincing vocational expert, you have a very good chance.

---

## TIP

You can say you want to go into public relations, accounting, or whatever all day long and still not convince the court that it's practical. But if you have a vocational counselor *testify in court* that you were tested and proved qualified to enter the field and should succeed, that's another thing entirely. That's *proof*. Make sure your vocational expert has good credentials.

---

## Income Taxes and Your Alimony

Alimony, both temporary and permanent, is usually deductible by your husband as an expense on his income tax return. At the same time, you will have to pay taxes on any alimony you receive. So sayeth the Internal Revenue Code. How does this work?

Let's look again at Richard and Jean. When the judge directs Richard to pay Jean $50 per week as temporary alimony, or $2,600 per year, on April 15 of the following year Richard will deduct $2,600 from his gross income as a proper deduction on his personal tax return, the same as a business expense. Therefore, assuming that Richard will be paying 25 percent of his income as taxes, the $2,600 does not cost him $2,600 but approximately $1,950 annually or approximately $37 per week.

At the same time, Jean will have to include the $50 per week (not $37 per week) as additional income on her income tax return. Her income tax return will now read as follows:

| | |
|---|---|
| Salary (part-time programmer) | $10,000 |
| Temporary Alimony | $ 2,500 |
| Total Income | $12,600 |

Let's assume that Jean will face a 20 percent income tax rate on her base salary of $10,000, or a total tax of $2,000. She must pay 20 percent on total income of $12,600, or an additional $520, so that her total tax bill is now $2,520. Therefore, Jean *does not receive $2,600 as alimony but $2,600 less $520, or $2,080*, which, of course, is not $50 per week but closer to $40 per week. (These tax calculations apply only to alimony awards, *not* to child support, which is neither deductible by a husband on his income tax return nor includable by a wife on her income tax return.)

The higher the award of temporary alimony or permanent alimony, the larger the tax impact. A few years ago, when individual income tax rates were as high as 50 or 60 percent, wealthy husbands were quite willing to pay higher awards of alimony and smaller awards of child support because they got the benefit of a 50 percent or 60 percent deduction and were actually paying about one-half of the alimony award to their wives; the government paid for the other half.

# TABLE 16.1
## POST DIVORCE ALIMONY (FACTUAL APPLICATIONS)

| Your Husband's Situation | Your Situation | Will You Get Alimony? |
|---|---|---|
| 1. He makes $75,000 net after taxes. His health is fairly good. | You are fifty or older. You never worked during the marriage but have always been a homemaker. You have no vocational qualifications. | Absolutely, probably indefinitely. You will not be required to accept a job washing dishes or working in the stockroom of a department store. |
| 2. He earns $75,000 a year after taxes. | You make $20,000 a year after taxes, but you're raising three children from a former marriage. Your first husband is not contributing very much to their support. Your health is getting worse. | Probably, until the youngest child becomes emancipated. |
| 3. He earns $50,000 net. | You earn $15,000 net but you've got a major debt problem:<br>• student loans<br>• loans from your parents for divorce expenses<br>• the judge has decided you'll have to pay your own counsel fees and expenses. | Probably, until you can develop a career (college, graduate school, etc.) and then for a few years thereafter until you pay off your debts and become self-supporting. |

188

| Your Husband's Situation | Your Situation | Will You Get Alimony? |
|---|---|---|
| 4. He earns $75,000 net but has been ordered to give you the marital home ($100,000, no mortgage) and $50,000 in cash. He's also paying the children's college expenses. | You haven't worked for ten years, and you're in fair health. The children are away at school. The home is larger than you need. | Probably a small award, say $2,500 a year for five years. (If you sell the home you'll have $150,000 to invest at 7%, and you'd get $10,000 or so a year.) You'll have to look for work. |
| 5. He earns $75,000 net. He is sending all three children through college—average, $10,000 per child. | You earn $12,000 net. | Probably an award of $50–$100 per week for 3 to 5 years. The children's education comes first. |
| 6. He earns $50,00 net and works 50–60 hours a week or more. He is in fair health but has high blood pressure. | You've got a college degree in marketing but you've never used it. Your children are in their teens. You play a lot of tennis and bridge. | No. |
| 7. He earns $50,000 net. | You earn $30,000 net. There are no children. | No. |

It's important to realize that you will have to pay taxes on any alimony award you get, and you must consider this before you agree to anything by way of settlement.

---

## TIP

If you're negotiating for temporary or permanent alimony, *ask* your husband to pay the taxes on your alimony as well.

---

Using Jean again by way of illustration, her attorney could ask Richard's attorney for an award of $50 per week plus an obligation on his part to pay Jean's income taxes on the alimony every April 15. While husbands don't like to do this, some will go along to settle that aspect of the case. Your attorney should try it.

### Will You or Won't You Get Permanent Alimony?

Again, it depends. The trend seems to run in favor of granting temporary or permanent alimony where there is a *disparity* in the economic situation of husband and wife, not merely to award alimony for the purpose of "rehabilitation." What's meant by "disparity"? I don't mean that alimony will be granted automatically if your husband makes more money than you do. What I refer to, however, are those cases where there is a marked or *significant disparity* in the amount of money he makes and the amount of money you make and, further, where your "economic horizon" is bleak.

Table 16.1 (see pages 188–89) shows some factual applications of post-divorce alimony.

If you identify with Situation 6 (tennis and bridge), I strongly suggest you make every effort to seek employment *before* you get to court. Why take the chance that the court will find that you have the capacity to be a brain surgeon and could therefore earn $200,000 a year? Get the best job you can (even if it's only part time), and then the court won't day-dream about your earning potential (you can play bridge or tennis on weekends).

## CHECKLIST: GETTING PERMANENT ALIMONY

1. Know your alimony factors by heart. Write a narrative for each factor and be ready to testify on each one at length.
2. Work on your income and expense statement (this time without your children's expenses), and *make sure you don't exaggerate any item.*
3. If you can work, get a job.
4. If you can't work, make sure you have medical testimony to back you up.
5. Alimony is taxable to you—you'll have to set some aside each week for your income taxes.

That's how you get permanent alimony. Now, we'll look at how you keep it.

## Seventeen

# Permanent Alimony: How to Lose It

This chapter is about *court-ordered* alimony—that is, payments the equitable distribution judge orders your husband to pay after the final hearing. These are different from *negotiated* alimony payments, which your husband agrees to make as part of an overall settlement without going to court.

### COURT-ORDERED ALIMONY IS SUBJECT TO REVOCATION OR MODIFICATION

The same divorce code that entitles you to alimony also says that, under three general conditions, you may lose all or part of it. Loss of alimony can occur if you remarry; if circumstances change; or if you "cohabit." All conditions do not rule in every state, so your attorney will tell you whether any apply to you.

But not every case goes to court; some are settled by negotiation. For instance, early settlement, though rare, is possible if your husband is reasonable, fears going to court, or wants to remarry before the final court hearing. Out-of-court settlement may lead to an agreement, called a property settlement agreement or contract, providing certain terms your attorney has negotiated and your husband has accepted. The judge then issues a divorce decree on the basis of this agreement, and there is no litigation. But let's see how you can lose *court-ordered* alimony.

192

## STORY

Gregory and Lee were married for twenty-five wonderful years. Gregory, a successful architect with an internationally known firm, had earned over $100,000 a year for the past ten years. Lee and the three children enjoyed a life of luxury. Unfortunately, Gregory never saved any money; it all went for their high priced life-style. By the time the last child had graduated college, Gregory's income had increased to over $200,000 annually, but there were no assets to speak of. The family home had been sold because Gregory wanted to rent an apartment and use the house proceeds for a trip around the world. There was no pension plan, no large bank accounts, no real estate. "Where did all the money go?" asked Lee. "High living, honey," smiled Gregory. They bought new furniture for the apartment, Gregory sent a check for six months' rent to the agent, then called Amy. "Let's go, babe," he said. And go they did.

After Lee filed for divorce, she realized that her claim for equitable distribution wasn't worth anything because there weren't any marital assets to speak of. Gregory had a job, not a business. In her case the real battle was over alimony.

Now let's assume that Lee memorized the alimony factors in her state, she was an excellent witness, and her attorney and CPA proved that Gregory's net income was around $150,000. On top of that, her physician testified that Lee had no earning capacity (arthritis), and her vocational expert said that it was too late for her to go back to school. The judge was in her corner and Lee knew it. Upon receiving the judge's final adjudication Lee was overjoyed to learn that Gregory had been directed under court order to pay her $1,000 a week, indefinitely. If he refused to pay he could be jailed for contempt of court. Barring an appeal, the order was final. (Gregory didn't appeal.)

Six months later Lee met the nicest guy; eventually they got married.

End of story, *end of alimony.*
*It's not fair!*
But that's what the law says.

*How to Avoid the Future Loss of Alimony by Remarrying*

If your husband is willing to settle out of court, try to negotiate a final property settlement that provides that you don't lose your alimony if you remarry. You want that clause written into your settlement agreement. Your husband won't be thrilled about this clause, but may agree to it if he wants to get the divorce over with. (By the way, you can't get a similar "remarriage clause" from the court.)

Another option is to negotiate for lump-sum alimony, payable at the time of your divorce decree. If your husband is facing $500 a week of alimony payments for 10 years, or $260,000, and you believe you may remarry within that period, try to settle for a lump-sum payment of, say, $150,000. This way you keep the lump sum, whether you remarry or not.

Where there are major assets to be distributed and you want big alimony, try to negotiate a "more assets, less alimony" settlement. For example, if there is a vacation home worth $50,000 in the marital pot, your attorney can suggest that your husband deed that property over to you, in return for which you will accept only $100 a week as permanent alimony rather than the $400 you would ordinarily be entitled to. Then if you remarry you lose only the $100 alimony payment; you still own $50,000 worth of real estate.

So much for losing alimony by remarrying (except that you should know that *your husband can remarry* and there's no effect on your alimony award).

Ready? 1-2-3: "It's not fair!"

## If There Is a Change in Economic Condition

What if Lee *doesn't* remarry? What happens when six months after the final adjudication, Gregory suffers a heart attack? Gregory's lawyer files a *petition to modify award of alimony*, which says that Gregory can't work, that his firm is paying him only $300 per week in sick pay, that he has no disability insurance, and that he owns no assets. After a court hearing, Lee's alimony will be reduced to $25 or $50 a week, if not entirely terminated.

A drastic change in your ex-husband's health can't be "negotiated-out." Your settlement contract may say your alimony can't be modified "for any reason," but under these facts the court will disregard that clause.

To avoid this, your lawyer can write a health clause into your settlement agreement so that your alimony award can't be modified even if your husband's health declines—*if his assets and earning capacity remain unaffected.* This way, if he gets sick but his assets and income remain healthy, you won't lose your alimony.

## In Some States You Can Lose Your Court-Ordered Alimony by Cohabitation

In some states, the divorce code says that a *court award* of alimony (distinct from a *negotiated award* ) will terminate if the receiving spouse "cohabits" with a person of the opposite sex not a member of his or her family. Most state courts define cohabitation simply as living together as man and wife.

Although philosophically irrelevant and difficult to apply, such language in the divorce code permits a former husband to hound you to death over your life-style. Unhappy with paying alimony, he may resort to interrogating the kids: "Does Mom have a boyfriend? Does he sleep over? How often?" Yuk. He may even hire a private detective to watch your home. If one night you and your friend decide he will sleep over, is that cohabitation? No. Nevertheless, you find yourself back in court answering a *petition to terminate alimony by reason of cohabitation.* Your husband will lose, but consider what this does to your peace of mind and what it does to your children. *It's Not Fair!*

How can you avoid this outrageous and obscene part of the divorce law? Aside from complete abstinence, you can:

- Avoid any appearance of cohabitation until your alimony runs out—your boyfriend just doesn't stay over;
- File a petition for an *increase* in your alimony award if you learn that your husband's economic situation improves (of course it'll cost you money for counsel fees, but your ex-husband may drop his "cohabitation" crap);
- Try to settle with your husband and negotiate for *nonmodifiable alimony* (which you won't lose even if you remarry or your

boyfriend moves in lock, stock, and barrel). If your husband wants out, he'll probably agree.

## In Some States "Misconduct During the Marriage" Is an Alimony Factor

Alimony is an economic, not a moral, concept. It simply refers to your need for support and maintenance from your ex-husband for a period of time following the divorce. It should be a mathematical and legal calculation, nothing more, but in these states it doesn't work that way:

| | |
|---|---|
| Alabama | Missouri |
| Arkansas | North Carolina |
| Connecticut | Pennsylvania |
| Florida | Rhode Island |
| Georgia | South Carolina |
| Idaho | Tennessee |
| Kentucky | Virginia |
| Maryland | West Virginia |
| Massachusetts | |

The judge may consider what is deemed your misconduct during the marriage a factor in determining whether you are entitled to alimony and if so how much. Your husband's misconduct may be weighed as well.

If modern divorce law is no fault, no longer should a husband and wife fight over who did what to whom. It's all economics, right? Wrong, at least in seventeen sovereign states.

Let's say you're fifty-five, have been married for twenty-five years, raised six children, washed floors in the early years to help support the family, now suffer from varicose veins and can't support yourself. Your husband earns $75,000 a year after taxes. Your lawyer says you need $20,000 a year as alimony for life. In applying the alimony factors of your case, your claim is solid; you should get $400 a week for the rest of your life. *You're entitled!*

But if you live in Birmingham, St. Louis, or Harrisburg and one night years ago told your hubby about an isolated indiscretion, misconduct becomes a factor. His lawyer now cross-examines you about your "adulterous disposition" and the judge allows it. *It's not fair!*

The judge probably will not turn down your claim for alimony under these facts. A solitary act of misconduct doesn't count for much in light of your twenty-five years of being a good and faithful wife.

Would it be different if you'd had an affair with your next-door neighbor for twenty-four years? Probably. The trial judge in a divorce case is an eight-hundred-pound gorilla; he or she can do anything: consider your misconduct as a basis to deny you alimony at all; cut your demand in half; or whatever he or she *feels* is just. Sure, you can file an appeal to the higher court if you don't like the award, but who needs the additional expense, delay, and aggravation?

To make it worse, not only can misconduct be considered in a sexual context; it can be anything your husband throws at you under the general heading of misconduct. So in "no-fault" litigation you may find yourself denying that you were a poor cook, didn't do windows, or disliked his mother. The misconduct states do not define it, so it's up to the judge to *interpret* it. Here are some simple rules on misconduct:

1. *Tell your lawyer everything.* Don't hold anything back because *you* think it's not misconduct.
2. If your husband also played "true confessions," tell your attorney what he said; let *him* worry, too.
3. Never think for a moment that your husband won't testify against you about "that party" or "the nude encounter" or "that night in Miami." He will.
4. If you are cross-examined about your "moral lapses," don't waffle; tell it like it happened. **It is better to confess to a single act of adultery or a short-lived affair, than to destroy your entire case by lying.**

Remember that misconduct as an alimony factor applies to your or your husband's conduct only *during the marriage*, not after separation.

If you separated at 10 P.M. and commenced a torrid love affair with a tango dancer at 10:30, it would be irrelevant. The judge would not hear any evidence about it (other than to determine what time you started!).

In general, "misconduct" won't affect your case. Most judges will quickly see that your husband is just trying to bash you a little and will stop it. If you need alimony to maintain yourself, you'll get it as long as the other alimony factors are on your side.

But as I said before, don't lie. As this next story shows, you must tell your attorney the entire truth about your marital history, or you can be in big trouble.

### STORY: WANDA THE WHIPEE

Many years ago, I was in a large firm. One day one of my young associates came in to see me.

Tom:  Hey, boss, I've got a problem. You've got to help me.

Me:   What's up?

Tom:  Well, a woman came in last week and began to tell me some story about kinky sex, and frankly, it's all over my head. I never learned about this stuff in parochial school, and I don't think I can handle it.

I smiled. He was a bright, eager, young attorney who had just been sent up to the domestic relations front.

Me:   Tell me about it. I'll see what I can do to help you.

Tom:  Well, we filed for wife support, and she has to prove that she left the house for some good reason and did not desert him. [This, of course, was before equitable distribution.]

Me:   So?

Tom:  Well, when I asked her why she left, she said it was because of his sexual habits. She said he beat her, kind of.

I tried to look serious and bosslike.

Me:   You'll have to tell me what she said.

Tom:  (hesitantly) Well, she said that he would get dressed up in funny black clothes and boots and whip her. She's very embarrassed to talk about it in court. I think she wants you to try the case.

Me:  Well, Tom, I'll be glad to try it, but I don't have the time to prepare the case. So here's what we'll do. You get the case ready for trial and put the case on my calendar, and I'll go over to the courthouse and try it for you. But I want you to be there with me so you can learn how to do it. By the way, have you asked her to locate the paraphernalia?

Tom:  What paraphernalia?

Me:  You know—the whip, the boots, the black hood.

Tom:  What do you mean?

Me:  Well, Tom, it's one thing for her to say, "He beat me with a whip," but what happens when he says, "You're out of your mind! I never did such a thing," and she can't prove it. Why don't you ask her to see if she can locate the cardboard box in his closet where he keeps his stuff.

Tom:  How do you know there's a cardboard box in his closet? And how do you know there's a hood? I don't get it.

Me:  Tom, I've been practicing domestic relations law for some twenty years. Tell her to go back into the house—she has a right to do that—and get the cardboard box and put it in our office safe. Make sure that you bring it over to the courtroom on the day of trial. I'll try the case; you just get it ready.

So young Tom called Wanda and explained that she had the right to go back into the marital home to retrieve the cardboard box with the paraphernalia (it turned out to be a large, brown shopping bag, not a cardboard box). Wanda called Tom the next day and triumphantly told him that she now had the proof. But she didn't tell him everything.

Early one morning, about a month or so later, I noticed on my calendar that I had to try Wanda's support case at 1:30 that afternoon. I called Tom and reminded him to bring the brown bag over to the courtroom so that we would be prepared. In the meantime, Tom was busily preparing Wanda for her fateful testimony before the judge.

Wanda came into my office with Tom at about 12:30, and I had a brief chat with her about her testimony.

Me:  Wanda, you can't be embarrassed about this. You'll have to tell it just like it happened. I'll put you on the stand and ask you how much you need for support and then I'll ask you to describe the circumstances under which you left the house. You'll tell the judge just why you left, and then I'll ask you if you've ever seen the shopping bag before. Then I'll hold the items up, one by one, and you can identify them. At that point, Wanda, your husband's lawyer should ask to stop the case, and you'll get the support you need.

Wanda looked at me with an almost imperceptible look of fear in her eyes. I'd seen it before—it was apprehension about going to court. Sure, that's what it was.

Wanda took the stand at 1:35 and her case went just fine for the first three minutes. She told the court her name and where she lived. She briefly described how much she needed for support and maintenance. Then in response to my question, she told the court she had to leave the marital home because her husband beat her, and she described the details to the shocked courtroom. She then identified the brown paper bag as having been the one in her husband's closet. I turned to my opponent, winked, and said, "Now, Wanda, what did your husband wear when he beat you?" She almost whispered, "High black boots!"

Everyone in the courtroom, the judge included, looked at her husband, who had about size fifteen feet, as if he were some piece of refuse found in a garbage dump.

I now whispered to breathless Tom, who was sitting next to me, "Hand me the bag." *For the first time* I reached into the brown shopping bag, fiddled around for a few seconds, and pulled out two high-heeled black boots, size five and a half.

Because I couldn't think of anything else to say, I held the boots high up in the air and said, "Now, Wanda, are these the boots your husband wore when he whipped you?"

Of course, the courtroom exploded with laughter. The judge, an old friend of mine, decided to rescue me from my lack of preparation.

Judge:   Can I see counsel in my chambers, please? And, you don't have to bring the, er, clothing with you.

   Well, of course, Wanda was not the whippee, but the whipper. But she hadn't told me that. After all, she was ashamed.
   You might be interested in learning that the husband gave in at that point! Why? Well, *he* was too ashamed to get up on the stand and explain why he permitted his wife to use the paraphernalia. If I recall, she'd asked for $300 a week, he offered to give her $200, and everybody left the courtroom somewhat satisfied, although I had egg on my face for at least two or three years after that sorry episode.

The moral of this story: tell your lawyer everything, no matter what it is. Remember Wanda the Whippee.

## Negotiating Tips for Permanent Alimony

1. Never negotiate a settlement where your husband says, "Let's divide the assets 50–50. I want to be fair." Counter with: "OK. I want to be fair too. I'll take 50 percent of the marital assets and 50 percent of your net income as permanent alimony."
2. Remember that your husband gets a tax break on the alimony he pays you. If his tax bracket is at 25 percent, his $300-a-week alimony payment actually costs him $225. You won't get $300 because you'll have to pay income taxes on your award. Negotiate his paying your income taxes on the alimony payments.
3. If you enjoyed a $25,000 standard of living prior to separation and you can earn only $15,000 a year, generally you're entitled to a $10,000 alimony award, especially if you do not receive *income-producing assets* as part of your equitable distribution award.

## Chronology: Henderson v. Henderson, May 1987

Margo:  Sidney, do you realize we've spent over ten hours on my statement of income and expenses?

Me:  I sure do, but remember that Fenster will spend a lot of time cross-examining you on these items, so it's better if you're prepared. As a matter of fact, let me take another hour or so and cross-examine you as if I were Fenster to see whether you can remember what I've taught you about cross-examination.

Margo:  But we've done that before!

Me:  I know, but you'll be in front of the judge soon and you've got to be ready.

Margo:  OK. Go ahead.

Me:  (imitating Fenster's deep, theatrical voice) Now, Mrs. Henderson, your expense statement indicates an item of $687 per month for a mortgage and another $300 or so for utilities. That's almost a thousand a month, right?

Margo:  Yes, sir.

Me:  Well, can't you rent a garden apartment for $500 or so? I mean, you don't need a four-bedroom home, do you?

Margo:  Mr. Fenster, my husband and I and the children have enjoyed our home since June 1975, almost 12 years. My husband left, as you know, on January 1. I don't see why that should affect *our* needs, sir. After all—

Me:  Wait a minute, Mrs. Henderson. I—

Margo:  Mr. Fenster, you just interrupted me. If you don't mind, I'd like to complete my answer.

As I was saying, we lived in a four-bedroom home when we lived together; he could afford it then, and he can still afford it. Our needs haven't changed, we still require a home. Just because he left doesn't mean we should live in an apartment, does it?

I stood up and applauded. Margo was grinning. She was ready.

## CHECKLIST: PERMANENT ALIMONY

1. Make sure to ask for permanent alimony in your divorce complaint or counterclaim;
2. If the only major assets are your home and your husband's pension (no business or profession), go for big permanent alimony.
3. As you approach your final hearing, prepare for your alimony testimony; know your alimony factors by heart;
4. It may be advisable to negotiate for lump-sum alimony or more property and less alimony, so you won't lose your court-ordered alimony by remarrying; undergoing a change in economic circumstances; or cohabitating.
5. It may also be wise to negotiate for more child support and less alimony to reduce income taxes on alimony payments.
6. Permanent alimony may include all college or vocational school expenses.
7. If you have a serious health problem you will need your physician to testify at your alimony hearing.
8. You'll need a vocational guidance counselor as an expert witness to prove you have negligible earning potential.
9. If there's "misconduct" in your past, tell your attorney everything!
10. Your statement of income and expenses is extremely important in your temporary and permanent alimony hearings. Know it by heart and expect to be cross-examined on every item. Don't exaggerate!

So much for temporary and permanent alimony. Let's get on to child support.

# Eighteen

# Child Support

The temporary child support (and temporary alimony) order you got within the first few weeks of separation relieved you of some anxiety during litigation. You should now press for a permanent award of child support. You can probably get more money from the court, and the increased payment will be retroactive to the date you filed for divorce. Also, if your temporary support order is *unallocated* (simply specifying $200 a week for wife and children for example), you can reduce taxes with an order allocating your husband's payment between child support and temporary alimony. (Unallocated orders are taxable as alimony; child support isn't taxable.)

Child support is not, in and of itself, part of the divorce code. The obligation of parents to support their children predates all divorce laws; such obligation arose from the common law the colonists brought from England. It must be discussed because, where children are involved, child support is such an integral, albeit separate, part of the termination of most marriages. Other than being heard as part of your temporary alimony hearing, your child support hearing will not be a part of your divorce litigation (unless you ask the court to enter a higher award of child support in a final hearing). Therefore, the kind of wife you were or the kind of husband he was will not enter into the child support equation.

The issue of child support usually will be heard early in the litigation, in many cases by a judge who has no part in your divorce fight. *If you have young children, the order of child support may be the most important facet of your divorce case.*

## STORY

Andrew and Louise had been married for twelve years when they separated, and both had successful careers. Andrew operated a plumbing and heating concern with a partner, and Louise had a small but profitable travel agency. Their three children were 10, 7 and 5 years of age. Andrew's net income was $50,000 a year and Louise's about $25,000. Both were in good health. The major assets up for equitable distribution were the marital home ($125,000, mortgage $35,000), Andrew's 50 percent partnership interest (valued by Louise's expert at $100,000), and Louise's travel business (valued by Andrew's expert at $25,000). I told Louise that she would probably get the marital home and furniture and that she and Andrew would keep their businesses. Minor assets (small bank accounts, IRAs, cars) would be split 50–50. I also told Louise that she was not a good candidate for permanent alimony because of her business. "Your battle," I told her, "will be for large child support—not for equitable distribution or alimony."

So I went after Andrew with a hammer and a tong for a large order of child support. We never even asked for alimony. I had Louise testify in great detail about how her own income would be eaten up running the home and paying for her own expenses after the divorce. She'd also prepared a detailed income and expense statement for the children that showed their weekly needs to be $500. Andrew couldn't do much about her testimony except listen.

It worked. The judge awarded her $300 a week for her children. She didn't get permanent alimony, but the $15,600 a year for her nontaxable child support made up for it.

## FIGHT FOR A LARGE CHILD SUPPORT ORDER

In fighting for a large child support order, your attorney will need to know every aspect of your children's needs, from religious education and skiing instruction to eyeglasses and orthodontia. Present and future medical/dental expenses, camp fees, swim club fees, pet expenses, teen tours, hobbies, and allowances all need to be taken into account. (Child support is more than just food and clothing.)

This does not mean you can use child support to sandbag your husband after the separation. (The court usually will not tolerate Jeff's sailing lessons if he has never been on the water before.) The court will award you a fixed weekly sum for all reasonable and necessary expenses of raising the children keeping in mind that some of the things you might like to do for your children may not be possible during the divorce litigation. It's all a matter of balance and common sense.

*Nevertheless, you should not compromise on child support.* Make sure you list all of their needs at your *first* hearing. If you have forgotten anything or an unanticipated need crops up, you'll have to file a *petition to increase child support order* and go through another court proceeding to modify the original award. (So will your husband if he wants to decrease the order.)

Also keep in mind that although in most states any permanent alimony received will terminate upon remarriage, child support will terminate *only* as the children are emancipated—that is, marry, go off to college, or get a job. Therefore, while you and your attorney may be reasonable in the settlement negotiations with regard to equitable distribution, permanent alimony, or counsel fees, you should not be "reasonable" when it comes to child support. For instance, it's morally and legally wrong for your husband to become the rich father and you the poor mother when summer vacation comes along. If you, your husband, and the children vacationed at the seashore every summer for the past few years, don't be "reasonable" by giving that up. List vacations as an item of need in your income and expense statement for the children (more about that later), the cost to be based on *your* taking the children on the same, or similar, summer vacation.

Invariably your husband's attorney will lay a trap for you when he cross-examines you on this subject:

Fenster:   Now, Mrs. Henderson, I note in your income and expense statement that you require $200 a month for entertainment and vacations.

You:       Yes, sir.

Fenster:   Do you realize that comes to $2,400 a year?

You:       That's correct.

Fenster:   Well, Mrs. Henderson, did you spend $200 a month for that item last month?

You:       No, Mr. Fenster, we didn't have it to spend last month.

Fenster:   How about the month before?

You:       No, we didn't have it to spend the month before either.

Fenster:   Then why should my client pay it to you now, Madam?

You:       Mr. Fenster, when we lived together as a family unit we spent at least that much for entertainment and vacations, 80 percent to 90 percent of which was for the benefit of the children.

           I believe it is in their welfare for them to continue enjoying entertainment—movies, athletic events, cultural activities, summer vacations, and so forth, despite the fact that their father and I are getting divorced. Their needs haven't changed one bit.

Fenster:   But—

You:       I'm not finished, sir. Now I can't afford to provide the $2,400 a year for this need of theirs. My husband can. Therefore, in answer to your question, your client should pay this item now because it is what we spent *before* the separation, it is what we need *now* and, finally, Mr. Henderson *can afford* to pay it.

Children should not be punished because their parents can't get along. Jeff may need a new baseball glove or Jennifer may need a new pair of jeans whether their father lives at home or not.

## Your Children's Income and Expense Statement

It's up to you to establish on the witness stand what your children's needs are. Once you're certain what's fair and reasonable, don't settle for less, which is where your income and expense statement comes in. So that it can be filled out properly, supply your attorney with a chronological history of your children's expenses from the time they were born. In many cases the children's expenses were also *your* expenses (house, utilities, transportation, telephone, vacations, etc.), so you'll have to allocate your household expenses and your children's on one income and expense statement. You must write down their direct expenses—food, clothing, medical and dental expenses, summer camp, athletic equipment, tutoring, instruction, etc.—as well as household expenses.

Make sure you separate your needs from theirs. Review old bills to break them down.

## Medical Expenses for the Children
In establishing medical or dental needs, talk to your husband first: "Roger, I've been told that Jennifer needs orthodontia. Will you come to the dentist tomorrow?" If he refuses, get the doctor to write a report and send it directly to him, inviting him to discuss the treatment and its cost. Insist that your husband provide the children with *full* medical, dental, and psychiatric coverage, not just the portion covered by insurance. He should pay for office visits, tests, or anything not covered.

If you have to fight over medical expenditures, bring the doctor to court to testify, as a letter is unacceptable evidence unless your husband's attorney agrees in advance and reviews it—which many won't do, preferring instead to put you to greater expense and trouble. (Still, once your lawyer tells your husband's attorney that Dr. So-and-so will be testifying for you, there will be an agreement to use a letter instead.)

## College Expenses for the Children
When it comes to getting college expenses for your teen-age children be reasonable, but also be prepared. First, calmly discuss these costs with your husband before you even get to court. *This is a must.* Second, if your husband earns $50,000 net and you need $15,000 a year for your support and another $10,000 for the children, then you have to be prepared to compromise on a state college rather than a private one, or cut back on your alimony demand. He has only so much income to share.

However, if your husband is unreasonable, stubborn, and un-yielding ("I didn't go to any fancy college and I made it, didn't I?"), be prepared to fight it out.

Get a written synopsis of all college expenses and incidentals (tuition, room, board, books, fees, transportation, etc.) and send it to your husband's attorney for a stipulation that he will not require testimony from your child on the witness stand. If he won't agree, prepare your child to testify that he or she has been accepted to such-and-such college, that the total cost is $X$ dollars per semester, that there won't be enough time to study and work full time, that part-time work will provide only $Y$ dollars a week, and that the family income precludes getting a federal loan. It is the rare father who is so warped that he will require his child to testify in a support proceeding. However, once in a while a psychopathic personality who loves money more than his children will insist on it. It's tough on the child, but it's also necessary. Your child will have to testify.

## THE CHILD SUPPORT PROCEDURE

In most counties, you'll have to file your income and expense statement or budget with the domestic relations office of the family court. You and your husband probably will have to attend a preliminary conference before a hearing officer of the domestic relations office (not a judge) who will ask some basic questions about your job, benefits, taxes, etc. Even though both attorneys will be present, this is only an intake conference designed to settle the "easy" cases. If your case can't be settled, however, the hearing officer will make a recommendation for child support, which your husband must obey.

In large counties, the next step in the support proceeding will be a hearing before a "master," an attorney appointed by the court to hear all cases of temporary alimony and child support. The master is a court official, not a judge. Both you and your husband will testify and will be cross-examined. Your accountant and other financial witnesses may testify as well.

The master's decision is not the final word, and if either you or your husband objects to the master's recommendation you can ask the court to hear your case. For instance, if the master believes you can earn $12,000 a year and awards you only $50 a week for child support, you can appeal (called filing *exceptions*) for redetermination by a judge.

In smaller counties a judge will hear your case directly within a few months after you ask for child support. In most counties, child support hearings will be a full trial before a judge, with a court reporter transcribing the testimony so that you and your attorney will have a complete record of the proceedings.

### How Long Will the Trial Take?

By now you know what I'm going to say: It depends. If you and your husband both work the case could take an hour or so. On the other hand, if he has a business, you haven't worked for a while, and your child needs orthodontia, therapy, or anything else you and your husband can't agree on, you can count on up to five days of trial—not necessarily *consecutive* days. Consequently, it could take months.

### You Can't Lose

No matter how long it takes, you must realize that you can't lose in a child support proceeding. Even though you may ask for $250 a week and get only $150, or the judge may decide that you have an earning capacity that precludes your getting temporary alimony, still you can't lose. Not only will your husband be on the defensive under cross-examination by your attorney, you will get your first real chance to show him that you won't break. Moreover, *your husband's economic situation will be recorded for the first time in black and white.*

---

### TIP
Don't compromise on child support. Go all the way!

---

### Keeping Your Husband Honest When You Negotiate for Child Support

1. Don't let your husband get away with "Look, take $100 a week and I'll make it up—you know I love them." I'm sure he

loves his children, but insist on full child support reflecting their actual needs.

2. Don't take less child support and more alimony. Remember, alimony payments terminate if you remarry, and it will cost you to go back for more child support if you lose your alimony or have it decreased for any reason.

3. Don't fall for suspended child support while the children visit or vacation with their father. You're entitled to fifty-two weeks a year in child support. (That's the law!)

4. Don't be afraid to go to court over child support; it's not sinful or immoral.

5. Don't be unreasonable, however: you needn't fight over wedding expenses for your eight-year-old daughter.

6. Don't forget that the children's expenses will increase as they get older. Therefore try to get a cost-of-living increase every two or three years.

7. Don't agree to voluntary child support—that is, a private agreement not subject to court order. Your husband may say that it's humiliating for him to pay for his child's support through the court system. Let him be humiliated and insist on a court order. Suppose he makes voluntary payments for three months, then gets a job in Bahrain! Good luck!

8. Don't be afraid to enforce punctual payment of child support. If late payments become a problem, take him to court. Don't be shy about it. Your husband needs the education, and your children need the money.

9. Don't assume that the burden of child support is entirely your husband's. If you have earning capacity, you have a duty to help support the children.

10. Don't concede under cross-examination that you can easily earn *X* dollars a week doing part-time work. You might be awarded that much *less* when your support order is computed—whether you're working or not.

## Child Support Orders Are Never Final

A child support order can be modified by the courts at any time. Suppose a mother and father fight over child support, go to court, and endure three months of hearings. At the end, the judge may issue a comprehensive order such as the one shown in Figure 18.1.

## FIGURE 18.1
### SAMPLE CHILD SUPPORT ORDER

ORDER

   The parties have three children, Timothy 15, Betsy 12,
and Mark 10. The father's net earning capacity is $45,000
per year. The mother has a limited annual earning capacity
of $2,500.

   The children attend public school. Timothy is an
accomplished athlete. Betsy requires orthodontia treatment
with $1,200 remaining unpaid. Mark has been taking karate
and swimming lessons.

   The reasonable needs of the children require $12,500
per year, of which the mother can supply $2,500. Accordingly
the court issues the following order:

   1. Father shall pay to the Domestic Relations Office
      the sum of $200 per week for the support of
      Timothy, Betsy, and Mark;

   2. Father shall also pay for Timothy's athletic
      equipment up to $350 per year; for the remainder
      of Betsy's orthodontia treatments ($1,200); and
      for Mark's swimming and karate lessons up to $500
      per year;

   3. This Order shall decrease by $50 when Timothy
      reaches the age of 18, becomes employed, graduates
      from high school, or leaves for college (whichever
      is the last event to occur); by an additional $50
      when those events apply to Betsy; and shall terminate
      as these events apply to Mark;

   4. The parties shall attempt to negotiate an amicable
      solution to mother's request for Timothy's college
      needs. If the parties cannot accomplish this, the
      Court will hear this dispute within 60 days of
      this day.


                              _____
                              Thomas A. White, Judge

   The order is spelled out clearly, but what happens if Mark
develops problems requiring psychiatric treatment, his mother gets
a full-time job at $12,000 a year, or his father suffers a drastic cut
in salary?
*Either party can file a petition to modify the original order,*

resulting in a new hearing, additional testimony, additional attorney's fees and, finally, a new order. There is no statutory limit on the number of times an order can be modified. If Mark's father gets a big raise in salary or his business becomes more profitable, his mother can go back and ask for more child support. The prevailing order can be amended/renewed as circumstances change until the children are emancipated.

## CHECKLIST: CHILD SUPPORT

1. Ask immediately for a separate child support order as soon as possible. Never agree to voluntary payments not paid through the court.
2. Try to negotiate an amicable order with your husband; if you can't, go to court.
3. Give your attorney all necessary information about your children's needs so he can help you prepare a complete income and expense statement. Remember to allocate fairly all household expenses between you and the children.
4. If you have some earning capacity, get a job.
5. Never accept larger alimony payments in lieu of smaller child support payments.

So much for the law and background of child support. The bugles are blowing for the first real battle. Let's go!

# Nineteen

# The First Battle:
# Margo Wins Round Two

## *Chronology: Henderson v. Henderson, June 1987*

If you recall, Margo asked for temporary alimony and child support in her complaint for divorce filed January 16, 1987, a few days after she received Fenster's "Dear Madam."

Shortly thereafter Roger agreed to a temporary order of $200 per week. He also agreed to pay the mortgage, utilities, all unreimbursed medical and dental expenses, and to give Margo the use of the car and his gasoline credit card. A judge signed the stipulation thereby making it a court order but "without prejudice," meaning Margo could ask for more and Roger could try to cut it back when the case was heard in court.

I then asked that the case be scheduled for May, hoping by then I'd have some discovery, but when we appeared we were told to file written questions. The judge (Greene) did not authorize face-to-face questioning with Roger on the "hot seat" under oath. (Remember, in Margo's state there was no compulsory financial disclosure.) So there would be no support hearing in May.

I filed the interrogatories on June 1. Roger's answers to the interrogatories, filed on the last possible day, gave me no information. Fenster made sure of that.

Nevertheless, when Margo's alimony case was scheduled for June 26, I decided to go ahead, discovery or not, hoping I could prove "economic sin" by cross-examining Roger on subpoenaed documents. Also, the case had been assigned to Judge Harriet Jackson, so we wouldn't have to worry about "Mr. Husband" Judge Greene anymore. This is what was racing through my mind as I got the notice from the Court Administrator.

*Good News:* Judge Jackson is "Judge Straight-down-the-middle." She doesn't favor husbands or wives—she just calls them as she sees them.

*Good News:* June 26 is only a few weeks away. I'll get Roger on the stand real soon. I can't wait.

*Bad News:* Judge Greene's order denying the oral depositions I needed said I could ask for them again if Roger's written answers were vague. They were vague, all right, but I can't get back to Judge Greene, have him change his mind, and take Roger's depositions by June 26. I'll be going into battle stone-cold.

The judge's schedule for June 26 showed only two hours for the case—how could I get to Roger's earning capacity in two hours? After all, Margo had to testify about her needs and be cross-examined first. Even though I'd be "flying blind" I didn't want to ask for a postponement. So that I'd have at least *some* records to work with, I subpoenaed Roger's personal and corporate income tax returns for the past five years, his canceled checks (personal and corporate) for the past two years, and the financial statements for the past five years prepared for HEI by his CPA and, finally, the HEI books and records for the same period.

My biggest problem, however, was time! I had two hours to put Margo on, establish her needs, and then convince the judge that Roger's $25,000 a year was only the tip of the financial iceberg.

The only relevant papers Margo had been able to find were the invoice for Roger's Mercedes (he'd paid $34,500 for it in mid-1986) and a 1986 corporate tax return for HEI. Well, ready or not, here I come.

### Chronology: Telephone Call, June 5, 1987—10:30 A.M.

Roger:   Joe, I just got your letter. How come we got a lady judge?

Joe:   She's a judge, Roger. What's on your mind?

Roger:  I had her checked out. She's tough—they call her "Stone-balls"
        Jackson.

Joe:    Nah, ya got it wrong—"stone-wall," not "stone-balls."

Roger:  I hear she's tough. Can ya get someone else?

Joe:    Don't worry. I can handle her. Anyhow, I can't change the
        assignment. Let's get ready for court.

## *Chronology: Telephone Call, June 5, 1987—11:00 A.M.*

Margo:  Sidney, is that good news—a woman judge?

Me:     I don't think it's good or bad news, Margo. Harriet Jackson is
        a fair, tough but unbiased judge. I think you'll do well in front
        of her.

Margo:  Well, does she favor women? I mean, after all . . .

Me:     Forget it, Margo. She's a good judge. I'm pleased we got her—
        but don't expect her to treat you any differently than she treats
        Roger. And don't forget you're not working. She may not like
        that. But she's got a mind like a steel trap, and that's all that
        counts.

## *Chronology: Henderson v. Henderson, Testimony, June 26, 1987, 9:30 A.M.*

When we walked into the courtroom on June 26, I once again
sensed Roger's arrogance. He was used to getting his way. I could
almost read his mind as he stared at me ("You won't touch me, you
SOB!"). Fenster smiled and glad-handed everyone as usual, but I
felt he was nervous beneath the surface.

Margo took the witness stand and testified very convincingly.
She was scared, of course, but more important, she was angry. The
judge liked her. I was proud of her—all the rehearsing had paid
off.

Margo:  Your honor, based on our previous standard of living, our
        present needs, and the fact that my husband can afford to pay
        this sum, the children require $350 per week and I need $250
        per week as temporary alimony, plus the items my husband is
        now paying by agreement.

With regard to my earning capacity, I haven't worked for nine years and feel that the emotional turmoil we are going through makes it impossible for me to work at the present time. I'm also raising two preteen children.

Then Fenster began his cross-examination.

Fenster:  Now Mrs. Henderson, you appear to be an intelligent woman. If my mathematics are correct, you're asking the court to direct my client to pay you $30,000 a year as direct support, plus mortgage, utility, and insurance payments of another, say, $8,000 to $10,000—that's $38,000 to $40,000 a year when the income tax return *that you signed* shows his wages from HEI at $25,000 gross. Can you explain that, Madam?

Margo had been well-rehearsed for this question. She smiled coolly as she answered.

Margo:  In the first place, Mr. Fenster, your mathematics are correct but your knowledge of my husband's financial situation is not.

Secondly, I am not asking for $30,000-plus for *me*, sir, but for me and my two young children who live with me. They are, as you know, nine and seven years old.

Thirdly, you point out that I signed the joint income tax returns. Of course I did. I did everything that Roger told me to do, including signing his income tax returns *in blank*.

Finally, you asked me to explain how he can afford to pay $30,000 plus on an income of $25,000. The answer is quite simple, Mr. Fenster—

Fenster:  (feeling gored) Your honor, would you tell the witness to stop making speeches. She's not responding to my question. I object.

Judge:  Well now, Mr. Fenster. I think she's responding very well, nor do I think she's making a speech. You asked her a four-part question, and I think she should be permitted to answer all four parts, don't you?

Fenster:  (looking gray) Uh, yes, ma'am.

Judge:  (smiling at Margo) Please continue, Mrs. Henderson.

Margo:  Thank you, Your Honor. (turning to Fenster, with a ferocity I hadn't seen before) What you don't know, Mr. Fenster, is that Roger *draws* $25,000 a year from his business and then takes what he wants from the business to pay for everything else. He—

Fenster:  But Mrs. Henderson, you—

Margo:  (fighting back) You interrupted me, Mr. Fenster. I haven't finished the question you asked me.

Judge:  Let her finish, counselor.

Margo:  Let me give you some examples of how Roger paid between $75,000 and $100,000 to run the household before he left. (counting off on her fingers)

- He paid for all restaurant, travel, and entertainment by using his company American Express card even though none of these things had anything to do with his business.
- He paid for all repairs to the house from the business, including a $15,000 addition two years ago.
- All of our gasoline, car repairs and auto insurance were paid through the business.
- He took cash from certain customers, didn't report it, and used it for expenses when we traveled. He said the IRS couldn't trace it that way. He kept the cash in a cigar box in the bedroom closet.
- He paid our day worker through the business.
- He bought his Mercedes through the business.

    Mr. Fenster, I could go on for another hour, but I realize that we don't have much time this morning. I'll stop there but I have more to tell the court if there's time.

Fenster:  I have no further questions.

Me:  Now Mrs. Henderson, please tell the court again what you are asking for today as alimony pendente lite and child support.

Margo:  (slowly, to the judge, giving it everything she had): $350 a week for the children plus all their unreimbursed medical and dental expenses. $250 a week for me as temporary alimony plus all my unreimbursed medical and dental expenses. Plus all the items Roger agreed to in the order signed by Judge White on January 21. Plus summer camp or day camp if the children decide to go. And if it's proper, I ask that this order

be made retroactive to January 16, 1987, when I filed my
complaint in divorce.

Me:    No further questions.

Fenster:    I have nothing further.

Judge:    Thank you, Mrs. Henderson, you may step down. Your next
witness, Mr. De Angelis?

It was now 10:45. If I let Fenster call Roger to the stand there
wouldn't be enough time for me to get to him. Fenster would make
sure to drag his direct examination out beyond 11:30. I had to go
for Roger now.

I turned to Roger and said, "Your Honor, I call Roger Henderson to the stand on cross-examination." (Ordinarily, Fenster would
have called Roger to the stand as his witness and Roger would have
gone through his script. But I felt that by calling him, which I had
a right to do, he would get flustered right away. He did.)

Me:    Mr. Henderson, please try to answer my questions as directly
and precisely as possible.

Roger:    (sneering) Sure.

Me:    You own all of the stock of HEI, don't you?

Roger:    Yeah.

Me:    There is no independent board of directors, is there?

Roger:    Uh, no.

Me:    You and you alone decide what to pay out of the corporate
treasury, isn't that so?

Roger:    Well, my accountant—

Me:    Mr. Henderson, didn't we agree that you would answer the
questions *directly*?

Fenster:    Objection, your Honor, Mr. De Angelis is badgering the
witness.

Me:    Mr. Henderson, am I badgering you?

Roger:    (arrogant) No way.

Me:    Answer the question, Mr. Henderson.

Roger:    Yeah, I decide what to pay—unless we don't have any money.

Me:    Well sir, in the summer of 1986 was your company out of
money?

Roger:    (puzzled) We're always short.

Me:    Were you short of money in the summer of 1986?

Roger:  (treading water) I guess so.

Me:    Was your company short of funds in mid-1986?

Roger:  Uh, yeah we were.

Me:    If the court please, I would like to mark a corporate income tax return for 1986 as Plaintiff's Exhibit Number Three.

        Now, Mr. Henderson, do you recognize this document?

Roger:  Sure, it's the Form 1120 corporate income tax return for Henderson Electronics, Inc.

Me:    Who prepared it?

Roger:  Howard Picker, our CPA.

Me:    Is it correct?

Roger:  (still puzzled) Sure.

(I moved in for what I thought would be the first "kill.")

Me:    Then, sir, can you explain this item under depreciation called Automotive Equipment—$6,450 in your company tax return?

Judge:  (looking at a copy, getting interested) What page is that, Mr. De Angelis?

Me:    Page four, Your Honor.

Roger:  Well I'm not an accountant, but the IRS says that a corporation can depreciate equipment. It's perfectly legal.

Me:    I didn't ask you if it was legal, sir, but now that you've brought up the subject of legality, tell the court what automotive equipment was depreciated for $6,450.

(Fenster looked concerned, and Roger turned green.)

Roger:  Yeah, it was the company car.

Me:    For which the "company" paid $34,500?

Roger:  Yeah, I think so.

Me:    And the make of the "company car" is . . .

Roger:  It's a used Mercedes.

Me:    1986?

Roger:  Yes.

Me:    Now tell us again why your company deducted $6,450 on page four of its 1986 corporate income tax return?

Roger:   I told you—it's a proper deduction.

Me:      (it was now or never) So the company, HEI, owns the 1986 Mercedes?

Roger:   (now chartreuse) Yeah.

Me:      And the title to the Mercedes is in the company name, right?

Roger:   Uh, sure.

Me:      Then can you explain why the invoice from Classic Motors, and we'll call it Plaintiff's Exhibit Number Four, dated July 14, 1986, lists *you* as the purchaser, not your company?

     And further, why the state bureau of motor vehicles lists you as the owner of the Mercedes?

Roger:   You'll have to ask Mr. Picker.

Judge:   He's asking you, Mr. Henderson. Answer, please.

Roger:   (now drowning) I don't know.

Fenster now stood up and attempted to rescue Roger from the obvious, but it was too late. Fenster screamed that it was irrelevant, that it was argumentative, that I was badgering poor Roger, and that I should ask Picker these questions, not Roger. The judge was unimpressed by Fenster's theatrical outrage.

Judge:   No Mr. Fenster, you objection is overruled. I understand what Mr. Henderson and his accountant did here. It seems to me that every American taxpayer is helping to pay for Mr. Henderson's Mercedes. Go on, Mr. De Angelis.

By now, the judge knew what had happened. Roger (and Tracey) wanted a new Mercedes in July 1986. HEI paid for it, and Roger insisted that the car be put in his name. Picker knew it was wrong, but he went along because HEI was an important client. Neither Roger nor Picker ever thought that the transaction would be scrutinized in a courtroom less than a year later.

All this time I was feverishly scanning the subpoenaed HEI cash disbursements ledger Fenster had turned over to me only this morning. I felt like a fighter pilot in the middle of a dog-fight. There were enemy planes all over the place.

As Fenster did his screaming number with the judge, I flipped through the monthly HEI checks. Most of them were run-of-the-mill—Roger's net salary, wages, utilities, etc. But the ledger showed Roger getting $200 a week, and the explanation was in a column called "Officer's Loans." I smelled blood.

| | |
|---|---|
| Me: | Before we leave the Mercedes, Mr. Henderson, would you kindly explain why your corporation pays you $200 a week over and above your monthly salary? |
| Roger: | Uh—it's a loan I made to the corporation. They're paying it back. |
| Me: | When did you make a loan to HEI? |
| Roger: | (now with a funny look on his face) I dunno—a few years ago. |
| Me: | How much did you lend the company? |
| Roger: | (looking for a life preserver) Uh—I think—uh, it was $34,000 or so. |
| Me: | And the company paid that money over to Classic Motors so you could have a Mercedes. |
| Roger: | I'm—uh—not sure about that. |
| Judge: | Did they or didn't they, Mr. Henderson? |
| Roger: | I think they did—Picker knows for sure. |
| Me: | So you lent $34,000 to HEI and now they're paying it back, right? |
| Roger: | Ask Picker. |
| Me: | (on a hunch) Well, neither you nor Picker can find a check for the $34,500 right? |
| Roger: | I guess. |
| Me: | Where did you get the cash, Mr. Henderson, the $34,500 in greenbacks? |
| Fenster: | Objection! Your honor . . . |
| Judge: | Overruled, Mr. Fenster. Go on, Mr. De Angelis. |

Now I had opened up the cigar box full of cash. I was beginning to have fun.

I decided to leave the '86 Mercedes and went on to another subject. I showed Roger an HEI canceled check for $5,000 dated January 5, 1987, made out to Fenster, Clark and Williams, marked "retainer—corporate advice." I glanced at the clock. It was almost 11:30. I showed Roger the check and gave the judge a copy.

Me: Mr. Henderson, you left the marital residence on January 1, 1987, did you not?

Roger: Yeah, she threw me out.

Me: Well, whether you were thrown out or you just flew away, you then hired Mr. Fenster to represent you on January 5, 1987, the first Thursday after the Christmas–New Year holiday, isn't that true?

Roger: I'm—uh—not sure. I don't recall.

Me: Well, let me help you with your memory. Please look at Plaintiff's Exhibit Number Five.

Roger: (grimacing at the check) OK.

Me: Is that the check you used to retain the Fenster firm for your divorce matter, sir?

Roger: It says "retainer corporate advice."

Judge: Please answer the question, Mr. Henderson.

Roger: I don't remember.

Me: Well sir, do you have a canceled check from your personal checking account for $5,000, also dated January 5, 1987?

Roger: I guess not.

Me: So Plaintiff's Exhibit Number Five is how you paid for Mr. Fenster's services in this matter, correct, sir?

Roger: I guess so.

Judge: (interrupting) Mr. Fenster, what does your client's personal return for 1986 show?

Fenster: Well, Judge, the corporate tax return—

Judge: Anything wrong with your hearing, Joe?

Fenster: No, Your Honor. It shows $25,000.

Judge: Have it admitted into evidence along with the plaintiff's exhibits.

Gentlemen, I've heard enough evidence. It's about 11:30 and I have a long list today. I think we'll have an early lunch. (to the court reporter) Transcribe the record as soon as you can, Mrs. Stevens. (to the lawyers) Get me short briefs by Wednesday. I'll hand down a decision by July 14. Thank you gentlemen.

After court adjourned Margo and I walked to the corner coffee shop for lunch.

Margo:  How'd I do?

 Me:  You were great!

Margo:  I've never been so scared in my whole life. I thought I was going to faint.

 Me:  Do you know who's really scared, Margo?

Margo:  Do I ever!

We both laughed.

## Chronology: Hiding Under the Table at the Smithdale Cafe, June 26, 1987, 3:00 P.M.

Fenster:  Thanks for lunch, Rog.

 Roger:  (after three martinis) OK, Joe. Look, I don't like this crap. Why didn't you stop that stuff about the Mercedes?

Fenster:  Wait a minute, Roger, I don't make the rules. It was relevant evidence. The whole transaction stinks. Anyhow, De Angelis does that stuff all the time.

 Roger:  Whaddya think the judge will do?

Fenster:  I don't really know—$300, $350, maybe less.

 Roger:  Well, whatever, how long do I have to pay it?

Fenster:  Roger, you'd better have another drink. You have to pay it until the divorce is final. If there's an appeal you pay until the appeal is decided.

 Roger:  How long could it take?

Fenster:  Two, three years, maybe more.

 Roger:  Why can't I get a divorce now and do the money crap later?

Fenster:  Like I told you before, Rog, in this county the courts wait until the whole case is over before they issue a final decree. That's true in most jurisdictions. Anyhow, you won't get a divorce until Margo gets her economic settlement—equitable distribution, alimony, counsel fees, and so on.

 Roger:  But Tracey wants to get married, Joe, she's putting pressure on me. I told her I'd get a divorce in ninety days because we have no fault.

| Fenster: | You told her wrong, Roger. Tell Tracey to relax. It'll take a couple of years. |
|---|---|
| Roger: | It's not going like I thought. |
| Fenster: | It never does, Rog. |
| Roger: | Why can't we settle the damn case? |
| Fenster: | Because De Angelis says "no discovery, no settlement talk"— you remember. |
| Roger: | Well Joe, I'm not blaming you, but I don't want to go broke on this case. Let's give 'em the records they want and maybe Margo'll settle. She looked nervous today. |
| Fenster: | I didn't think so. |
| Roger: | She'll break—you'll see. Anyhow, tell De Angelis he can look at the damn records. Let's try to get this over with. Christ! He got the worst stuff already. Why did Picker let me put the car in my name, damn it? |
| Fenster: | I think it's a smart move. If we get the same judge for the equitable distribution hearing, she'll make you give De Angelis everything. Maybe we can still lose a few papers here and there. I'll call De Angelis tomorrow and tell him he can have discovery. But promise you're not hiding anything, Rog. |
| Roger: | No, that's it. Do your best, Joe. |
| Fenster: | I always do, pal. Give my regards to Tracey. And tell her to be patient. |

### *Chronology: Henderson v. Henderson,*
### *June 26, 1987,*
### *4:30 P.M.*

I had to go to the courthouse in the afternoon for a short hearing on another case. When I got back, Marge told me Fenster had called. "He said you could take Roger's depositions next week if you were available, and he wants to depose Margo."

| Me: | I'm not surprised. |
|---|---|
| Marge: | How'd it go, do you think? |
| Me: | I'm not sure, Marge, maybe $400, $450. |
| Marge: | Good. Margo deserves it. |

I called Fenster and we set up a date for Roger's depositions.

Fenster:  How about talking settlement now?
  Me:  After discovery, Joe.

Only a day after we filed our briefs, I received Margo's alimony and support order in the mail (see Figure 19.1).

## FIGURE 19.1
## MARGO'S TEMPORARY ALIMONY AND SUPPORT ORDER

```
In the Family Court of Smith County, _____


Margo Henderson                     Support Case - No. 87-1059
          Plaintiff
     vs.

Roger Henderson
             Defendant

                        ORDER

     And now this 2nd day of July, 1987, after hearing in
open court, it is ordered and decreed that Roger Henderson,
Defendant, shall pay the following amounts to the Domestic
Relations Office of this County:

     For alimony pendente lite for petitioner, Margo
Henderson, $250 per week;

     For child support for the minor children, Jeffrey and
Jennifer Henderson, the sum of $350 per week;

     The Defendant shall also maintain complete medical and
dental insurance for his wife and children and shall also be
responsible for their unreimbursed medical and dental expenses.

     The respondent shall further continue paying for those
items listed on the Stipulation dated January 20, 1987, with the
exception of the telephone and utility expenses, which shall
henceforth be the obligation of the petitioner, Margo
Henderson.


     This order shall be effective as of January 16, 1987.  Any
arrearage created by this order shall be paid at the rate of
$50 per week in addition to the Order set forth above.


                    By the Court,


                    _____
                    Harriet S. Jackson, Judge
```

I called Margo immediately. She was so excited she could hardly listen.

First I explained the judge's mathematics. She would get $600 a week but she'd have to pay telephone bill and utility expenses—they'd run about $75 or so a week—but she could manage easily. Roger was still under an order to pay the mortgage, the various insurance payments, and allow her to use his gas credit card. The court had hung Roger and made him pay another $50 a week for the arrearage. At that rate, Roger would have to pay the extra $50 a week for 108 weeks. So the total was $650 a week for the next two years.

Then I explained to Margo that Roger couldn't take an appeal from the alimony part of the order because the alimony order was temporary and in our state a temporary order can't be appealed. He could appeal the child support portion, but I doubted he would go to the expense.

I told her the good part last. No matter how long it took now or what delay there was, Roger would have to pay the $650 plus until the arrearage was paid and then $600 plus until the case was over.

Me:    Margo, I don't think Fenster will play defense any more. Roger will be paying over $35,000 a year and he has to come to the conclusion that he wants the case over with quickly. No more delay.

A few years ago a client bought me an imitation-brass plaque she'd found in a "hokey" souvenir shop in Atlantic City. I don't remember the inscription, which was in Latin, but I do remember the translation:

When you've got them by the balls,
their hearts and minds will follow.

## Twenty

# Discovery and Depositions: Looking for the Smoking Pistol

Pretrial discovery is perhaps the most important legal procedure prior to going to trial. A divorce attorney who neglects to take pretrial discovery for his client is probably guilty of malpractice, particularly when he represents the dependent spouse and there is some question about the husband's *real* income along with a suspicion of hidden assets. Although no judge is present during the proceedings, discovery is a legal proceeding. What your lawyer discovers during the pretrial procedure may become more important than the eventual trial before the judge. If your attorney tells you he doesn't think discovery is necessary, tell him to write you a letter explaining why—you'll get discovery very soon.

After the judge came down with her $600 plus a week order, Roger suddenly wanted to get the case moving—fast. Depositions were set to start on July 10 at 10:00 A.M.

The first thing I did was to send Fenster a list of documents I wanted to examine and copy by no later than July 3. (I made sure Fenster understood that this list of documents was only my *initial* request.)

After sending Fenster a letter confirming the deposition date, I prepared another stipulation, this one signifying Roger's agree-

228

ment to supply documents and be deposed. Roger, I knew, felt the noose tightening around his neck.

The Henderson documents were delivered to my office on Friday, July 3 at 4:00 P.M. My friend Fenster assumed I'd go sailing Monday and Tuesday, come back to the office late Wednesday morning, and then be too busy to look at them before the depositions.

But as much as I love sailing, I had a job to do. So I pleaded with Barbara Gordon, the CPA we'd engaged, to meet me at my office on Monday night.

At about 7 P.M. on the night of the sixth, Margo, Barbara, and I began going over all of the tax returns, financial statements, canceled checks, and other documents Fenster had delivered. My conference table was completely covered by papers and mushroom pizza.

Most of Roger's business checks were run-of-the-mill stuff. However, Barbara kept those that were in the "slush-fund" category in a separate pile, called the "Funny Pile." Margo and I reviewed all of Roger's personal checks. I was looking for the "smoking pistol," a hidden asset, hidden income, or evidence of "fancy" accounting.

On July 10, Roger and Fenster came to my office. The court reporter set up her transcribing machine, Roger touched the Bible, swore he would tell the truth, then started to light a cigar.

|  |  |
|---|---|
| Me: | Mr. Henderson, I hope you don't mind, but I would prefer that you not smoke during these proceedings. |
| Roger: | (to Fenster) Can't I smoke? |
| Fenster: | Wait till the break, Rog. |
| Roger: | Shit! |
| Me: | Mr. Henderson, would you kindly explain the "Loans from Officers" item of $34,500, which appears in the balance sheet of Henderson Electronics as of December 31, 1986? |
| Roger: | (blinking) You'll have to ask the CPA. |
| Me: | Sir, I'd like you to answer the question, please. |
| Roger: | I really don't know what it is. |
| Me: | Well, tell me this—who is the officer who made the loan to the company? |

(Roger turned to Fenster and they began whispering to each other while looking at the balance sheet. I waited patiently. Hell, I already knew the answer to the question.)

Roger:  I loaned the money to the company for working capital—they were short.

(Fenster had now turned slightly away from Roger and was staring at the paintings on the wall.)

Me:     Did you make this loan during the year 1986?
Roger:  I think so.
Me:     From your personal funds?
Roger:  I guess.
Me:     Then you would have a canceled check from your personal account in Smithdale National to HEI for $34,500?
Roger:  I suppose I do.
Me:     May I see it, please?
Roger:  It's gotta be in that package of checks we delivered last week.
Me:     (with a straight face) Mr. Henderson, suppose you take these canceled checks, all in consecutive order, and find the check for $34,500.

(Glumly Roger looked through the pile of checks and, of course, couldn't find one for $34,500.)

Roger:  I can't find it.
Me:     But the company states on its books that you loaned them $34,500 during 1986, doesn't it?
Roger:  I guess so.
Me:     You are the president of Henderson Electronics, Inc., correct?
Roger:  Uh-huh.
Me:     Is there any other company officer who loaned HEI $34,500.
Roger:  I don't think so.
Me:     So you gave the company $34,500 in cash?

Fenster:   Don't answer that, Mr. Henderson! (Agitated, Fenster points his finger at me.) Look here, De Angelis, you just accused my client of income tax evasion and you can't back it up. I want you to know I'm reporting you to the Disciplinary Board of the Supreme Court.

Me:   Sure Joe, go right ahead. And while you're performing that civic duty why not stop in at the fraud division of the IRS and report your client's income tax hanky-panky.

Court Reporter:   Shall I transcribe that last exchange?

Fenster:   Nah.

(Of course by now Roger knew that I knew, but there was nothing he could do about it—he was on the hook and couldn't get free. Every word he said was under oath and transcribed in black and white. In the meantime, Margo watched it all, completely fascinated.)

Me:   Let's turn to another subject, sir. I see HEI gives checks to you each week for $200 marked "repayment of loan." Can you explain them, please?

Roger:   Yeah, that's to repay me for the money I put up, the loan of $34,500.

Me:   So you loaned the company $34,500 and they pay you back at the rate of $200 a week, or $10,600 a year. Is that it?

Roger:   Uh-huh.

Me:   I understand, sir. But tell me, what did HEI do with the $34,500? (I winked at Joe Fenster.)

Roger:   I don't know—pay bills, I guess.

Me:   Would it refresh your recollection, Mr. Henderson, if I were to remind you that HEI purchased a 1986 Mercedes in July 1986, from Classic Motors for the sum of $34,500?

Roger:   (wishing he were anywhere else) If you say so, counselor.

Me:   Well did they or didn't they, Mr. Henderson?

Roger:   OK, they did.

Me:   Mr. Henderson, isn't it true that you gave your bookkeeper, Thelma Rickels, $34,500 in cash on July 14, 1986, told her to deposit it in the company checking account in Smithdale National, then had her write a check out to Classic Motors on the same day for $34,500 so you could own a Mercedes, and then told her to put the deal on the books as a loan so you could get back the $34,500 tax free?

Roger:  No, that's ridiculous.

But everybody in the conference room, including Roger, knew it wasn't ridiculous. I pressed on.

Me:     Mr. Henderson, do you own any assets other than those you've listed on your statement of assets, even in someone else's name or in a corporate or partnership name?

Roger:  No.

Me:     Are you sure?

Roger:  No—nothing else.

Me:     In this state or any other state?

Roger:  No—nothing else.

Me:     Sir, do you owe any money to any banks?

Roger:  No.

Me:     Did you ever have any bank loan in the past five years?

Roger:  (unaware of where I was leading) Yeah, a few years ago we were short of cash and the company wanted to buy a large quantity of components, so we borrowed $40,000 or $50,000 from Citizens. But it's paid back.

Me:     (leading him on) Well, did the company use these funds to buy the components?

Roger:  Absolutely—it's in the records.

Me:     So you paid the loan back in full?

Roger:  Absolutely.

Me:     And when did the company make that loan, sir?

Roger:  Oh I guess '82, '83. I'm not sure exactly.

It was getting late and I was beginning to get weary of chasing this cat through the jungle, but there was one other area I had to cover before we quit.

Me:    Mr. Henderson, I note that HEI has been sending checks to your father, Ralph Henderson, for the past few years. Our CPA, Ms. Gordon, says these checks total $35,000. What's it all about?

Roger:    Consulting fees.

Me:    I beg your pardon?

Roger:    My father is a consultant and the corporation pays him for his services.

Me:    What's his salary?

Roger:    What?

Me:    What—is—his—salary?

Roger:    I dunno.

Me:    Who would know?

Roger:    What?

Me:    Would Peter Pan know how much his salary is? (Roger sneers, doesn't answer.) How much did he get so far this year? Take your time and try to answer the question.

Roger:    He gets paid on a per-job basis. I'll have to check the books to see how much he got.

Me:    What kind of consulting does he do?

Roger:    Financial planning.

I called a short recess and took Joe Fenster aside.

Me:    Joe, where's the $35,000?

Fenster:    How the hell would I know?

Me:    Shall I subpoena the old man for next week?

Fenster:    Nah—I'll talk to Roger.

He and Roger whispered between themselves. They looked like two nervous bridesmaids at a wedding. Then he came back to me.

Fenster:    We'll stipulate the $35,000 is in a mutual fund in the name of Ralph Henderson.

Me:    And will you—

Fenster:    Yeah, we'll agree to a court order tying it up till the final hearing. Are you finished?

Me:    Yep, I've got enough for today. It's your turn. Thank you, Mr.
        Henderson. That's all I have.

It was about 4:30 P.M.

At 4:45 Fenster started asking Margo some rambling questions, trying to establish that she could earn $25,000 a year as a teacher and that her parents were extremely wealthy and would leave her hundreds of thousands of dollars when they passed away. But Margo and I had spent almost four hours in preparation for her depositions. Joe didn't touch her.

They left around 5:30 and Margo, Barbara, and I hung around in the conference room and discussed the day's events.

Me:    I hate to give you false hope, Margo, but I think it's all over.
        Roger is mortally wounded and will die soon.
Margo: What do you mean?
Me:    Can you afford to pay for me to fly to Atlanta next week?
Margo: What? Why—what's there?
Me:    Barbara, show Margo the check.

Barbara Gordon reached into her briefcase and showed Margo one of the canceled checks on Roger's personal checking account that we'd examined Monday night. It was dated March 21, 1983 (see Figure 20.1).

Margo looked at both sides of the check, then shook her head.

Margo: I don't understand.
Me:    I think I do, Margo, but I believe I've got to go to Atlanta and
        talk to Mr. Connor, and then I'll know for sure.
Margo: Know what?
Me:    What the hidden asset is and how much it's worth.
Margo: What makes you think he's hiding an asset in Georgia?
Me:    I'm not sure he's hiding an asset anywhere, Margo, but I think
        it's important to find out.
Margo: Well, can't you just have a Georgia lawyer take Connor's
        deposition like you took Roger's? It would be cheaper—after
        all, it'll cost me a lot of money for you to fly to Atlanta.

## FIGURE 20.1

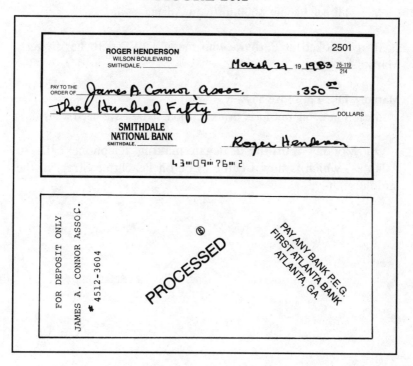

| | |
|---|---|
| Me: | Margo, I can't take anybody's depositions in Georgia or even in this state without Fenster and Roger being present. I have a hunch that the check Roger wrote to an architect in Atlanta may lead us to something fairly important. |
| Margo: | What makes you think he's an architect? |
| Me: | Atlanta telephone books. |
| Margo: | But can't you just ask Roger about the check? |
| Me: | Sure I can, but I want to keep my suspicions under wraps for a while. |
| Margo: | But what's so strange about a check for $350? |
| Me: | Well to begin with, you can see the check was folded—it's creased three times. Second, check #2501 was out of turn. During March of '83 Roger was up to check #3700 or #3800 in his personal checkbook. Number 2501 had been in his wallet a long time, for an emergency. |

Margo:  Even if it was in his wallet, so what?
  Me:   I'll need about $600 to fly to Atlanta—OK?


Margo looked at Barbara who made a "V" with her fingers.
Margo shrugged.

Margo:  OK, I'm broke anyway.
  Me:   I'm going out for a drink. C'mon, ladies. We need a break.


On Monday morning I began making telephone calls to
Atlanta—which is how I came to be on Peachtree Street in the
middle of July.

# Twenty-One
# Discovery II: The Smoking Cannon

Lawyers have a network of lawyer friends around the country, attorneys they deal with either on the same or opposing side in other cases. Even if they haven't shared cases they're part of the legal profession and always come to each other's assistance when help is needed. This network is especially effective between matrimonial attorneys. I needed some information in Atlanta, and it took just four telephone calls to get it.

First I called the chairman of the family law section in Atlanta and got the names of three top divorce lawyers. The first one was in court; the second one was in a conference and his secretary couldn't help. The third, George Griffith, understood exactly.

G.G.: So you think you got the fox cornered in the henhouse?

Me: I'm not sure, George; that's why I need to know about Jim Connor.

G.G.: Well Sidney, he's top-notch. Our leading architect—flawless reputation, honest as they come. Matter of fact, I've met him once or twice at charity functions.

Me: Will he talk to me without going through depositions—whaddya think?

G.G.:  I'll find out who represents him and arrange it. I suppose it would help if I came along?

Me:  Of course. Incidentally, George, I think I should have Mrs. Henderson retain you as co-counsel in Georgia. She doesn't have any money, but—

G.G.:  That's not necessary, Sidney. You can help me up North now and then. Suppose we meet at my office on Friday and take Jim to lunch. You payin'?

Me:  You got it, brother. Thanks a million!

George called back the next day. He'd spoken to Connor's attorney who agreed to his client having lunch with George and me, provided I agreed not to take his depositions or try to subpoena him for court. I could ask him anything I wanted and he would answer truthfully, but he would not supply any documents. "Fair enough," I said.

Atlanta was as hot as blazes in mid-July, but it was perfectly cool in Connor's luncheon club. Connor was a Georgia gentleman—tall, thin, white-haired, soft-spoken, intelligent. I looked at him and knew he would be straight with me. After small talk, George Griffith got down to the subject.

G.G.:  Jim, Sidney here represents a Mrs. Margo Henderson in a divorce suit. Her husband is a Mr. Roger Henderson. Sidney would like to ask you a few questions about Mr. Henderson.

J.C.:  (smiling, very friendly) What can I do for you, sir?

I showed him a copy of the canceled "wallet check" dated March 21, 1983.

J.C.:  Well, it was sure made out to my firm and deposited into our account. I checked with my office manager after George called yesterday, and it shows up in our books as payment for an initial conference back in '83 for the Orlando Development Company.

I felt a jolt of adrenaline. My coffee cup began to shake.

Me:  Orlando Development Company? What kind of job was it, Mr. Connor?

J.C.:  A strip shopping center, Sidney—some 100,000 square feet—on the outskirts of Orlando. A small job for us, really, but I guess they heard about us 'cause we'd just done a big mall nearby.

Me:  Mr. Connor, can you remember who the principals of Orlando Development were?

J.C.:  Sure can. There was this Dr. Frank Henderson, a high-pressure dentist from Orlando who seemed fairly savvy in real estate development, and his brother, your man.

G.G.:  Well now, we surely do have the fox cornered in the henhouse.

Me:  Mr. Connor, do you have any recollection indicating the initial cost of the project—land development costs, landscaping—the whole package?

(I had to put the damn coffee cup down on the table.)

J.C.:  Well, Sidney, I anticipated you'd be asking me that one. Our proposal shows about 2.5 million—whether they actually spent that or not I don't know. Of course, it would be heavily mortgaged.

Me:  George, Mrs. Henderson really must retain you now. Can you find out whether Orlando Development was registered either here in Atlanta or down in Tallahassee? And of course, any papers filed showing the participants.

G.G.:  Be glad to. And I'll send you certified copies—take me about a week or so. Course now, maybe our fox just paid for the initial conference and put everything in the dentist's name. Maybe he doesn't show at all.

Me:  I don't think so, George. Back in '83, Roger Henderson had no idea he'd be in a courtroom four years later. I don't think he was that careful. But find out as soon as you can. And send Mrs. Henderson a retainer agreement and a bill. If she can't pay it right away, I'll make certain you get paid at settlement—my personal guarantee.

Anyhow, I've got to fly to Orlando to see what's actually built there. Thank you, gentlemen, it's been a great lunch.

J.C.:  First trip to our fair state, Sidney?

Me:     No, sir. I had the pleasure of digging a few foxholes in the red
        clay up around Fort Benning a few years ago—'43 I think.

G.G.:   Seems to me you're still digging, Mr. D.

Me:     I guess so, George, but I get more than $18 a month now.
        Anyway, I think we may have the smoking pistol for sure—
        maybe even the smoking cannon.


   The Orlando Shopping Mart was the prettiest sight I'd seen for a
long time. It was only a "strip" shopping center—twenty or
twenty-five shops anchored by a supermarket—but all the space
was rented and the parking lot was full. As far as I was concerned,
it could have been five blocks of Rodeo Drive.
   Before I went to the airport for my flight home, I learned that
Dr. Frank Henderson was an extremely wealthy dentist, who spent
more time developing land than he did pulling teeth. I asked my
Orlando friend to get me the ownership of the center, a copy of the
deed and mortgage, and a series of 8×10 color shots of the place.
All I was missing was an 8×10 of Roger standing in front of the
development wearing his $350 wing tips and smoking his cigar.
To be sure, the Florida State Office of Fictitious Registration
would have his "picture" on file (when you start a business in a
company name, you have to register the name and the principals
with the state).
   On the flight back I made up my mind to tell Margo that
Roger's brother was involved but that we'd have to wait for
George's detective work to find out if we had Roger on the gallows.
I didn't want to build up her hopes although I suspected Roger's
name *was* filed as a partner. Back in 1983, the Henderson marriage, though not great, wasn't yet on the rocks, and Roger had no
real need to keep the Mart a secret from Margo.
   Divorce lawyers can't tell the future, but they can sure put the
past together, even if all the pieces aren't available. I could just hear
the telephone conversation between Frank-the-dentist and his
brother back in 1983:

Frank:   Rog, this seven acres in Orlando is available. Thirty thousand
         an acre. I think we could get the zoning—one of my patients is

on the zoning commission—and we can probably get 100 percent financing. Whaddya say to 50–50?

Roger:  Sure Frank, I'm in, but—uh—well, I'm involved with someone up here and it's pretty serious. If Margo finds out I—

Frank:  Hey, Rog—how in the hell can she find out? We'll file the papers here in Florida.

Roger:  Then how would I get my share?

Frank:  Any way you want, brother. Talk to that clever accountant you got, he'll figure it out. But don't tell Margo anything.

Roger:  But what if she talks to Betsy?

Frank:  Betsy don't know shit. Talk to your accountant and I'll have my attorney form a partnership, OK?

Roger:  OK, Frank.

The next day I told Margo about my busy day in the South and what I had learned. She understood its importance but not why I didn't just call Fenster and confront him.

Me:  No Margo, I don't want Fenster and Roger to know what I think I know. I want to get Roger cold on the stand and show him the 8×10 glossy and ask him if he knows anything about it. If I confront Fenster, he and Roger will have time to cover their tracks.

Margo:  But Roger will lie and say it's Frank's asset, won't he?

Me:  Of course he will. But it will be up to me to prove that he's lying and then the judge will head the lynching party.

Margo:  I don't know, Sidney. Roger's always outsmarted everybody else. He always wins, too.

Me:  He won't win this time. But let's wait till we get the papers from Tallahassee. I can't imagine Roger allowing Frank to own 100 percent of the center. My guess is that he's listed as a 50 percent partner.

Margo:  Call me as soon as you hear.

On Friday morning, July 24, I found out that I had been wrong—*dead wrong*! Orlando Development had been registered as a fictitious name in Tallahassee all right, but the only owner listed was Dr. Frank Henderson! (See Figure 21.1.)

## FIGURE 21.1

---

**AFFIDAVIT UNDER FICTITIOUS NAME STATUTE**

STATE OF FLORIDA            )
COUNTY OF _ORANGE_          )   **ss:**

The undersigned, under oath, says; It is the intention of the undersigned to engage in a business enterprise under the fictitious name of _ORLANDO DEVELOPMENT COMPANY_

located at _Davisville and Tate Roads_
in the city of _ORLANDO_, _ORANGE_ County, Florida.

Those interested in said enterprise, and the extent of the interest of each, is as follows:

| Print or type name | | Interest |
|---|---|---|
| Frank Henderson, DDS. - 100% | Signature | _Frank Henderson_ |
| | Address | _Bay Drive, Orlando, Florida_ |
| | Signature | |
| | Address | |
| | Signature | |
| | Address | |

Sworn to and subscribed to before me, at _Orlando, Florida_ , this _3rd_ day of _August_ , 19_83_ .

JEAN C. TURNER, Notary Public
Orlando, Orange County, Fla.

**Notary Public, State of Florida at Large**

My Commission Expires _Oct. 19, 1988_

[Proof of publication of this intention to register, is filed herewith, pursuant to the provisions of Chapter 20953, Laws of 1941 (865.09 FSA) ]

---

I called Margo with the bad news. Her reaction was as expected: "Roger always wins. I told you so." I was beginning to believe her.

Another sleepless night. Something told me that Roger had an interest in the center. Other than the check for $350 and the conference with Jim Connor there was something else.

I hate to call Marge at home but . . .

Marge, sorry to bother you at one in the morning, but there's something about the *Henderson* case that bothers me. When Vicki comes in tomorrow, tell her to get Roger's depositions out of the file and put them on my desk.

The next morning I rushed to my office and re-read Roger's depositions. I found what I was looking for and called Barbara Ann Gordon.

Me:    Barbara, call Picker and tell him we need all the Citizens Bank paperwork when HEI borrowed the $45,000 in '83.

B.G.:   I don't get it. The loan was paid in full. I checked the cash disbursements. They paid some $60,000 for a shipment of components—it's all kosher.

Me:    You may be right, but ask Picker if you can write to the bank and get a copy of the loan application. Don't make a big fuss about it, be casual. Don't mention why you want them. Just get his authorization to get the records.

B.G.:   You on to something?

Me:    I hope so. Get back to me soon.

Well, it looked like Roger had outsmarted all of us, but still, I wasn't ready to give up. What I didn't know, however, was that Margo was.

## Twenty-Two

# "I Can't Take It Anymore!"

### *Telephone Conversation, Mid-July, 1987, 9 A.M.*

Roger: Joe, this is Roger. Howard called last night and says that the lady accountant wants some bank records. What's going on?

Fenster: I don't know—you tell me. Anything in the records that could hurt you?

Roger: Absolutely not. We borrowed some $50,000 to buy a carload of small components, and we paid it back.

Fenster: Did the money go for the components? You didn't buy a boat or something like that, did you?

Roger: Joe, you're gettin' to sound like De Angelis. Look, the deal was straight. Nothing like the Mercedes.

Fenster: Then I don't know what he's up to.

Roger: Do me a favor, Joe. Call him and find out when she wants to settle this damn thing—and find out what he wants with the damn bank records. Christ, Tracey is getting nervous, and I am too.

Fenster: I'll do better than call, Rog, I'll stop in to see him—call you later.

Marge walked into my office with a twinkle in her eyes. She's

244

been with me for over twenty years, and I can tell when something's good or bad just by looking at her.

| | |
|---|---|
| Marge: | Guess who's out front without an appointment? |
| Me: | The President, who wants to talk to me about an appointment to the Supreme court? |
| Marge: | How about Joe Fenster, who wants to talk about Henderson? |
| Me: | Send him in and hold my calls. |
| | |
| Joe: | How ya doin', pal? |
| Me: | I'm fine Joe. What's up? |
| Joe: | Nothin'—just stopped in to see if we could settle *Henderson*. |
| Me: | Well Joe, I'm always glad to see you but our discovery isn't complete. We're still waiting for the appraisal of HEI and the warehouse. And Barbara Gordon says she needs some bank records to finish her report. |
| Joe: | Yeah Sid, what's that all about? They paid the loan off—nothing out of the ordinary. Whaddya fishing for? |
| Me: | Well, Joe, Barbara has this theory that Roger didn't use the proceeds of the loan to buy components and she wants to check it out, that's all. |

(No reason to tell my opponent about my hunches, is there?)

| | |
|---|---|
| Joe: | I don't get it—what difference would it make if the company bought tomato soup with the bank loan? The money came in and the money went out. |
| Me: | You're probably right, Joe, but I'm going to file a petition to take the bank's depositions— |
| Joe: | Wait a minute. Suppose I get Roger to sign an authorization to Citizens to give you any records you want. So long as anything you copy, I get a copy. |

*[Translation: Roger doesn't want you to bother the bank. While Roger may not need to borrow any money right now, he may have to in the future so why tell the bank he's in the middle of a divorce case.]*

Me:    That's fine, Joe—I'll prepare the authorization and get it over to
       you this afternoon.

Now Joe got down to the purpose of his visit.

Joe:   What will it take to settle this case, Sidney?
Me:    I don't know yet.
Joe:   Look, Roger wants this over. He's authorized me to wind this up
       today. Tell me something, what are your fees to date—approxi-
       mate?

*[Translation: Roger's fees are choking him and he's afraid you're
on to something. So why not tell Margo to take the house and child
support and we'll pay you whatever you want for your fees (in
other circles it's called a bribe, but we'll call it attorney's fees.)]*

Me:    That's not the point, Joe. I'll get my fees through the courts or out
       of the settlement. It's what Margo gets that's important.

*[Translation: Screw you, I don't bribe!]*

Joe:   All right. Roger wants this over. Got a hellava deal for you.
       Suppose he gives her the house and one-half of the mortgage
       payments for five years—and your fees.
Me:    (getting bored) Joe, let's wait until all of the facts are in—as soon
       as they are I'll come over to your office with a written proposal.
Joe:   Doesn't she want to settle?
Me:    Sure she does, but she wants to be able to look at her hand before
       she bets. You understand, don't you?

Joe understood perfectly. He grimaced, limply shook my hand,
and walked out. I called Margo.

Me:     No, it isn't over yet Margo. It was just a crude attempt to buy
        me.
Margo:  That scares me, Sidney.
Me:     What—that he tried to buy me? That shouldn't surprise you.

Margo:  No, you warned me that he'd try when things got rough for
        him. What I'm worried about is he'll try to bribe the judge.

Me:     Impossible, Margo, not in this county.

Margo:  He's always done it. He always buys whatever and whoever he
        wants.

Me:     Not now, Margo. But even if he could—and he can't—you can
        always appeal.

Margo:  Sure. What with? I'm just getting by now—if you call not
        being able to repair the transmission on my car "getting by"!

Me:     Margo, I know it's tough for you, and I know you're just
        making it financially. But you've got to remember that the
        closer we get to the end, the tougher it gets. It's like climbing
        that mountain I drew for you.

Margo:  I know what he's trying to do, Sidney, and I know I couldn't get
        by without alimony for a while, but how long will this case
        last? When will it end? I can't take much more. And how will I
        ever be able to pay you? I just got your bill for that trip to
        Atlanta and it looks like I spent almost $2,000 for a wild goose
        chase!

It was perfectly normal for Margo to be frustrated. She had always
perceived Roger as King Kong when it came to business, the kind
of guy who would do anything to get his way. I also realized that
the *Henderson* case (equitable distribution, permanent alimony,
counsel fees, divorce) would not be scheduled for at least a year,
and there would be more and more counsel fees as we prepared for
the final hearing. And of course, I felt lousy about the trip to
Atlanta.

Me:     Margo, I understand your feelings. Look, why not come in this
        afternoon and we'll have another blackboard session. And re-
        member, it's *your* case. If you want to settle at any point it's your
        option, but before you make any decision let's review the facts. See
        you about four.

Margo didn't look too great. There was a settled tension about her
eyes, and I suspected she'd met with Roger again but was ashamed
to talk about it. I was right.

Margo:  Yes, he called right after you met with Fenster and he was screaming. He said I was a greedy bitch and you were worse and all you cared about was getting money from me. And that he didn't care if it took ten more years, he'd fight me tooth and nail. That's one of his favorite expressions, Sidney—"tooth and nail."

Me:  I know what he's like, Margo. A few weeks ago I checked our courthouse computer and found out that Roger or his company has been sued five or six times on allegations of fraud, double-dealing, sharp practices—you name it.

But your case is different. You are entitled by law to certain financial considerations, whether your husband is a wimp or Jack the Ripper. The marital assets get identified, valued, and distributed. The court considers whether you're a candidate for post-divorce alimony, and finally, the judge will ask me what I did for you, how much I charged, and whether Roger has to pay my fees or part of them, including the trip to Atlanta.

As I analyze Roger's position on marital assets, he says the pot is worth $240,000 or so. Our position is that they're worth more like $400,000, maybe $450,000.

Margo:  (sighing) You may be right, but it looks like another Seven Years' War to me.

Me:  Well it *looks* like the Seven Years' War, but—

Margo:  Not to mention the thousands of dollars for appraisal fees and the money for the appraisers to come to court. No Sidney, I can't make it. I want it over.

Me:  Margo, I know how depressing it appears to be to you. But you can't give up now.

Margo:  What do you mean?

Me:  Well, Roger's net marital assets show $240,000. If he succeeds in proving those valuations, or if you don't prove otherwise, your 50 percent—if you got 50 percent—would be $120,000. But he values the house at $150,000, so you'd have to sell the house and give him $30,000.

On the other hand, if you can prove $400,000 (and HEI may be worth far more than our projected $100,000), you would be entitled to, say, $200,000 of distribution—the house at $100,000 (your valuation) and another $100,000 from him.

And if you went to court you'd have a good shot at alimony after the divorce. Hell, you need some $7,500 a year just for the mortgage alone. Why give up now?

Margo: But Roger'll pay half the mortgage for five years—Fenster said so.

Me: I realize that, but you may be entitled to *all* of the mortgage payments until the kids are 18.

Margo: Sure I may, but then I may not. Nothing is black and white except the fees and appraiser costs. Everything else is "it depends."

Look Sidney, it's not your fault. You told me when I first came in that it's not fair, and I've come to realize how true that is. Roger wants to take the kids to California for the month of August, and I can't afford to take them anywhere.

You've done your best—I know you have—but I can't take it anymore. I'm going to meet Roger tonight and get the best settlement I can. I'm sure he'll agree to pay your bill.

Me: I'm not pressing you for fees.

Margo: I know you're not—(crying) I just want to get it over with. I can't take it anymore!

Me: Will you wait till next Monday?

Margo: (smiling through her tears) You expecting the tooth fairy?

Me: Maybe.

Margo: I'll call you Tuesday morning. That's it.

It was about 5:30 when Margo left and suddenly, I felt drained. I'd worked so hard for her, for her children, and it seemed a shame to have her give up now. My intercom buzzed.

Marge: Do you want your calls?

Me: Not really, I'm exhausted. Margo wants to throw the towel in.

Marge: Well maybe you'd better call Barbara Gordon back before you leave. She said it might be important.

Marge was right. The Citizens Bank papers had come in, a whole stack of them. I rushed out to my car and headed for Barbara's office. The adrenaline was pumping again.

# Twenty-Three
# Roger the Sinner

I drove quickly, too quickly, to Barbara Gordon's office a few miles away, my mind cluttered with the *Henderson* case. Could Margo hold out much longer? She was right—nothing was black and white, and it wouldn't be until we got to a judge for the final hearing, in a year or so.

I knew that Margo could do far better in court than she could with Roger in a cocktail lounge, but I wasn't sure I could tell her how *much* better. I knew Roger would make a lousy witness, but I couldn't compute how much the "sleaze factor" would affect the judge who would hear the case. And I didn't know who would hear the case. Would it be Mr. Husband, Judge Greene, or someone with no gender ax to grind? My anxiety over Margo and my curiosity over Roger's bank records had me flying over the turnpike.

Now what did I hope to find? All I had to go on was Roger's given propensity for lying when it was advantageous for him to do so and the fact that he had to borrow some $50,000 six years ago to buy some components. That and my hunch that Roger wasn't in Atlanta in 1983 to see a prominent architect just to say hello and have a mint julep. I wasn't at all sure I'd be able to get anywhere with Dr. Frank. Even *if* our court issued an order under the

250

Interstate Deposition Act—and they might not—it would have to be enforced in the Florida court. (We'd have been in the Supreme Court of Florida for three or four years on that one.) And anyhow, Frank would have no trouble convincing our judge that he was just a "small-town dentist" who got lucky in real estate and that Roger had no interest at all in the Orlando Mart.

Finally, I had to face an economic fact of life. Even if Roger owned a hidden 50 percent interest in the mart, there would be precious little equity in the project. Built in 1984 or so for about $2,500,000, it was undoubtedly mortgaged to the hilt. Most of the mortgage payments made on the mart since 1984 had ·gone to interest and real estate taxes, not to principal. Anyhow I had to be kidding myself. No matter what, Margo couldn't afford a Florida real estate appraiser.

As soon as I arrived, Barbara Gordon showed me the large manila folder she'd received from Citizens National. Most of it was useless stuff—computer printouts of the loan payments, interest charges, and internal bank records. There was a letter from Roger outlining that he needed the money to buy a closeout on a discontinued line of components (I knew that) and a copy of a letter to Roger telling him the bank couldn't approve the loan on the credit of HEI—"insufficient credit history," meaning they'd never borrowed money from a bank before. Then it got hotter. Another letter told Roger he'd have to co-sign the loan as an individual, not just as company president, if he wanted the money. I held my breath as I read through the letter. Bingo! They wanted him to give them a personal financial statement.

OK. We were almost home. Where was Roger's personal financial statement? Had he told the truth or, as I suspected, lied through his teeth? There were only two possibilities. Roger could tell the truth and give a truthful financial statement or Roger could lie and try to convince the bank that his real name was Onassis. I made a mental bet with myself. The SOB never did anything straight. He *had* to lie!

It was about 9:30 at night and I hadn't eaten anything since noon. I was tired, hungry, and slightly dizzy, but at that point I felt nothing but pure concentration.

The statement was all by itself in a scotch-taped brown manila envelope with the word "Confidential" stamped on the front. I opened the envelope and scanned Roger's financial statement of September 1, 1984 (Figure 23.1).

## FIGURE 23.1
## ROGER'S CONFIDENTIAL STATEMENT

**CITIZENS NATIONAL BANK**
Citizens National Bank Building
Smithdale

August 10, 1984

Mr. Roger Henderson
c/o Henderson Electronics, Inc.
Wilson Blvd. Commercial Center
Smithdale, _____

Re: <u>Demand Loan</u>

Dear Roger:

I am pleased to advise that the Loan Committee of Citizens National has approved the Loan Application of Henderson Electronics, Inc. for a demand loan in the amount of $45,000, with interest at two points over prime, upon the following terms and conditions:

1. As President of HEI you will execute a financing statement prepared by our loan department which would confer upon the Bank a lien upon all of the assets of HEI, including its receivables; copies enclosed.

2. As an individual you would sign a confidential statement, our Form No. 700, listing your assets and liabilities as of September 1, 1984.

3. As an individual you would have to co-sign the demand note as a guarantor. Your wife would also co-sign.

As soon as we receive this documentation we will complete the transaction and deposit the funds into an account with the Bank.

If you have any questions please call me.

Very truly yours,

John T. Durant,
Vice President
Commercial Loan Department

JTD:am
cc: Loan Committee
Enclosures

(PERSONAL)

## TO – CITIZENS NATIONAL BANK, SMITHDALE

Name_____ Roger Henderson

Account Officer___ Durant

Business or Occupation __electronic components__

Branch Office No. Main Street

Location__ Wilson Boulevard Commercial Center

The following statement of condition as of __Sept. 1__ 19__84__ is submitted for the purpose of procuring, establishing and maintaining credit with you in behalf of the undersigned or persons, firms or corporations in whose behalf the undersigned may either severally or jointly with others execute a guaranty in your favor. The undersigned warrants that this financial statement is true and correct and that you may consider this statement as continuing to be true and correct until a written notice of a change is given to you by the undersigned.

**Fill all blanks, writing "no" or "none" where necessary to complete information.**

| ASSETS | IN DOLLARS (Omit Cents) COST | MARKET | LIABILITIES | IN DOLLARS (Omit Cents) BALANCES | PAYMENTS |
|---|---|---|---|---|---|
| Cash | $ 2,500 | $ | Notes Payable - Banks Secured | $ | $ |
| Government and Listed Securities | | | Notes Payable - Banks Unsecured | | |
| (Schedule A) | | | Notes Payable - Relatives | | |
| Unlisted Securities | | | Notes Payable - Others | | |
| (Schedule A) | | | Accounts Payable | | |
| Accounts and Notes Receivable | | | Unpaid Income Taxes | | |
| Trade | | | Other Unpaid Taxes and Interest | | |
| Relatives and Friends | | | Real Estate Mortgages Payable | | |
| Others | | | (Schedule B) | 60,000 | |
| Cash Value Life Insurance | 1,500 | | Chattel Mortgages and Other | | |
| (Schedule C) | | | Liens Payable | | |
| Investment in Businesses | | | | | |
| (Show Book Value in 'Cost' Col.) | 14,700 | | Other Debts - Itemize: | | |
| Real Estate Owned | | | Credit Card Bills | 2,200 | |
| (Schedule B) | 840,000 | | | | |
| Vested Interest in Deferred | | | | | |
| Compensation Plans | | | | | |
| Automobile(s) | 15,000 | | | | |
| Other Personal Property | 2,500 | | | | |
| Other Assets - Itemize | | | | | |
| Profit Sharing | | | | | |
| Plan | 51,000 | | | | |
| | | | Total Liabilities | 62,200 | |
| | | | Net Worth (Cost/Market) | 865,000 | |
| TOTAL ASSETS | 927,200 | $ | TOTAL LIABILITIES and NET WORTH | 927,200 | $ |

**Sources of Income:**

Salary $ 25,000    Dividends $_____    Interest $_____    Commissions $_____

Real Estate Income $_____    Other $ 15,000 (estimate) Orlando Shopping Mart

**Contingent Liabilities:**

As Endorser, Co-Maker or Guarantor $ None    on Leases or Contracts $ None

Legal Claims $ None    Other None    $ None

**General Information:**

Defendant in Suits or Legal Actions? None    Explain:_____

Assets Pledged or Restricted? None

Income Taxes Settled Through What Date? 1983    Additional Assessments $ None

**(Complete Schedules and Sign Statement Officially on Reverse Side)**

Form No. 700

**Schedule A**  U. S. GOVERNMENT, LISTED AND UNLISTED SECURITIES OWNED

| No. of Shares or Par Value of Bonds | Description | In Name of | Market Value |
|---|---|---|---|
| | | | $ |
| | | | |
| | | | |
| | | | |
| | | | |
| | | | |
| | | | |
| | | | |

**Schedule B**  REAL ESTATE OWNED

| | Description and Location | Date Acquired | Title in Name of | Market Value | Mortgage Amount | Mortgage Maturity | Insurance |
|---|---|---|---|---|---|---|---|
| (1) | 576 Oak Drive, Smithdale, | 1980 | Roger & Margo Henderson | $150,000 | $60,000 | 2000 | $ |
| (2) | 50% Interest-Orlando Shopping Mart, Shop. Center, Orlando, Florida | 1977 | Orlando Develop. Company | $750,000 (Equity) | | | |
| | | | | | | | |

**Schedule C**  LIFE INSURANCE

| Name of Company | Amount | Cash Value | Loans | Beneficiary |
|---|---|---|---|---|
| Eagle Life Insurance Co. | $250,000 | $1,500 | $0 | Margo Henderson-Wife |
| | | | | |
| | | | | |
| | | | | |
| | | | | |
| | | | | |

**NAMES OF BANKS, FINANCE COMPANIES OR OTHER SOURCES WHERE CREDIT HAS BEEN OBTAINED**

| Name | Date | High Credit | Basis |
|---|---|---|---|
| None | | $ | |
| | | | |
| | | | |
| | | | |
| | | | |
| | | | |

The undersigned certifies that both sides hereof and the information inserted therein has been carefully read and is true and correct.

*September 1,* 19 84
Date Signed

*Roger Henderson*
Signature

Signature

So Roger swore, in writing, that he owned 50 percent of the Orlando mart in September 1984. No real surprise. The deal with brother Frank was simple: Frank would "own" the Mart 100 percent. The deed would be in his name, he would sign the mortgage, and he'd get all of the profits—at least on paper.

What protected Roger in case Frank died? Very easy—an undated blank deed in Roger's safe deposit box signed by Frank conveying 50 percent of the partnership to Roger for $1.00.

How did Roger get his 50 percent of any profits? Any way he wanted—in cash, in an off-shore account, or in a "special account" in Frank's name in Orlando.

Who knew about this secret deal? Roger, Frank, Frank's attorney in Orlando, Howard Picker, and Tracey. *Not* Margo. *Not* Fenster (Roger even lied to his own attorney).

But the best part of the statement of September, 1984 was Roger's valuation. *He swore his 50 percent interest was worth $750,000!* Of course he was lying. The Mart couldn't possibly be worth $1,500,000 on the day it was constructed. It may have cost $2,500,000 to build, but the mortgage was $2,500,000. So there was no equity on September 1, 1984.

But the best thing about the statement was that neither Fenster nor Roger knew I had it. Either Roger *forgot* that he filed the statement or he forgot that he fudged the value of the Mart. Like the crook who drops his driver's license at the scene of the crime, Roger had his eyes on the deal, not on doing it right.

Why, you might ask, did Picker and Fenster agree to give Barbara Gordon the bank records in the first place? Why didn't they refuse to give Barbara an authorization signed by Roger allowing the bank to turn over a copy of its complete file? Finally, why didn't they examine the file *before* they turned it over? Obviously because Roger never told them about the statement and, it would seem, because the two of them had become infected by his arrogance. One other reason. When I took Roger's deposition, I led him and Fenster down the primrose path by asking him whether he'd used the proceeds of the loan to buy components. Roger thought that was a dumb question. It was. So Roger felt invulnerable on the bank loan. (He'd forgotten or never read that "the dominion of arrogance shall perish from the earth.")

And let's not forget Roger's psychology in 1984. He could do anything he wanted. Margo was a wimp. No one would ever find out. His people—Frank, Frank's lawyer, Picker, Tracey—wouldn't tell. He was pulling one over on the bank, that was all. He'd get his $45,000, buy the components, make a hefty profit, pay the bank loan off, and take Tracey to Maui, all in one easy motion. Who in the hell would ever find out?

Margo was in my office on Tuesday promptly at 9:00 A.M.

Margo:   You look tired.
  Me:    I am—I looked at bank records and depositions till 11:00 P.M.
Margo:   Find anything?
  Me:    I want to show you something that Roger signed in September of 1984.

(Margo glanced at Roger's statement.)

Margo:   Will this get us to court earlier?
  Me:    No.
Margo:   Will you show this to Fenster and get a better settlement.
  Me:    No.
Margo:   Why not?
  Me:    If I did that, Fenster and Roger would have a year to come up with some cockamamie story about the statement. We'd lose all surprise.
Margo:   Then what's so great about this $750,000? I won't get any part of it for five years—if then.
  Me:    Margo, all you've got to do now is be patient. Don't meet with Roger—you might slip and mention the Mart. We'll get to trial in a year or so, and I'll call Roger as a witness and show him his statement to Citizens. That afternoon, at about 5:15, Fenster will call and ask what you want to settle for.
Margo:   What do I want?
  Me:    Well, how's the house, Roger to pay off the entire mortgage— that's about $50,000, $50,000 in cash—all of my fees and your costs, $350 weekly child support, plus college tuition, $250 per week for you as alimony (no cohabitation, no modification

downward if you start to earn money) until you remarry, health insurance, life insurance, and a new car?

Margo:  What makes you think Roger'll do it?

Me:  Experience. Common sense. Knowledge of the divorce law.

Margo:  But in the meantime I have to live on what I'm getting, right.

Me:  Right.

Margo:  You don't think I should give in, do you?

Me:  Roger thinks you should, but I don't.

Margo picked up Roger's statement again and re-read it, this time more carefully.

Margo:  The bastard! I wanted to go on a vacation in '84 and he told me we'd have to borrow the money because he was broke. A few weeks later he told me he had to go to Hawaii for a sales convention. I stayed home.

She paused again, deep in thought, then said, "F __ __ __ him—no lunch!"

As soon as Margo left, I dictated a notice to the court administrator. In the case of *Henderson v. Henderson*, the Plaintiff was ready for trial.

# Twenty-Four

# Getting Ready for "D" Day

## Chronology: Henderson v. Henderson, Fall 1987

Preparing for the *Henderson* trial wouldn't begin in earnest until the early part of 1989; we didn't expect a trial date from the court administrator until May or June. But there were two matters left that demanded attention. First, there was the little item of $35,000, which had gone out in HEI checks to Roger's father for "consultation fees." When Barbara Gordon saw the checks, properly endorsed by Mr. Ralph Henderson, she raised her eyebrows. "I don't believe it, Sidney." Neither did I. However, the court wouldn't let me take Mr. Henderson's depositions. The judge said I could subpoena him for trial, all right, but it was "harassment" to drag Roger's father in for pretrial depositions. Well, I'd have to wait until the trial for his explanation of just what he did for HEI to get $35,000. In the meantime, we finally got Roger's Profit-Sharing Plan documents and found that he had $80,000 salted away.

But the biggest question mark was how much Roger's HEI stock was worth. Howard Picker had prepared a balance sheet for HEI as of December 31, 1986, the day before Roger and Margo separated. It showed various assets totaling $100,000, various liabilities of

$80,000, and a net worth of $20,000. So Picker could swear that HEI was only worth $20,000 on December 31, 1986. But our expert, Jay Fisher, had carefully analyzed the HEI profit and loss statements for the five years prior to December 31, 1986, and had found that annual sales were $500,000 and annual expenses only $400,000. Therefore, HEI showed a net profit of $100,000 a year for the past five years. Fisher believed that HEI would be likely to earn $100,000 a year indefinitely. He also knew that HEI (Roger) owned the building in which it did business. So Fisher, using IRS 59/60 and after interviewing Roger, came up with a *fair market value* of $250,000 to $300,000—the amount another buyer would have to pay for HEI.

Not only was Fisher's theoretical analysis sound, but he'd also searched for sales of similar businesses and had discovered similar multiples—two and a half to three times the average net profit.

I felt like we'd discovered gold. Fisher had testified in hundreds of business valuations all over the country, and he was good. And he knew by heart the IRS regulations applying to business valuation of closed corporations, IRS 59/60 and IRS 68/609.

---

## TIP

Where a husband operates his own business, the most important expert a woman will require is an experienced business valuation appraiser. A divorce lawyer who doesn't understand IRS 59/60 (and its companion ruling, 68-609) might as well be deaf and dumb.

---

From Margo's point of view the marital assets were now in excess of $1,000,000! I had a large chart (see Figure 24.1, page 260) prepared for trial, outlining the marital assets.

Now I was ready for trial. Margo wouldn't talk to Roger, so Fenster had to deal with me. He stopped me in the courthouse every so often and offered the house, half the mortgage payments, plus my fees. I listened and politely told him that I'd get back to him. Accordingly, I wrote this letter (see Figure 24.2, page 260) on three or four occasions in late '87.

## FIGURE 24.1
## OUTLINE OF MARITAL ASSETS
## (FOR COURT DISPLAY)

| | | |
|---|---|---:|
| 1. | House (net equity) | $ 97,000 |
| 2. | Furniture and contents | 5,000 |
| 3. | Bank accounts | 7,500 |
| 4. | Cash in cigar box | 12,400 |
| 5. | Roger's Mercedes | 20,000 |
| 6. | Margo's Cutlass | 6,000 |
| 7. | Roger's 1/2 interest - Orlando Mart | 750,000 |
| 8. | Roger's stock - HEI | 250,000 |
| 9. | Profit-Sharing plan | 80,000 |
| 10. | Mutual Funds (held by Roger's father) | 35,000 |
| | TOTAL | $1,250,000 ($\pm$) |

## FIGURE 24.2

**SIDNEY M. DeANGELIS**
Attorney At Law
Main Street Professional Building
Smithdale

```
Joseph Fenster, Esquire
Suite 500
Fidelity Building
Smithdale, _____

                    Re:  Henderson v. Henderson

Dear Joe:

        Your most recent offer is respectfully
refused.

        Try, try again!

                         Cordially,

                         SIDNEY M. DeANGELIS

SMD:e
cc: Mrs. Margo Henderson
```

## Telephone Conversation, March 10, 1988, 9:00 A.M.

| | |
|---|---|
| Roger: | Joe, I gotta talk to you. What the hell's going on? De Angelis writes these snotty letters to you and you keep asking him for a bottom line settlement figure, but all I get outta this are big bills you send me. So far I've paid you over $60,000 and we haven't even been to trial yet. Now what the hell—. |
| Joe: | Cool it, Roger, There's nothing I can do to force Margo or her lawyer to send us a written demand. Her lawyer's a prick, you know that by now. I guess we'll hear from him soon and then we can start to negotiate. |
| Roger: | That's what you've been telling me for a year, Joe—"we'll hear from him soon, we'll hear from him soon." Look Joe, I don't mind paying your fees but Christ! I gotta get out of this. Tracey says—. |
| Joe: | Roger, I don't care what Tracey says. I represent you, not her. |
| Roger: | Listen to me, Fenster, I got news for you. If Tracey tells me to dump you, you're dumped. She wants the thing settled. We got honeymoon plans this Christmas and I got the feeling if there's no settlement there's no Tracey. And with her legs, she'll have no trouble finding someone else to pay the freight. |
| Joe: | Roger, if you want another lawyer, come in today and get your goddamn file—I'll have a final bill ready for you. |
| Roger: | Oh shit! Get me a settlement figure, Joe—I'm not gonna change horses now! |

## Telephone Conversation, March 10, 1988, 11:00 P.M.

| | |
|---|---|
| Roger: | Margo, this is Roger. Sorry to call you so late—kids OK? |
| Margo: | Yes, Roger, they're fine. Why are you calling at this hour? |
| Roger: | Look Margo, I want to get this thing between us over with. It's no good for you or for me. We'll spend a fortune for those bloodsucking lawyers. Can I come over tomorrow night? |
| Margo: | Roger, I can't discuss settlement with you. That's what Sidney says, and I listen to him. Call your lawyer. |
| Roger: | But you and I don't need the lawyers to settle—you know what you want. |
| Margo: | Call Fenster and tell him to call Sidney. |
| Roger: | Margo, listen to me. *I want to meet you and settle this case!* |
| Margo: | Call your lawyer Roger, and please don't raise your voice to me. |

Roger:   I'll be over at 9:00—OK?

Margo:   (calmly) Call your lawyer, Roger. Good night. (She hangs up)

Roger, up to his old tricks, called Margo a few more times to try to get her to settle the case without my help. Each time she told him where to go.

There was nothing much we could do during 1988 except wait for trial. In April, I asked for updated tax returns for 1987, and of course, Fenster told me that Roger got extensions and the returns weren't due until September.

From time to time I had to file more discovery motions. For instance, I wanted to see what Roger's books and records showed during 1988, and, of course Fenster refused. First Picker was on vacation. Then he was using the books for the income tax returns. Finally, I got a court order for the 1988 books. Did I get copies? No-o-o-o-o-o. I went to Picker's office, and the books were there all right, but the copy machine was "broken." Sure it was.

Then Picker's wife got sick, poor thing. The last excuse was that aliens from outer space had eaten the records, or something like that. I finally got them, but they had been sanitized. After all, Picker had to give up creative accounting while we were in litigation.

In the meantime, we waited for the magic letter from the court administrator—a date for trial. I couldn't walk into the court administrator's office and kick his butt in order to get an earlier date. All Margo and I could do was wait.

Eventually 1989 rolled around and in January we got a trial date for March 15. But more important, the case had been assigned to the Honorable Harriet S. Jackson and not to Bernie Greene. I called Margo immediately.

Me:      We've got to start dress rehearsals. We open in two months.

Margo:   We're going to do this, aren't we, Sidney?

Me:      Yes we are Margo, we're gonna do it.

## PREPARING FOR YOUR DAY IN COURT

Let's re-examine what you and your attorney have done up to this point to prepare for your final divorce hearing.

You have given your attorney all of the facts about your marriage and your finances; consequently, your attorney knows as much about your life up to this point as you do. You have also made backup folders for every item that will become an issue at trial, especially where the equitable distribution and alimony factors are concerned. Examples:

1. If your driveway has to be repaved, you've already secured a written estimate from a paving contractor.
2. If your automobile isn't safe to operate, you've secured a written estimate to lease a new car.
3. If it's your intention to advance your education, you've already secured a written statement of the tuition, cost of books and related expenses, and the college brochure, which shows the court how long it will take to complete your education and what it will cost.
4. If necessary, you've updated your income and expense statement.

Moreover, you've given your attorney a list of every witness you believe will be helpful in your case and included names, addresses, telephone numbers, and brief synopses of what the witnesses will say. You've called these witnesses and told them to expect a call from your attorney. You've also assisted your attorney in the preparation of an equitable distribution chart.

You've rehearsed and rehearsed your testimony and demeanor (how you'll behave) in preparation for direct examination by your attorney and cross-examination by your husband's attorney.

You and your attorney have gone to the courthouse and watched another equitable distribution hearing in progress (if, in your county, these cases are open to the public) to see what actually happens in the courtroom and assess the wife's testimony. What did she do right? What did she do wrong?

Finally, you've discussed with your attorney what you owe him in professional fees and expenses, and you have a typed list of all the expenses you have incurred for expert witnesses, depositions, copies, and the like. Your attorney has had a final bill typed up— final, at least up to the day of the trial. Your team is now ready for "D" Day.

Before I begin telling you about "D" Day, I should remind you that it may not take place in front of a judge at all, at least not at the outset. Remember, in many states divorce cases are heard first by a Master. The Master is an attorney selected by the court to hear all divorce cases in the hope that he or she will be able to settle many of them before they ever get to a courtroom. You will want to win your case before the master even though you may have to win it all over again before a judge. If you or your husband is dissatisfied with the master's recommendation, exceptions to the master's ruling can be filed and your case will go to a judge.

In some counties the judge will disregard the masters proceedings and start from scratch; in others the judge will not hear any testimony at all but merely review the transcribed record of the master's proceedings for any technical or legal errors. Your attorney will explain which system your court follows.

Suffice it to say that "D" day, whether it takes place before a master or a judge, is similar to June 6, 1944, when American, British, and Canadian troops stormed the Normandy coast and invaded Hitler's Europe. What's the connection? *Planning.*

The accomplishment of any task, whether military invasion or divorce litigation, is based on months, sometimes years, of planning, conferences, documents, expert counseling, and rehearsal. When training is complete, the sun rises on "D" Day.

Then everything goes wrong. All of the theories, all of the plans, and all of the neatly drawn charts are thrown away. But the troops who wade through the surf and onto the beaches have no other choice but to keep their heads down and plod ahead.

Pardon me for this overly dramatic comparison of war and divorce litigation. The divorce attorneys who read this book will know exactly what I mean. *You* will, too, if it happens to you. All that you can do at this point is depend on the experience and competency of your attorney. As the commander-in-chief of your team, he or she will know what is going right and what is going wrong. Your attorney will know when there are mistakes and how to correct them and will know how to take advantage of the mistakes that the "enemy" is making. Just keep cool and plod ahead. Remember your training—stay cool, and "keep your head down."

## You As a Witness

In the beginning you will note that your attorney and your experts seem relaxed and confident. They are professionals, veterans who have been in the trenches dozens, perhaps hundreds of times. But your apprehension chokes you. You are afraid that you will faint; that you will not remember your name or the date of your marriage; that your attorney will forget something; that one of your experts will be late; that you will not be able to testify as you sit in the witness chair facing your husband; that the judge will scowl if you stutter or falter; or that you will have to go to the bathroom in the middle of your testimony.

Such fears and apprehensions are real. Unless you've had acting experience you're bound to feel stage fright. But you're probably worrying more than you need to. Let's talk about a few of your fears.

Will your attorney make a mistake? Yes. Even if this happens the lapse will be corrected before the trial is over. Remember that the trial will not be over in an hour or two hours, but will probably last throughout the entire day—in most cases several days. If at the end of the day your attorney suddenly remembers an important exhibit, a sidebar will be requested, where the two attorneys and judge speak on one side of the bench, away from the court reporter: "Judge, I am very embarrassed. I just realized that I forgot to introduce a very important exhibit regarding the appraisal of my client's jewelry. May I re-open my case and submit it?" In 99.9 percent of the cases the judge will say, "Sure, go ahead," whether your husband's attorney likes it or not.

If one (or more) of your experts doesn't make it on time your attorney will proceed with your case and hope the expert shows up later. Failing this, there will be another sidebar conference, and usually the judge will arrange for another hearing.

What happens if you make an error in your testimony? No problem:

You:    Your honor, I met Roger when I was 19 and I had just graduated from college.

        (Your attorney knows you just made a minor error; you were 22 when you graduated. He also knows that it doesn't make much difference but will make a note of it.) His next question to you will be as follows:

Me:   Mrs. Henderson, you have just testified that you met Roger upon your graduation at the age of 19. Is that correct?

You:   I am sorry. I was 22. Please excuse me.

Everyone will. No problem.

What if you become so nervous you lose your concentration and can't continue? If the judge notices, a recess will be called and you'll be able to leave the courtroom and pull yourself together. If your attorney notices, a short recess will be requested so you can get a cup of coffee or some fresh air. If you have to go to the bathroom, whisper to the judge or an attendant so you can be excused. If you cry, you will cry. Proceedings will halt momentarily, you'll be handed some Kleenex, you will apologize, and go on. None of this will affect the outcome of your case.

The most important thing for you to remember is this: *no one in the courtroom knows more than you do about the facts of your life*, not the judge, the court reporter, the sheriff, the two court attendants, your husband, his attorney, or even your attorney. Therefore there is no reason for you to be afraid.

**You have the only copy of the script.**

How should you dress? As if you were going to worship or to a school luncheon to meet your children's teachers.

What if your husband stares at you? Smile and turn away. Don't be intimidated by his presence or by any "look" on his face. You have come a long way to get to this point. He has been unfair, and you're entitled to go after those rights guaranteed you by the law of your state. Don't be intimidated by his presence. (Pretend he's not there!)

## How to Behave on the Witness Stand

Here are a few simple rules to guide you in answering questions while you're on the witness stand.

*Answer the question!* One of my biggest problems in preparing some clients for trial is a natural tendency to ignore the question and start to talk about everything except the answer. I understand

and respect the situation they face in the hostile setting of divorce litigation. In almost every case they have never been in a court-room before and soon feel the enormous pressure exerted by this terrible husband-wife conflict. Nevertheless, our adversary system of divorce litigation is the only system we have, and the rules must be followed. If you're asked a question, concentrate on the question and answer it precisely. If you don't, you will only confuse everybody or worse, turn the judge off. Here are some examples of "good" and "bad" answers:

> Me: Now Mrs. Henderson, when was the last time you actually worked for someone and received a salary?
>
> *Bad Answer*: Well my husband never really wanted me to work. He said that he wanted me to stay home, take care of the children, and—he wanted me to give parties for his colleagues—keep the house looking good so he could impress the people he did business with. I'm really not qualified.
>
> *Good Answer*: I last worked in 1978.

If you're asked a question requiring a numerical answer, give the numerical answer; if you're asked a question requiring a color as an answer, name the color; if you are asked a question requiring a name, give the name. *Do not drift; be precise.*

If your husband's attorney asks you a three- or four-part question, don't answer it; don't even try. Simply say, "Mr. Fenster, I can't answer the question because it consists of three or four parts. Would you mind slowing down, sir, and asking me one question at a time?"

Don't ever wonder why your husband's attorney is asking you a particular question, what he's driving at. Often *he* doesn't know. Relax. It is not your job to understand your husband's attorney during cross-examination. He may be incompetent or malicious. Don't look at your attorney pleadingly; he or she may not object simply to show the judge that these questions are senseless. In any event, you don't need your attorney's help on cross-examination. Example:

| | |
|---|---|
| Husband's Attorney: | Mrs. Henderson, isn't it true that you sell cocaine, LSD, and amphetamines to elementary school children? |
| You: | (quickly and calmly) No. |

That's it. Don't think for a minute you don't understand why he asked you such a stupid question. After the proceedings are over that day, you and your attorney will be able to laugh at the cross-examination. Until then, listen to the questions, answer, and don't be distracted by wondering why such dumb questions are being asked.

Be as precise as you can. Here are illustrations of poor, fair, and good answers with regard to precision. Your attorney is questioning you:

| | |
|---|---|
| Me: | Mrs. Henderson, you have testified that Roger took you and Jennifer to California in 1983. Can you tell the court how much that vacation cost and who paid for it? |
| *Poor Answer*: | Well, it was a lot of money, I know that. We could buy anything we wanted, and it seemed that there was plenty of cash to spend. We just did what we wanted, that's all. I just don't know. |
| *Fair Answer*: | Well, I'm not sure. I know that the hotels were at least one hundred dollars a day, and we rented a car. We ate out every night. Well, no, sometimes we went out for pizza. And, you know, we had the airfare and spending money, so it must have cost a couple of thousand dollars. |
| *Good Answer*: | Your honor, in the summer of 1983, Roger, Jennifer, and I flew to Los Angeles so that Jennifer could visit Disneyland. The expenses of the trip were paid for by Roger. The night before we left, he showed me an envelope of one-hundred-dollar bills. He told me that there were thirty of them and that we had three thousand dollars for all of our expenses. He also told me that the airplane tickets and hotel all had been paid for through the business and therefore we would have the |

three thousand dollars in cash to spend as we wished.

We stayed at a hotel in Anaheim and, as I recall, we had a suite that cost $180. We stayed there for five nights. The cost for hotel rooms was $900.

Roger rented a car at a cost, if I recall, of fifty dollars per day. We kept that car for six days.

We ate all of our meals out, and I have prepared a schedule of how much I estimated we spent for breakfast, food at Disneyland, and dinner in the evening. The total for food for the six days was approximately $500.

In addition to those expenses that I have enumerated, Roger would give me a hundred-dollar bill in the morning for "walking-around money." I used this money for gifts, film, cold drinks, and incidental expenses as we went through the park.

In preparation for trial, my accountant came across the airplane tickets, and we found out that they cost $900.

Therefore, sir, the cost of the trip was approximately $3,500. The airfare and hotel were paid for by Roger's corporation. Roger paid for everything else with cash.

## Specifics on Testifying (Direct and Cross-examination)

1. Insofar as possible when you answer questions, talk to the judge. Do not talk to your husband, his attorney, or your attorney. Remember, the one who decides the case is the judge, so talk directly to the bench

2. *Avoid* "I guess," "probably," "I'm not sure, it was a long time ago; how can I remember that far back?" If you know the answer to something, state it. If you don't know the answer say, "I don't know" or "I don't remember." There is no in-between except "to the best of my recollection." Learn the difference.

3. Avoid "Well, everybody knows that he makes more than he reports" or "His own sister told me that he doesn't report all of his income." While the law says that you cannot testify what

someone else told you, you *can* tell the court what *your husband* told *you*.

4. In reciting your husband's conversations with you, *always use the first person*.

|                     |                                                                                                                                                                    |
| ------------------- | ------------------------------------------------------------------------------------------------------------------------------------------------------------------ |
| Your attorney:      | Mrs. Henderson, will you please tell the court what, if anything, your husband told you about his personal income tax return?                                       |
| Wrong:              | He said he needed me to sign the return because it had been prepared by the accountant and he didn't want me to ask any questions.                                  |
| Right:              | He said, "Margo, I want you to sign this return. Howard prepared it and I don't want you to ask any questions about it. Just sign it, honey."                       |

OR

|        |                                                                                                                                                                                          |
| ------ | ---------------------------------------------------------------------------------------------------------------------------------------------------------------------------------------- |
| Me:    | Will you tell the court what your husband said about hiring a car when you were in London?                                                                                                |
| Wrong: | He said he wanted a black limousine. He said he didn't want a gray one. He said he didn't care what it cost.                                                                              |
| Right: | We were at the car rental agency and my husband said to the clerk, "Look, I want a black limousine. I don't want a gray one or any other color. I don't care what it costs, it has to be black." |

5. If you begin your answer with "I don't know" or "I don't remember," you have already shot yourself in the foot. If you don't remember or don't know, you can't testify. Avoid conversational embellishments that, perfectly proper in a social gathering or when you are with your family, have no place in a courtroom.

6. You will put out of your mind all debilitating emotions for that day—hatred, anger, venality, vengeance, or vituperation. (Avoid those three "Vs.")

Your husband's lawyer is not angry at you, nor is he your enemy. He is merely doing his job. Yes, he will try to confuse you. Yes he will try to trip you up on your direct examination; that's his job. Relax and answer his questions directly. Don't get cute. As you sit through the cross-examination you will realize you have nothing to worry about; that as long as you answer the questions directly, and precisely, your husband's attorney will only founder.

However, avoid the following:

Husband's attorney:   Now, isn't it true, Mrs. Henderson, that at no time during the marriage did you ever say to your husband that you wanted to go to graduate school?

*Wrong Answer*:   Look, Mr. Fenster, he was never around. How could I ask him about anything?

*Right Answer*:   Mr. Fenster, my need to attend graduate school has arisen only since the separation. When we lived together as a family Roger supported us completely, and I was content to be a homemaker and mother. Now I want to develop my own career.

Learn to *counterpunch*, a technique to be practiced with your attorney who can play the part of your husband's attorney. An example of counterpunching:

Husband's attorney:   Now Mrs. Henderson, isn't it true that all during these years when you say your husband had this unreported money, you signed the income tax returns?

You:   Yes Mr. Fenster, I signed the returns, *but* I signed them because he told me to sign them and I believed that it was my duty as his wife to sign them. I never believed that they were true and correct. Furthermore, I signed them in blank.

This is the wonderful "yes-/but" answer, which you should learn to spring on your husband's attorney in cross-examination. You don't always have to answer a question with a simple yes or no; sometimes a yes-/but explanation is in order, often causing your husband's attorney to stop his cross-examination sooner than he had planned.

Keep in mind that you're not on trial for first degree murder. You are not a criminal, you have not been arrested, nor has the world put you on trial for some vague, undefined crime.

You're a witness in a divorce litigation. The courts will not allow you to be treated discourteously. Nor will the court allow your husband's attorney to tread on you. Nor will *you* allow him to tread on you.

Example:

| | |
|---|---|
| Husband's attorney: | Now Mrs. Henderson, isn't it true that you knew all along your husband's automobile was a company car? |
| You: | Yes Mr. Fenster, I knew it was a company car— |
| Husband's attorney: | (interrupting) And isn't it true that you enjoyed the benefit of that car for the past four years? |
| You: | (not accepting the cutoff) Mr. Fenster, as I was about to say before you interrupted me, yes I knew that he was charging the car through the business for the past four years, but when I asked him if it was legal he said, "Margo, don't worry about it. They'll never find out." |

(This is also a wonderful counterpunch.)

Learn to answer the tricky questions, designed to confuse you, without getting confused. Here's a story I tell all of my clients on this point.

When I first started to practice law I was an assistant county prosecutor, and many of my cases involved drunken driving. In one case the testimony I presented showed that the Defendant had been seen weaving in and out of traffic and had hit two cars, stopping only when he hit a parked truck. The testimony further described the Defendant as staggering out of his car carrying a half-empty bottle of liquor then staggering to the sidewalk where he urinated. The young police officer who described this was clear and convincing, and there was no doubt in my mind that the jury would find the Defendant guilty. The Defendant's attorney, of course, knew the client was guilty and that he could not shake the young officer's testimony, so he asked the "fire hydrant" question:

Defense Attorney: Now Officer Kelly, you say you witnessed every-thing that happened that day. Is that correct?

Officer Kelly: I have already described what I witnessed, sir. Yes.

Defense Attorney: Well now, sir, will you tell the jury how close the nearest fire hydrant was?

Officer Kelly: (Perplexed, wondering what the question had to do with the case but afraid to say he didn't know, then going out on a limb) The closest fire hydrant, sir, was approximately twenty feet away.

Of course, there was no fire hydrant twenty feet away, and Officer Kelly should have said, "I don't have any idea where the closest fire hydrant was. I was watching the Defendant come out of the car with the liquor bottle and urinate, and I placed him under arrest." The jury felt that Officer Kelly wasn't credible and found the defendant not guilty.

If your testimony against your husband is what I call lethal and your husband's attorney knows you have convinced the court that your husband is making more money than he reports or whatever it is that you're trying to prove, he may well resort to the fire hydrant question.

Examples:

Husband's attorney: Now, Mrs. Henderson, you have stated that you were at a meeting with your husband and another businessman when they were discussing the value of the business. Is that correct?

You: Yes, sir.

Husband's attorney: Was this meeting in the conference room or in your husband's office?

You are puzzled. You can't recall whether the meeting was in the conference room or in your husband's office. You can't even remember whether your husband had a conference room at that point in time. You are afraid to say, "I don't know," because you are fearful that the judge will disregard your testimony. Nonsense.

You:   Mr. Fenster, the conversation was in my husband's place of business. I don't know in which room it took place, but I remember my husband saying that he wanted a half-million for his business.

If your case continues to another day, whenever possible, ask your attorney to get the notes of testimony before you resume your appearance. Read your testimony with a magnifying glass, carefully going over your mistakes, and make notes of the things you want to correct. (Your attorney will be doing the same thing.)

When possible, also read your husband's testimony so you can contradict what he said where necessary. Remember that the courts will always give you an opportunity to complete your testimony and that it will not necessarily have to be completed within one day or one hour. The courts are very flexible in this regard.

The most important single piece of advice with regard to your testimony on "D" Day is to remember that it is one of the most significant days of your life. You must be cool, speak clearly, and be mindful that much of your financial security depends on your appearance and demeanor. You can do it! All you have to do is be prepared.

Once your testimony is completed (direct and cross-examination), as far as you're concerned your case is over. Your attorney's work, of course, has just begun. Expert witnesses must be called, exhibits marked and admitted into evidence, and preparations made to cross-examine your husband and his witnesses. You can help your attorney as the trial proceeds by keeping notes and making your own observations. If you notice, for example, that one of your husband's witnesses appears frightened or apprehensive or you overhear a comment by your husband to a witness, make a note to give to your attorney at the end of the day.

One of the most appreciated bits of advice I have ever received during a hearing was in a bitter case where my client had been on the stand for two days of direct and cross-examination. It was now up to me, and I was going after her husband with a trifle too much zeal because his arrogance was showing and it was beginning to get to me. My client noticed that the judge was becoming a little upset with my raising my voice and pounding the table. She slipped me a little note: "Remember your Zen mode—relax."

You can communicate with your attorney throughout the rest of the trial, either by writing notes, whispering, or speaking at recesses or after the day's testimony. Your observations may prove helpful.

For the most part, once you testify on direct and cross-examination, you're through. Occasionally, as the case nears conclusion, your attorney may want to call you back for rebuttal (when you answer a few of the things your husband's witnesses brought up). By that time you'll be a seasoned witness, able to handle yourself without any of the previous apprehensions.

Divorce litigation is a slow process. Unlike on TV, there's no "verdict" immediately following the commercial. All that the judge will do when the testimony is eventually over is ask, "Is that all, counsel? If that is the end of the case I will now close the testimony and will invite the attorneys to submit briefs within thirty days after the notes of testimony have been transcribed. Thank you very much." It isn't Judge Wapner or "Divorce Court."

One final comment about the trial and your fears. Do you know who is the most frightened dude in the entire courthouse on the day of the trial? Well, it's your tough guy husband, that's who. After all, the worst thing that happens to you is you get frightened, or have to go to the bathroom. The worst thing that happens to him, dear, is that he pays. And pays. And pays.

Let him worry about the trial. All you have to do is get ready for it and then enjoy it.

## Twenty-Five

# Henderson v. Henderson: "D" Day Minus Ten

### Chronology: Henderson v. Henderson, March 1989

Throughout the spring of 1989, Margo and I went through rehearsals at least once a week. My paralegal, Vicki, and I began to assemble all of the exhibits we would introduce at the trial, and finally I met with each expert witness to review his or her report. Our list of major witnesses included the following:

1. Jay Fisher, who would value Roger's interest in HEI;
2. Barbara Ann Gordon, who would testify that Roger's earning capacity approximated $100,000 a year and that his draw of $25,000 was but the tip of the iceberg;
3. A residential real estate appraiser, who would testify that the Oak Drive residence had a fair market value of $147,500 (based on comparative sales);
4. A residential furniture appraiser, who would testify that a tag sale of Margo's furniture would bring approximately $5,000;
5. A pension- and profit-sharing expert, who would testify that the present value of Roger's profit-sharing plan was $80,000 (because he could roll over that amount into an IRA account and not pay income taxes until his retirement);

6. Dr. James Baker, a psychiatrist, who would testify to Margo's emotional health and her continued need for therapy;

7. Dr. Harold Kohler, a vocational consultant, who would testify about Margo's proposed career in public relations;

8. A commercial real estate appraiser, who would testify that the company warehouse, on the HEI books for $32,000, was actually worth $195,000;

9. Mr. Ralph Henderson (under subpoena);

10. Ms. Tracey Hall (under subpoena);

11. Roger (no subpoena necessary);

12. And, of course, Margo, who was prepared to testify at length that:

   a. She had no assets in her name, just some jewelry Roger had given her and a few dollars in her checking account (Fenster had agreed that we could use one jewelry appraiser, who valued Margo's rings, watch, etc. at $4,000);

   b. She could not work full time because she had to take care of the children and because she wanted to pursue a career in public relations (she had enrolled as a freshman at the university for the fall semester, in the School of Journalism and Public Relations);

   c. Her tuition, class fees, and books at the university would cost her $6,000 a year;

   d. She had no source of income other than Roger—no pension plan, no profit-sharing plan, no business, and had to depend on him for health insurance, life insurance, and maintenance while she got her degree;

   e. The standard of living she, Roger, and the children had enjoyed before the separation was based on an amount of $40,000 to $50,000 a year, all of which came from Roger's business, some of it in cash;

   f. She and Roger had lived the life-style of an upper-middle-class couple, enjoying a standard of living that included new cars for each of them every four or five years, vacations two or three times a year, tickets for concerts, shows, and sporting events;

   g. Roger paid for many vacations, home improvements, and even for some of her charge accounts in cash;

h. She required $350 a week, plus tuition, as post-divorce alimony in order to enjoy the same standard of living she had had with Roger (over and above child support);

i. She'd need this alimony for at least seven years because it would take that long for her to graduate, get a job, and reach the salary level of $35,000 to $50,000 annually;

j. She had been seeing Dr. Baker for some three or four years because of marital problems and would still need to see him for another one to two years because her emotional health was impaired; Baker charged $80 an hour;

k. She helped Roger develop his earning power by being a good homemaker, taking care of the children, giving parties for his big customers, attending trade shows and, in the beginning, taking care of the books, performing some secretarial work, and helping in the HEI warehouse, stopping only when she became pregnant;

l. Roger's father knew nothing whatsoever about the business, that he was a retired engineer who lived twenty miles away, and that he never worked for HEI as a consultant or in any other capacity;

m. Roger once told her that his business was worth at least "half a million" and that someday they'd sell out and be on "Easy Street";

n. Roger and his brother Frank, the dentist in Orlando, were extremely close;

o. The house on Oak Drive needed a new driveway, interior and exterior painting, and some roof repairs, all of which would cost some $6,000 or $7,000 (Fenster had agreed with our written estimates);

p. She could not depend on inheriting a great deal of money from her parents, who were only in their 60s and in good health (her grandparents had lived into their late 80s), and, furthermore, her parents had a very small estate, which they would probably consume during their lifetime;

q. Roger had been "going away" for weekends for the past five or six years, coming home with unlikely excuses, such as golfing, missed flights, business meetings, etc., and that it appeared to her that he was seeing someone; and that she'd heard him talking to Ms. Hall on New Year's Eve, confessing his love for her;

r.   She had paid me a retainer of $2,500 (borrowed from her parents), owed me $22,400, and was satisfied with my time records and the work I had performed on her behalf;

s.   She owed her aunt and her uncle $6,000 for the first year's college tuition, books, and class fees;

t.   She had sincerely tried to settle the case with Roger but was convinced he was not negotiating with her in good faith.

Everything was in order. Vicki and I had compiled a black loose-leaf notebook of the complete game plan, our order of witnesses, copies of the exhibits, and a short trial brief of appellate cases we felt were applicable to the *Henderson* case.

There was only one thing left to do. I'd always told Fenster I'd give him a written demand for settlement before trial, and I was ready to do that now. Before dictating the letter (which I wanted to deliver personally), I went to my blackboard for the last time before trial. The Henderson marital estate was worth $1.25 million!

Based on a total marital estate of $1.3 million and the application of the EDFs to the *Henderson* case, I figured that Roger had to be looking at a distribution of 50 percent, $600,000 (±) or 55 percent, $660,000 (±), depending on how Margo came across to Judge Jackson. This meant that Margo could expect the house, free and clear of the mortgage, and perhaps $300,000 or $400,000 over that if we went to trial and survived an appeal by Roger.

And yet I had an uneasy feeling about the case. First of all, the figures on my blackboard were not evidence, only *our* appraisals. Each one would have to be fought over in the trenches of litigation. And I had major anxiety about Margo's ability to hang tough.

More important, there was the specter of an appeal hovering over my calculations. If Roger got hit with $300,000 or $400,000 over and above Oak Drive, he'd appeal—no doubt about it. Then Margo would face another two or three years of litigation she couldn't afford. I did not believe that Margo could hold out until 1991 or 1992! Nor did I think she could face the possibility that the Superior Court could reverse the judge's decision *and send the entire case back to be re-tried.* It could happen! Nonetheless, I didn't expect Margo's trial to go past the second day. I felt reasonably confident that Roger would cave in fairly soon and that we'd have a negotiated settlement. Judge Jackson would probably never have to decide the case at all, so there would be no appeals to worry about. Actually, I had a gut feeling, a *strong* gut feeling, that Fenster would call me as soon as Roger's cross-examination was finished and suggest a settlement. But what if I was wrong?

Figure 25.1 is the demand I submitted to Fenster on March 10, the Friday before trial.

## FIGURE 25.1
## MARGO'S SETTLEMENT DEMAND

**SIDNEY M. DeANGELIS**
Attorney At Law
Main Street Professional Building
Smithdale

March 10, 1989

HAND DELIVERED

Joseph Fenster, Esquire
Suite 500
Fidelity Building
Smithdale, _____

Re: <u>Henderson v. Henderson</u>

Dear Joe:

Without prejudice, here is what Margo Henderson will accept in order to settle the divorce litigation:

1. A conveyance of premises 576 Oak Drive to Mrs. Henderson in her own name;

2. Roger to pay off the First Federal Savings & Loan balance;

3. Roger to assign all of the furniture and personal property located in 576 Oak Drive to Margo;

4. Roger to replace Margo's Cutlass with a 1988 automobile at a cost of not more than $15,000, this car to be titled in her name;

5. Roger to pay Margo $200,000 in exchange for her claims for Equitable Distribution, $100,000 of which will be due and payable upon the execution of the Agreement, $50,000 within one year, and the final $50,000 due one year after that (subject to collateral security as set forth below);

6.  Roger will continue to pay the existing child support Order in the amount of $350 per week, subject to modification only by reason of any circumstances of his health which prevent him from earning more than $20,000 per year.  Roger also to pay for all college expenses, graduate school, if applicable, and room and board, college fees, books and transportation to and from college;

7.  Roger to pay alimony to Margo in the amount of $350 per week for a period of seven (7) years, not to be modified by reasons of cohabitation or by reason of the fact that Margo becomes self-supporting during that period.  However, if Margo remarries the alimony Order would be terminated;

8.  According to my time records, present counsel fees are approximately $23,500.  If Roger accepts Margo's offer I expect that I would incur an additional twenty hours in preparing the Property Settlement Agreements and the collateral security documents.  Therefore, Roger would pay counsel fees in the amount of $25,000 upon the execution of the Property Settlement Agreement;

9.  Margo has spent approximately $6,500 for expert witness fees, appraisers, and miscellaneous Court costs.  She owes an additional $1,712.  Therefore, Roger would pay the total of those sums upon the execution of the Agreement;

10.  As collateral security for Roger's obligations herein, he would provide the following:

     a)  A decreasing term life insurance policy in the amount of $500,000, naming Margo as irrevocable beneficiary, to collateralize his obligations to pay alimony, child support, and college tuition and related expenses.

     b)  A $100,000 decreasing term life insurance policy naming Margo the irrevocable beneficiary, to collateralize his agreement to pay Margo the additional $100,000 as Equitable Distribution.

     c)  A $50,000 decreasing term life insurance policy naming Margo as irrevocable beneficiary, to collateralize his obligation to pay off the First Federal mortgage (in the event that he did not pay this upon the execution of the Agreement).

     d)  A second mortgage upon the Wilson Boulevard Warehouse in the amount of $100,000, to collateralize his obligation to pay Margo $100,000 over the next two years as Equitable Distribution.

     e)  A lien upon his 1986 Mercedes in the amount of $20,000 to further collateralize his Equitable Distribution obligation.

     f)  A financing statement upon all of the assets and receivables of H.E.I. to be recorded, and to remain so during the seven-year period he will be required to make alimony payments.

If this offer is acceptable please call me at once and I will prepare a Property Settlement Agreement based upon these terms.  If it is not acceptable we will proceed with the Equitable Distribution hearing scheduled for March 15, 1988.

                              Sincerely yours,


                              SIDNEY M. DE ANGELIS

SMD:e
cc: Mrs. Margo Henderson

Now of course I expected Joe to tell me to go to hell when he got the demand, but I didn't care. Marge typed it up and I dropped in on Fenster with no appointment.

### Chronology: Henderson v. Henderson, March 10, 1989

Me:       Hi Joe, I have a proposal for you. Here it is.

Fenster:  Well it's about time, De Angelis (reading). . . . You gotta be kidding—you outta your mind or what? Where the hell did you get these numbers? Are you takin' something? No way!

Me:       (smiling) See you next Friday, Joe.

I walked out. No use in arguing with Fenster anymore. The final battle was about to begin, and my troops were ready.

### Telephone Conversation, March 13, 1989, 11:00 P.M.

Roger:  Joe, sorry to call you at home, but that SOB subpoenaed my father and Tracey. I want you to stop it.

Joe:    I can't stop it, Roger. He's got the right—.

Roger:  I want those subpoenas wiped out, Joe—tomorrow!

Joe:    Can't do it, pal. Call me tomorrow. Good night, Rog.

### Telephone Conversation, March 14, 1989, 11:30 P.M.

Margo:  Sidney, I apologize for calling so late. Please forgive me, but I'm so scared I can't even remember my name and address.

Me:     It's natural, Margo. Take a hot bath and get some sleep.

Margo:  Will it go all right, do you think?

Me:     Sure it will.

Margo:  But I'm so scared.

Me:     Maybe so. But Roger—he's really scared, he's suffering from terminal fright, so relax. By the way, do me a favor, will you?

Margo:  What is it?

Me:     When you get to Maui, send me a box of Maui onions.

Margo:  (laughing) I'm glad I called. Good night. . . . Are you sure it'll go all right?

Me:     Depend on it.

I read some of my loose-leaf trial book and turned the lights out at midnight. It was "D" Day minus $9\frac{1}{2}$ hours.

# Twenty-Six

# "D" Day

March 15, 1989, was a clear, cold, and sunny day. Margo, Barbara Ann Gordon, and I had an early breakfast at the courthouse coffee shop and were in the courtroom at least an hour before the case would begin.

I wanted Margo to get acquainted with the feel of the courtroom; in addition I knew that Judge Jackson would be on the bench at 9:29, ready to go.

About 9 o'clock, Fenster, Roger, and Howard Picker walked in carrying boxes of records. They were laughing loudly and seemed to be enjoying themselves. Roger was wearing his $350 wing tips.

"Why are they laughing?" Margo whispered.

"Because they're on their way to the gallows. What else can they do?" I replied.

"You're sure of that?"

"Yep."

"I'm scared."

"So am I."

Scared or not I knew I was ready. I also knew that Harriet Jackson was a good judge for Margo. Some lawyers didn't like to appear before Jackson—she appeared crusty, humorless, even impatient. She certainly wasn't the kind of judge you could slap on the back with a "Hey, Judge, how ya' doin'?" But I was glad that we'd gotten her. Something told me she wouldn't take any crap from Fenster and that she'd find Roger's arrogance too much to take.

I'd appeared before Jackson a few times since her appointment but only for minor petitions and motions, not for a full-scale equitable distribution hearing.

At 9:29 Jackson stormed into the courtroom (she had a natural speed-walk), and gave Fenster and me her "Don't-give-me-any-crap-today" look.

I made a brief statement and then said, "My first witness will be Mrs. Margo Henderson." As she passed by me on the way to the witness stand I whispered, "Showtime!"

She was perfect. A little tense at the beginning, perhaps, but she went through all of the equitable distribution and alimony factors with no difficulty whatsoever. It was hard to tell that she'd been through hell over the past five or six years. Judge Jackson didn't interrupt her at all—just glanced down at her from time to time and made notes on her legal pad.

Margo testified until 12:30, when Jackson adjourned for lunch, telling us to be back at 2:00. As Margo and I walked out of the courtroom, she said, "That wasn't so bad, you know."

She took the stand again at 2:00 and I went to 3:30. I stopped then because everything was basically in the record, and also because I wanted to give her a break at 4:30 or 5:00 in case Fenster's cross-examination bothered her. It didn't. It didn't even get close.

Fenster:  Mrs. Henderson, can you explain why you're not working?
Margo:    Yes, Mr. Fenster. As you know I haven't worked since Jennifer was born. Then we had Jeffrey, and as the children grew up Roger insisted I remain at home to take care of them and our home. Over the past five or six years our marriage deteriorated, and I began to suffer from depression. Now I'm enrolled at the university for a graduate degree in public relations. I start in September.
Fenster:  You're the oldest student in your class, aren't you?

| Margo: | I don't think so. I met a woman in her fifties when I registered. |
|---|---|
| Judge: | Mr. Fenster, my sister is in graduate school and she's fifty-five. There's nothing wrong with that, is there? |
| Fenster: | No, ma'am. (but still not getting the message) Well, Mrs. Henderson, during the fourteen years of your marriage you never discussed graduate school with your husband, isn't that right? |
| Margo: | (ready for this one) Mr. Fenster, for those seventeen years I was Roger's wife, his friend, his confidant—I raised two children, I helped Roger with his business, we traveled, I went to his trade shows, I did what I could to help him. Now that he's gone, I have to develop a career for myself, one more financially rewarding than teaching high school so I can hope to enjoy the same standard of living we had before Tracey. |
| Fenster: | (loudly) Objection, your Honor! |
| Judge: | You don't have to shout, Mr. Fenster, I can hear you. Anyhow, there's no jury here. I can tell what's important and what's not. Objection overruled. |

(I was shocked. At no time had I ever suggested to Margo that she drag Tracey's name into an answer. Actually, Margo hated to refer to Tracey by name, usually referring to her as "that young slut." Anyhow, I was delighted that Margo was feeling her oats.)

Fenster began to realize that he'd dig himself into a deep hole if he kept on with his cross, so at 4:30 he looked up at the clock:

| Fenster: | Your Honor, I note that it is 4:30. How much longer did you intend to sit? |
|---|---|
| Judge Jackson: | As long as it takes you to conclude your cross-examination, Mr. Fenster. You realize that this case will take several more days of testimony. Let's go on until you've finished. |

(Fenster didn't like the judge's answer. He wanted to break and hope that Margo would be worried about the resumption of cross-examination and perhaps not be so cool the next time. Of course Judge Jackson knew that too.)

Judge Jackson:   You may proceed Mr. Fenster.
     Fenster:   I—uh—have no further questions, Your Honor.
Judge Jackson:   Court is recessed until 9:30 A.M. tomorrow. Gentle-
                 men, my secretary informs me that I had a full day's
                 trial scheduled for Tuesday, March 21, but that counsel
                 has advised it has been settled. We'll resume on March
                 21 at 9:30 A.M. Thank you.

    Margo had been on the stand for cross-examination for approxi-
mately fifty-five minutes. We had both expected her to be crossed
for a full day. She was flying high as we walked over to the coffee
shop for iced tea.

Margo:   Do you realize that for fourteen years I've been terrified that
        Roger would be mad at me if I talked back to him, that he
        might hurt me if I crossed him? That slimy SOB!
    Me:   I don't think Jackson likes him.
Margo:   Damn it, I wish we were coming back tomorrow morning!
    Me:   Well, you're finished with your testimony. By the way, Barbara,
        Vicki, and I have made a decision. We're going to call Roger as
        our next witness on the 21st.
Margo:   Oh boy, oh boy, I can't wait!
    Me:   Neither can I.

### *Chronology: Henderson v. Henderson,*
### *March 21, 1989, 9:30 A.M.*

---

    Me:   Mr. Henderson, I show you Plaintiff's Exhibit No. Twelve, your
        Statement of Assets and Liabilities. Do you recognize it?
Roger:   Uh-huh.
    Me:   Is it correct?
Roger:   (reading it carefully) Yes, it is.
    Me:   That's your signature, under oath, on the bottom?
Roger:   Looks like it.
    Me:   Have you left anything out?
Roger:   (with a sick look) No.

    I walked over to Vicki, who handed me a large envelope

containing the $8 \times 10$s of the Orlando Mart. I gave one to Fenster, one to the judge, and one to the court reporter and asked him to mark it as Plaintiff's Exhibit Twenty-Seven.

|  |  |
|---|---|
| Fenster: | (rising) I object, Your Honor, this photograph is irrelevant. |
| Judge Jackson: | How do you know that, counsel? It hasn't been identified yet. |
| Fenster: | Your Honor, I've never seen this photograph before. De Angelis should have shown it to me as part of his case. I object to its being marked. |
| Judge Jackson: | Mr. Fenster, did you file any pretrial interrogatories calling upon the plaintiff to supply you with copies of all documentary evidence, including photographs she intended to introduce? |
| Fenster: | No, ma'am, I didn't. But— |
| Judge Jackson: | Mr. Fenster, all that Mrs. Henderson's counsel is attempting to do is have the reporter put a numbered sticker on the photograph so we can refer to it properly. Please sit down and wait until Mr. De Angelis attempts to introduce it before you object. Proceed, Mr. De Angelis. |

I walked up to the witness stand, handed the photo to Roger, then backed away a few feet.

|  |  |
|---|---|
| Me: | Mr. Henderson, do you recognize the buildings depicted on this photograph, Plaintiff's Exhibit Twenty-Seven? |
| Roger: | (now agitated)Your Honor, can I talk to my lawyer? This is blackmail! |
| Judge Jackson: | Mr. Henderson, you are on cross-examination and you may not speak to your attorney. After the cross-examination is concluded, your attorney will be able to ask you any questions he wants to ask. Now, please answer the question and also, sir, refrain from characterizing a question put to you as "blackmail." |

Roger looked at me with clear murder in his eyes. I felt that he'd choke me if I got too close to him. So I asked the judge if I could approach the witness. The judge said, "Sure," so Roger and I were now "eyeball to eyeball."

|  |  |
|---|---|
| Me: | All right, sir, kindly look at P-27 carefully and tell Judge Jackson whether you recognize the buildings depicted there. |
| Roger: | (now determined to go all the way with the lie) Yeah, looks like a picture of my brother's shopping center in Orlando, Florida. He owns it outright—100 percent—it's all his. Dr. Frank Henderson. |
| Me: | Well Mr. Henderson, I didn't ask you who owns it, but now that you've volunteered that your brother owns it, can you tell us who put up the money to build it? |
| Fenster: | (standing up again) I object again, Your Honor, this is just intimidation by De Angelis. It's irrelevant what my client's brother owns. He isn't married to the plaintiff, my client is. |
| Judge Jackson: | (to me) Will you be following this up, Mr. De Angelis? |
| Me: | (softly) Yes, ma'am. |
| Judge Jackson: | I expected you would be. Objection overruled. |
| Fenster: | Your Honor, I'd like a ten-minute recess to review this matter with my client. |
| Judge Jackson: | It's only 9:40 Mr. Fenster. We'll break as usual, at 10:30. Go on, Mr. Henderson, answer the question. |
| Roger: | I forgot the question. |
| Judge Jackson: | He wants to know who put up the money to build the shopping center. |
| Roger: | My brother did—all of it—I didn't put up a thin dime! |
| Me: | Did you pay for any engineering studies? |
| Roger: | (feeling better) No. |
| Me: | Environmental studies? |
| Roger: | Absolutely not. It's my brother's deal. |
| Me: | Pay for anything at all, Mr. Henderson? |
| Roger: | Absolutely not. |

I signaled to Vicki, who brought me four copies of the "wallet check" for $350 made out to the architect. Everybody got one, and it was marked P-28. Fenster didn't bother to object this time.

Me: (showing Roger P-28) Is this your signature on this copy of a check?

Roger: Yeah, I guess so.

Me: Can you explain why you wrote a check to James Connor Associates on March 21, 1983?

Roger: Don't have the foggiest idea. I don't know anybody named Connor.

Me: Mr. Henderson, let's save the court and each other some time. Isn't it a fact that you and your brother Frank decided to build a small shopping center on a tract of land located on Davisville Road just outside of Orlando, Florida, sometime in 1977, that you and he purchased some seven acres for that purpose, arranged for zoning, financing, engineering and the like, from '77 to '83, and that on March 21, 1983, you went to Atlanta to see an eminent architect to retain him to design the center for you and your brother?

Roger: That's a damn lie!

Me: And further that you were so impressed with Mr. Connor who had just designed a big mall some few miles away that you retained him on the spot by paying him for the initial conference using a check folded up in your wallet?

Roger: Absolutely not.

Judge Jackson: Mr. Henderson, as you look at the check today is it your recollection that you retained Mr. Connor as an architect on March 21, 1983?

Roger: Absolutely not. I only put up the $350 because Frank didn't have a check with him. Frank paid it back, Judge. He gave me the $350 in cash a few weeks later. That deed is in Frank's name, you can check.

Me: Well, let's get right down to business, Mr. Henderson. Did you ever tell your wife that you owned a half interest in the Orlando mart—the one shown on p.27?

Roger:     (feeling stronger) No way!
Me:        Did you ever tell anybody you owned a 50 percent
           interest in the Orlando mart?
Roger:     (now worried) No—absolutely not.

I moved a little closer.

Me:        No one, Mr. Henderson?

He really wanted to choke me.

Roger:     No one.

I sighed, then looked up at Judge Jackson with a slight grin. I
walked over to Vicki, who handed me four copies of the financial
statement Roger had submitted to Citizens on September 1, 1984.
For a little fun, I'd told Vicki to put the copies of the statement in a
bright red manila folder, separate from all of the other exhibits.
As dramatically as I could, I extracted the statements from the
red manila folder, passed out copies, then had the court copy
marked as Plaintiff's Exhibit Twenty-Nine.
I then walked back to Roger, again getting permission to stand
close by him, and I handed him his copy.

Me:            Then, Mr. Henderson, can you explain why on Sep-
               tember 1, 1984, you stated, under oath, that you
               owned a 50 percent interest in the Orlando mart in
               Orlando, Florida, which you valued at $750,000?
Fenster:       (getting up and almost charging up to the bench) Your
               Honor, this is pure harassment! Everybody knows that
               people submit financial statements that sometimes
               exaggerate their assets. I object!
Judge Jackson: No, Mr. Fenster, this is not harassment, this is cross-
               examination. Secondly, I want it understood that I will
               not tolerate your signaling your client by suggesting
               possible answers to him while he is on cross-examina-
               tion. You know better than that. Now, Mr. Henderson,
               I'm curious—did you sign this statement to Citizens?

Roger:   (looking up at the clock, then at Fenster who was biting a fingernail, then back to the statement) I—uh—don't remember.

Me:   Well with all due respect, Mr. Henderson, that's not the end of it. Did you submit this statement to Citizens in order to secure a commercial loan of $45,000?

Roger:   I don't remember.

Me:   Sure you do, Mr. Henderson. As a matter of fact in your depositions, which you gave in July of 1987—I have a copy here—you were able to remember the bank loan all right. Here, sir, let's turn to page 78. Joe, can you get your copy? Didn't you say (reading)—"Yeah, a few years ago we were short of cash and the company wanted to buy a large quantity of components, so we borrowed $40,000 or $50,000 from Citizens. But it's paid back."

You remember that don't you, Mr. Henderson?

Roger:   Yeah, we borrowed the money.

Me:   But the only way you could get the loan was to co-sign it with the company and submit a personal certified financial statement. Isn't that what Citizens demanded as a condition?

Roger:   I don't know.

Me:   Well, let me refresh your recollection. (I signaled to Vicki, who gave me four copies of the Citizens–Roger correspondence) Here, suppose you read what we've marked as P-30, a letter written to you on September 10, 1984, from the Citizens vice president, John Durant.

Roger:   (who couldn't read anything at this point) Yeah, that's what it says.

Me:   So you filled out the statement, signed it, and swore to it, did you not, sir?

Roger:   Yeah.

Me:   Were you telling the truth on September 10, 1984?

Roger:   (now between the rock and the hard place) I was exaggerating. It isn't worth $750,000.

Judge Jackson:   *What* isn't worth $750,000, Mr. Henderson?

|  |  |
|---|---|
| Fenster: | I object, Your Honor. |
| Judge Jackson: | Sit down, Mr. Fenster. Answer my question Mr. Henderson. |
| Roger: | (not being able to respond, he looks at Fenster, then at me, finally at Margo—I almost felt sorry for him) |
| Me: | Can you answer the Judge's question Mr. Henderson. |
| Roger: | (faintly) I don't know. |

Up to now the courtroom had been very quiet. My cross-examination is usually conducted in a laid-back, soft tone of voice. Roger's responses were barely audible. Even Fenster had begun to speak softly as he realized his objections were getting nowhere. So when Judge Jackson exploded, her voice sounded like crackling gunfire.

|  |  |
|---|---|
| Judge Jackson: | I want to see counsel in chambers—right now! |

(Joe looked at me as if he'd just been given bad news from a cardiologist. Roger seemed stunned—I was afraid he was going to have a stroke. We followed the Judge into her chambers. She was standing by her desk. Steaming with anger, she started right in, not waiting for us to sit.)

|  |  |
|---|---|
| Judge Jackson: | Joe, I've heard enough. I've got a duty to uphold the law and I think that duty impels me to call the United States Attorney downtown and the United States Attorney for the Northern District of Florida and let them determine whether Henderson and his brother get indicted for criminal income tax evasion and conspiracy. I think you ought to tell your guy to settle this case today. |

Fenster got the message. His eyes fluttered a little and his voice was shaky but he managed an answer.

|  |  |
|---|---|
| Fenster: | How much—uh, when—uh, what time do you want us back? |

| Judge Jackson: | We'll adjourn until 2:30. Why don't you and De Angelis have conversation. |
| Fenster: | Sure. |
| Me: | OK with me. |

We walked back into the courtroom and whispered to our clients. Joe and Roger walked out first.

As Margo and I left the courtroom we spotted Roger and Fenster in the corridor, arguing with each other. I interrupted them.

| Me: | Joe, why don't you and Roger join Margo and me back at my office? Maybe we can work this thing out. |
| Fenster: | Can we talk now? |
| Me: | No. I have to go to the bathroom. See ya in ten minutes. |

I walked into the bathroom—I really had to go. While inside I heard the door open, then noticed that Roger was standing directly next to me. I tried not to look up. Then he spoke.

| Roger: | You wanna make $25,000 fast? Cash? No questions asked. |
| Me: | (still not looking up) You wanna go up to the district attorney's office with me and repeat what you just said to a county detective? |
| Roger: | Asshole! |
| Me: | See you in my office, Roger. Don't forget to wash your hands! |

A half-hour later we sat around my conference table, still feeling the tension of the morning. I decided to get it over with without any preliminaries.

| Me: | Joe, do you have my letter—the one I delivered last week? |
| Fenster: | Sidney, we can't come up with that—it's ridiculous—no way! |
| Me: | (getting up) OK fellas, see you at 2:30. |
| Fenster: | Wait a minute, will ya. Give me a chance to talk it over with Roger, OK? |

Me:    Sure, Joe. Margo, you come with me. Joe, we'll be in my office. Take your time.

In my office:

Margo:    Will you please tell me what's going on?
   Me:    I think it's over, Margo—but just sit back and relax. Joe'll be in here in a few minutes and we'll wrap it up. You'll have to give up on a few minor items.
Margo:    I don't understand!
   Me:    Margo, I think that Roger bailed out today. He doesn't want his father cross-examined, he doesn't want me to cross-examine Tracey, he doesn't want to explain the Citizens statement—he's afraid of the $200 a week—
Margo:    What $200 a week?
   Me:    Remember the $34,500 deal—the "loan" he made to HEI, the $200 a week they gave him as a tax-free "repayment" of a loan he made with hidden cash? The cigar box cash?
Margo:    Yes, I remember.
   Me:    Let me go on. He doesn't want to have Jackson go crazy with the $750,000. If Jackson gets mad enough she can easily find that the marital assets exceed one million and give you half. And he's beginning to have nightmares about the fraud division of the IRS. He's scared to death he and his brother will be indicted. So I think Roger wants to cut his losses—

There was a knock on my door.

Me:   C'mon in, Joe.

Fenster walked in carrying my letter of March 10. He walked over to me and put the letter down on my desk in front of me. He and Roger had scribbled some changes on it with a red pencil.

1. Roger would pay off the mortgage on Oak Drive in monthly installments, not in a lump sum.
2. Roger would pay my counsel fees in four installments over one year.

3. He would pay all of Margo's court costs, expert witness fees, and family loans within one year.
4. He would not replace Margo's Cutlass.
5. He wanted Margo to share the college expenses 50–50.
6. Everything else in Margo's demand was acceptable!

I asked Joe to leave for a minute and briefly discussed Roger's offer with Margo. I suggested she take it, provided Roger gave us additional collateral for the money he had to come up with within one year and for his obligation to pay off the mortgage on Oak Drive. I also advised her that Roger could sign a "financing statement," which would act as a lien on all of the HEI assets, including cash and receivables.

Me:    To make sure he lives up to his promises, I think he should also give you a second mortgage on his warehouse.
          If he goes along with the collateral we want, I'd give up on the new car but not budge on college expenses for the children.
Margo:  OK Sidney, I'll take it.

I walked back to the conference room and explained to Joe and Roger what we would take.

I then walked back to my office and Margo and I just looked at each other for a few minutes. Margo was biting her lip and still looked scared to death.

I felt it was over. I was certain that Judge Jackson had scared Roger out of his mind. I was right.

Joe came in and said, "We got a deal."

I told him it would take me about a week to draw up a formal property settlement contract incorporating our agreement and the collateral documents, but that we should go back to see Jackson at 2:30 and read our agreement into the record. Then Roger couldn't back out of it.

Judge Jackson wasn't surprised that we had settled the case. She patiently listened while Joe and I told her what the agreement was, and then she asked the usual questions.

Judge:   Now Mr. Henderson, you have heard your counsel and your
         wife's counsel state the terms of your agreement?
Roger:   Yes, Your Honor.
Judge:   Do you agree with those terms, that they're fair, and do you
         stipulate that you've been properly represented by Mr. Fenster?
Roger:   Yes, Your Honor.
Judge:   And are you now under the influence of alcohol or any drugs?
Roger:   (who had the odor of alcohol on his breath) No, I'm not.


The judge then asked Margo the same questions. Her face was
flushed with excitement as she answered each question.

I then addressed the court:


Me:      Your Honor, Mr. Fenster and I have agreed that the first
         payment of $100,000 to Mrs. Henderson, and the first pay-
         ment of counsel fees, costs, and repayment of loan, will not be
         due until May 1 to give Mr. Henderson some time to raise the
         funds. Would you therefore not issue any divorce decree until
         we advise the court that these payments have been received.
         They're to be certified checks.
Judge:   OK Mr. Fenster?
Fenster: No problem, Judge.


The judge then thanked everyone for settling the case, congratulated Margo and Roger, and then made our agreement an Order of
Court. (Of course, the court reporter was taking it all down. It was
in the record forever.)

It was 3:15. The case was over. When I got back to my office
Marge rushed into my office.

"How did it go?"

"Fine," I said, "just fine."

"Do you want your messages? I think you've got a few clients
waiting for you to call them back."

"No," I said, "I'm tired and I'm going home. And tomorrow I'm
going sailing. The cold air'll do me some good."

## *Chronology: Telephone Call, 11:30 P.M., March 21, 1989*

Me:    Yes?

Margo:  It's me, Sidney. (And she began crying.)

Me:    For god's sake, what's wrong Margo?

Margo:  You'll think I'm crazy, but—but—I feel sorry for Roger. He's never lost before. You know, we had some good times. We— (and she began to cry again)

Me:    Margo, I know how you feel. But you've got to begin thinking of yourself as Number One from now on. Get some sleep. And don't forget the onions.

# Epilogue

Roger's checks came in on May 1, as he promised. Earlier that week he'd signed the property settlement agreement and all of the collateral documents he'd agreed to in court. He and Tracey wanted that divorce decree as soon as possible.

On May 12, Judge Jackson signed the divorce decree (see Figure 26.1).

## Chronology: Henderson v. Henderson, Spring 1990

Margo was now a freshman journalism student at the university. She bought a new car with her money and hired an investment adviser to manage the rest for her. I warned her about getting married again without a prenuptial agreement. She said, "Never! Are you kidding? But if I do I'll call you first."

I went back to court with my other cases and saw Fenster from time to time. In October he told me that Roger had married Tracey and I told him to say "Good Luck" to Roger for me.

Vicki left to go to law school, and dear, faithful Marge continued to watch over me like a mother hen. Oh, yes, I wrote a long letter of thanks to George Griffin and Jim Connor in Atlanta and told them what had happened in court.

# FIGURE 26.1

## DECREE OF DIVORCE

```
            IN THE FAMILY COURT OF SMITH COUNTY _____

MARGO HENDERSON,                    :      NO. 87-1234
              Plaintiff
                                    :

     vs.
                                    :

ROGER HENDERSON,                           IN DIVORCE
              Defendant              :

                    DECREE AND ORDER

     AND NOW, this 12th day of May, 1989, the Court by virtue of
the authority vested in it by law, decrees that MARGO HENDERSON and
ROGER HENDERSON are hereby divorced from the bonds of matrimony, and
all the duties, rights, and claims accorded to either of the said
parties at any time heretofore, in pursuance of said marriage, shall
henceforth cease and determine, and the said parties shall severally
be at liberty to marry again as if they had never been married.

     AND IT IS FURTHER ORDERED, ADJUDGED, AND DECREED, pursuant to
"The Divorce Code," that the terms, provisions, and conditions of
a certain property settlement agreement between the parties dated
April 20, 1988, and attached to this Decree and Order as Exhibit "A,"
is hereby incorporated into this Decree and Order by reference as
fully as though the same were set forth herein at length.  Said
agreement shall not merge with, but shall survive this Decree and Order.

     IT IS FURTHER ORDERED AND DECREED that the alimony and support
provisions of the agreement attached to this Decree as Exhibit "A"
shall be incorporated into an Order of the Domestic Relations Section
of the Court of Common Pleas of Smith County, No. 87-1059, and all
payments thereunder shall be made through the Domestic Relations
Division of the Court of Common Pleas of Smith County.

     IT IS FURTHER ORDERED AND DECREED that the Custody Visitation
Agreement entered into in open court on January 22, 1987, in action
No. 87-756, as more fully set forth in Exhibit "B" attached to this
Decree and Order shall be the Order of this Court.


                         BY THE COURT,


                         _____
                         Harriet S. Jackson, J.
```

Husbands and wives came in and told me their troubles and the life of a matrimonial lawyer went on as usual.

From time to time Margo called to tell me about her college career and the children. Then in late fall she told me that she'd met a wonderful guy who ran an advertising agency in town—divorced, no children, madly in love with her. I congratulated her and reminded her about the prenuptial agreement.

Then, the following spring, my new receptionist buzzed me.

"There's a Mrs. Henderson to see you, Mr. D."

"Oh, send her right in."

I hadn't heard from Margo for a few months and wanted to hear about her romance. Did she want that prenuptial agreement this soon?

There was a knock on my door. I said, "Come on in, Margo," and a tall, gorgeous, blonde walked in with an anxious look on her pretty face. Her eyes were puffy and she seemed frightened. I quickly noticed two things—she was wearing an $800 suit, and it wasn't Margo. "Mr. De Angelis, my name is Tracey Henderson, and I want a divorce."


I realize there's a lot more you should know about your divorce, but we'll have to wait until we get together again. As I look back on our "talk," I'm sure you still wonder how a judge decides how much equitable distribution you get, whether you'll get post-divorce alimony, and if so for how long. I'm also sure you're not quite certain whether your husband will have to pay all or part of your lawyer's fees and litigation expenses. Don't let it upset you. I've practiced law for over thirty years and equitable distribution law since 1980, and I'm not always certain what a judge will do in a particular case.

But if I've been able to convince you of the importance of preparation, you'll be OK. Make sure you tell your lawyer everything that happened in your marriage, especially all of the economic facts, and then make sure he memorizes every single fact. And make sure you do your homework.

You're entitled to the economic security you enjoyed before. If you prepare your case on the basis of equitable distribution factors and alimony factors, and if your lawyer works diligently, you'll do all right.

I wish I could represent you, but I can't. However, I will be coming to your town soon. Maybe we can meet and talk about your divorce again. Even if it's over, at least I'll have some new stories for you. Take care and good luck!